OPENING UP THE BIBLE

Opening Up
the Bible

M a r y   B a t c h e l o r

A LION BOOK

Text copyright © 1993 Mary Batchelor
This paperback edition copyright © 1999 Lion Publishing

The author asserts the moral right
to be identified as the author of this work

Published by
Lion Publishing plc
Sandy Lane West, Oxford, England
ISBN 0 7459 4072 2

First edition 1993 (hardback)
This edition 1999 (paperback)
10 9 8 7 6 5 4 3 2 1 0

Acknowledgments

Bible quotations are from a number of different Bible translations,
as follows:
The Authorized Version of the Bible (The King James Bible), the
rights of which are vested in the Crown, are reproduced by
permission of the Crown's Patentee, Cambridge University Press.
Good News Bible, copyright © American Bible Society, New York,
1966, 1971 and 4th edition 1976, published by the Bible
Societies/HarperCollins, with permission.
New International Version, copyright © 1973, 1978, 1984 by
International Bible Society.
Revised English Bible, copyright © 1970/1989 by permission of
Oxford and Cambridge University Presses.
Revised Standard Version, copyright ©1989 by the Division of
Christian Education of the National Council of the Churches of
Christ in the USA.

All maps, illustrations and photographs are copyright Lion
Publishing, except those listed below. The following Lion
Publishing photographs appear by courtesy of the Trustees of the
British Museum: 14, 16 (top & right), 21 (below left), 35 (left),
38 (centre left & right), 49, 50 (below left), 51 (below right), 52,
58, 67, 71 (below left), 76 (above), 77 (above, & below right),
78, 80, 82 (below left), 100 (above), 101 (below right), 146, 158
(above, left, & below)

J.C. Allen: 16 (below), 70 (above)
Jon Arnold: 169
Biblical Resources Pilgrim Centre, Tantur: 64, 109 (above)
Colchester Museums: 156
Eretz Israel Museum: 25, 35 (above, right & below, right), 38
(top), 61, 137 (below, left & centre, right), 166 (above)
Hai Bar Reserve Museum (above, left)
Sonia Halliday Photographs: 59, 134, 137 (above right), 166
(below)
Robert Harding Picture Library: 20 (below), 63, 70 (below), 76
(below), 140, 141, 153
Hatay Archaeological Museum, Antakya, Syria: 51 (below, left),
110 (top), 137 (above, left)
Michael Holford: 101 (centre right), 149, 151, 160
Israel Museum, Jerusalem, Israel: 104 (below)
Museum of the History of Jerusalem: 43
Museum of Music & Ethnology, Haifa, Israel: 33 (below), 82 (far
right, & below), cover (far right)
National Maritime Museum, Haifa: 20 (above), 101 (above, left)
Willie Rauch: 13
Rockefeller Museum, Jerusalem: 23
Science Photo Library: 12–13
Zefa Picture Library (UK) Ltd: 21 (above & right), 22, 86 (right),
92, 100 (below), 101 (below left), 127 (left), 139, 161, 170

Drawings by Mark Astle, 26, 73, 144; Dick Barnard, 71; Vic
Mitchell; 77, Pauline O'Boyle, 71, 82, 87, 155; Stanley Willcocks,
45, 125

CONTENTS

A book that reaches the bestseller list usually contains suspense, adventure, love, and a whole range of human emotions, raw and subtle. The Bible — the world's bestseller of all time — has every one of these ingredients. In the Bible we read about men and women who are not fictional or idealized creations but flesh and blood people. Their feelings, their faults, their failures and successes ring true today. But their stories are not the main reason for the Bible's enormous popularity. It fascinates and draws readers because it deals with the deep-down questions to which everyone wants answers: Why are we on this earth? What is the purpose of life and what happens when it ends? How can we cope with the burden of guilt and anxiety? Is there a God?

In fact the Bible never argues for the existence of a God. It begins with the plain fact of God and tells us what he is like and how he reacts to men and women and wants them to respond to him.

Even a quick glance at the pages of a Bible makes it obvious that we are plunged into a world that is largely foreign to us. The culture is that of a bygone age and, for most readers, of faraway people. Yet millions find the Bible highly relevant today. Clothes and customs may vary but people are the same, deep down. They have always experienced the same human feelings of love, hate, jealousy, pity and greed. All share the mystery of life — are born, and go forward to certain death. All know a hunger — whether confessed or not — for something more than food, sex and creature comforts. All share the deep human urge to understand the meaning of life and to have their deepest needs satisfied.

There is another difficulty to be overcome when we read the Bible. It is a book written in a language other than our own. The Old Testament was written in Hebrew and the New Testament in Greek. We are seeing the original only through the skills and knowledge of translators, however expert.

Although we speak of the Bible as one book, it is made up of sixty-six different books. These vary in length, in content and in the form in which they are written. For example, some are poetry, some narrative, others wise sayings or letters. Their authors include kings, courtiers, priests, shepherds and fishermen, as well as many whose identity can only be guessed.

The writing of these separate books covers a time-span of very many centuries. Yet the Bible is a whole, not just a collection of separate parts. The books together make up a unity. The many different authors are all demonstrating in their own way what God has to say about his world and the people he has created. They show what God is like by the way in which he acts towards men and women and by making it clear that he wants to make a relationship with them of the closest possible kind.

The sixty-six books of the Bible are divided into two main groups, the Old Testament, which is made up of thirty-nine books, and the New Testament, which consists of twenty-seven. There are also a number of books known as Deuterocanonical, secondary to the books of Scripture themselves, which may be found within the contents of some Bibles. These books were not considered to have the same authority as the other Bible books. The word 'Testament' comes from Latin and means covenant or agreement. The Old Testament has God's ancient agreement with the people of Israel as its overriding theme. The New Testament is concerned with God's later agreement made, through Jesus, with people of every nationality who respond in trust to God.

But the God they respond to — or flout — has set out deliberately to find for himself the men and women he has created. People may begin to read the Bible in a desire to search for God. They soon discover in the Bible that God has already been searching for them and has found a way to bring them into close relationship with himself.

The Bible has something more to say about itself. Its own claim is that those who wrote it were inspired — or breathed into — by God's Spirit. So, its writers maintain, the words are more than the thoughts and inventions of men and women. The Bible is God's own word to his world.

M. K. BATCHELOR

BOOKS OF THE BIBLE

The text in our Bibles is divided up into chapters and verses. This division was a later addition, put in to make it easier to refer to any particular part of a book.
The list below is in Bible order.
Beside each title is the chapter in which the book is mentioned here.

THE OLD TESTAMENT BOOKS

The law books, sometimes known as the Pentateuch or five books:

Genesis	Chapter 1
Exodus	Chapter 2
Leviticus	Chapter 2
Numbers	Chapter 2
Deuteronomy	Chapter 2

The history books:

Joshua	Chapter 3
Judges	Chapter 3
Ruth	Chapter 3
1 and 2 Samuel	Chapter 3
1 and 2 Kings	Chapter 3
1 and 2 Chronicles	Chapter 3
Esther	Chapter 6
Ezra	Chapter 6
Nehemiah	Chapter 6

The poetry and wisdom books:

Job	Chapter 8
Psalms	Chapter 7
Proverbs	Chapter 8
Ecclesiastes	Chapter 8
Song of Solomon	Chapter 7

The books of the major prophets:

Isaiah	Chapter 4
Jeremiah	Chapter 5
Lamentations	Chapter 7
Ezekiel	Chapter 6
Daniel	Chapter 6

The books of the minor, or shorter, prophets:

Hosea	Chapter 4
Joel	Chapter 5
Amos	Chapter 4
Obadiah	Chapter 5
Jonah	Chapter 5
Micah	Chapter 4
Nahum	Chapter 5
Habakkuk	Chapter 5
Zephaniah	Chapter 5
Haggai	Chapter 6
Zechariah	Chapter 6
Malachi	Chapter 6

THE NEW TESTAMENT BOOKS

The four Gospels: accounts of the life of Jesus

Matthew	Chapter 9
Mark	Chapter 9
Luke	Chapter 9
John	Chapter 9

The first years of the Christian Church

The Acts of the Apostles	Chapter 10

Letters from Paul

Romans	Chapter 11
1 Corinthians	Chapter 11
2 Corinthians	Chapter 11
Galatians	Chapter 11
Ephesians	Chapter 11
Philippians	Chapter 11
Colossians	Chapter 11
1 Thessalonians	Chapter 11
2 Thessalonians	Chapter 11
1 Timothy	Chapter 11
2 Timothy	Chapter 11
Titus	Chapter 11
Philemon	Chapter 11

General letters

Hebrews	Chapter 12
James	Chapter 12
1 Peter	Chapter 12
2 Peter	Chapter 12
1 John	Chapter 12
2 John	Chapter 12
3 John	Chapter 12
Jude	Chapter 12

The visions of John

Revelation	Chapter 13

THE OLD TESTAMENT

1
BEGINNINGS
Genesis

'*In the beginning God created the heavens
and the earth.' Genesis 1:1*

With this magnificent and breathtaking
statement the Bible begins, taking us right
back to the start of our world. In those few
words the writer sets out the great
foundation truths that there is only one God,
who was in existence at the very beginning,
and that the whole of creation is his work. On
this everything rests, and from it the whole
biblical narrative flows.

The making of the world

Next comes a description of the creation,
beginning:

'*And God said, "Let there be light," and there
was light. God saw that the light was good and
he separated the light from the darkness. God
called the light "day", and the darkness he
called "night". And there was evening and there
was morning — the first day.' (1:3–5)*

Each dramatic creative act that follows
begins with the words: 'And God said, "Let
there be …"' and ends with the words: 'And
there was evening and there was morning'
and the number of the day.

The creation of the world is described for
us in the language of poetry and the events
are ordered into a perfect pattern. Poetry not
only conveys beauty, it is also a wonderful
vehicle for conveying truth. The statements
are not bald statements of fact in a scientific
sense, but represent truth with many layers
of meaning. They can be understood simply
at face value, or some of the underlying
meaning can be unpacked and appreciated
too. So the Genesis account is not trying to
set down a factual record of how God created
the world — say in seven literal days — but is
enabling the reader to take in the essential
truth about creation: sun, moon, stars,
plants, animals and human beings came into

being through the mighty power of God and
at his express wish and command.

Man and woman

As the account unfolds, the raging seas are
curbed, the world is clothed with trees and
plants, and living creatures fill the land, sea
and air. But when human beings are made,
God's creative purpose is described in a
different way.

'*Then God said, "Let us make human beings in
our image, after our likeness, to have dominion
over the fish in the sea, the birds of the air, the
cattle, all wild animals on land, and everything
that creeps on the earth."' (1:26)*

Men and women were made to resemble God in a way that the animal creation never could. They were to have the capacity to love, to remember, to choose and to be in relationship with God himself. They were also created to be God's agents, put in charge of the rest of creation, to manage it well. The writer does not see them as the products of blind chance or at the mercy of planets and stars. They are portrayed as the handiwork of a loving God who fashioned them to rule his world and — more amazing still — to enjoy his friendship. It is a perfect scene and the writer concludes his account with the words:

'God saw all that he had made, and it was very good.' (1:31)

A second strand to the story is the creation of woman as an equal partner for man. God brings the two together and the writer sums up God's pattern for marriage:

'For this reason a man will leave his father and mother and be united to his wife, and they will become one flesh.' (2:24)

The writer has described in the language of poetry the broad sweep of God's good creation. He has answered some of the deeper questions of how life came to be, of the purpose behind it. He has left us with a perfect world.

But we all know that life is not perfect. Even in the natural world there is disturbance and chaos, and among human beings there is greed, anger, exploitation and murder. So the writer next recounts, still in the language of poetry, how these alien elements entered that perfect world.

Tragedy

The first man and woman, Adam and Eve, lived in the beautiful Garden of Eden, caring for the plants and animals, in happy companionship with God. They were given complete freedom except for one condition:

'You must not eat from the tree of the knowledge of good and evil, for when you eat of it you will surely die.' (2:17)

These were God's words. The name of the tree gives some clue to its significance. Men and women would claim to know for themselves what was good or evil for them. It would destroy innocence and introduce harmful knowledge. To eat its fruit would result in death.

God spoke the word, the Bible says, that brought everything into being—macrocosm and microcosm—from the furthest star to the smallest flower.

The Orion Nebula is 1,600 light years from Earth. A common garden dahlia expresses the beauty of the Creator's design.

The account describes how the crafty serpent tempted Eve to eat the forbidden fruit. In another place in the Bible the serpent is said to be the name given to Satan, the enemy of God and humankind. Eve took the fruit because she saw that it was 'good for food and pleasing to the eye, and also desirable for gaining wisdom'. She gave some to Adam too, and when they had eaten their eyes were opened. Their innocence had gone. They were conscious of their nakedness before God and each other. For the first time they were ashamed to meet God and they hid from him. They had chosen self-assertion and disobedience instead of loving dependence on God their Maker — and by their action the whole of creation was put out of joint. From this tragic act flowed a host of bitter consequences.

God is pictured as talking to the serpent and to Adam and Eve, showing them the consequences of their actions. From now on the land would bring forth thorns and weeds. The relationship between the sexes would be spoiled by exploitation. Physical death — though not immediate — would follow. Spiritual death had already ended their close relationship with God. In a deeply significant act, Adam and Eve were banished from their garden paradise. Blood, sweat, toil and tears lay ahead.

The poetry of these first chapters of Genesis is followed by narrative accounts of the early descendants of this first man and woman. Their son Cain murdered his brother Abel, out of jealousy, and their descendants continued the downward spiral into sin and violence. At length:

'When the Lord saw how great was the wickedness of human beings on earth ... he bitterly regretted that he had made mankind on earth.' (6:5–6)

This seventh-century BC clay tablet is inscribed with an ancient Babylonian account of the flood.

Other Creation and Flood Stories

As well as the Bible's account, there are other early stories of creation and a great flood that come from Babylonia. Some of the ideas seem similar to the Bible accounts but the differences, especially in the concept of God, are very marked. The God of Genesis is one God, not many, and man and woman are the climax of his creation. In the Babylonian account, human beings were made as an afterthought and as a convenience for the gods, whom they could feed and wait upon. The God of Genesis acts in love and justice, not out of caprice or self-interest.

The flood

God determined to blot out his creation with a flood. But he found one good man, Noah, who trusted and obeyed him even in those dark days. At God's bidding Noah built a huge boat — the 'ark' — to preserve his family and members of the animal kingdom. Noah also attempted to persuade those around him to turn back to God — but to no effect. When the flood came, Noah and his boat with its precious cargo survived and eventually emerged to build an altar and give thanks to God. God pledged that he would never send another such flood and gave the rainbow as a sign of his unbreakable promise.

The tower of Babel

After the flood men and women continued to go their own way. They refused to spread out and populate the earth as God had instructed Adam and Eve and their descendants. Instead they settled in one centre and began to build a monument to their own pride and achievement. God confounded their plans, but it was clear that the majority were not prepared to go God's way.

Abraham

The second half of the book of Genesis moves from a broad canvas to bring the spotlight onto one particular man, Abraham, and his wife and family. God still wanted to make himself known to men and women and to bring them back from their disobedience into happy relationship with him. The way he planned was to choose one man — a single family — and to make of him and his descendants a nation in special relationship to God. God would make himself known to them, give them his promises and his laws. They, in turn, would make God known to the other nations of the world: this was God's plan, his purpose in choosing these people.

God's promise

Abraham and his wife, Sarah, lived in the city of Ur at the eastern end of what is known as the Fertile Crescent. This is a semicircle of land stretching from Egypt through Palestine

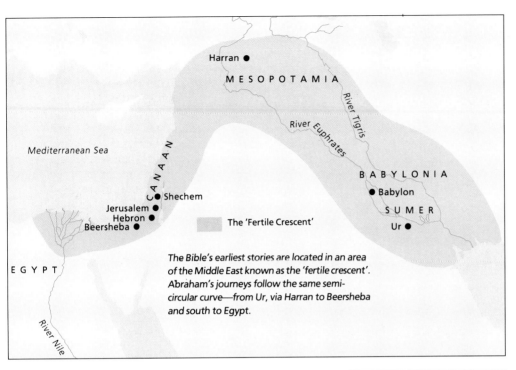

The Bible's earliest stories are located in an area of the Middle East known as the 'fertile crescent'. Abraham's journeys follow the same semi-circular curve—from Ur, via Harran to Beersheba and south to Egypt.

From the time they left Ur, Abraham and his family, with their flocks and herds, lived as nomads, moving from place to place on the way to Canaan and even when they arrived. These bedouin tents evoke the scene and the lifestyle.

and Syria, then down the River Euphrates to the Persian Gulf. In the midst of the comfort and culture of Ur, God called Abraham to leave his settled home and set out on a nomadic life, journeying towards the land of Palestine. God promised:

'I will make you into a great nation and I will bless you . . . all peoples on earth will be blessed through you.' (12:2–3)

Abraham obeyed God's call. For the rest of his life he would live as a nomad, moving as his flocks and family needed water, but staying in the land of Canaan which God had promised to his descendants.

God made a covenant or agreement with Abraham. In a solemn ceremony he promised that Abraham's descendants would be as numerous as the sand on the seashore or the stars in the sky, and that they would inherit the land of Canaan. There was one great difficulty in the way of God fulfilling his promise. Abraham and Sarah had no children and they were both old. Yet the promise involved their descendants.

After many testing years of waiting, when Sarah had passed child-bearing years, God's promise was fulfilled and a son, Isaac, was born. The Bible commends Abraham for his faith, because he continued to trust God even when it seemed impossible for the promise to be kept.

An even greater test of Abraham's faith was yet to come. When Isaac was a young man, God did the unthinkable and asked Abraham to offer up his son as a sacrifice. At

UR: THE CITY OF ABRAHAM

Abraham and his wife Sarah were living in the city of Ur, in the south of Babylonia, when God gave them new directions. They were to leave the security of the city with its great temple to the moon-god, and set out on a long journey to a new land God promised would be their own.

Excavations on the site of ancient Ur have uncovered the remains of the houses of well-to-do citizens: two storeys built around a paved courtyard. Vast quantities of clay tablets provide records of business life—the purchase of land, inheritance, marriage—and diplomatic affairs. And the ruins of a great pyramid-stepped temple witness to the importance of religion.

A lady-in-waiting to the queen of Ur once wore this elegant golden headdress (from the royal graves).

Many treasures have been unearthed from the royal graves at Ur, dating from some centuries before Abraham's time. This beautiful gaming-board with counters was among the discoveries made.

A marvellous example of the goldsmith's craft is this gold dagger and scabbard, made for display (from the royal graves at Ur).

The Bible's 'tower of Babel' was probably built up from a series of platforms in the same way as the temple at Ur, whose ruins are over 4,000 years old.

that time human sacrifice was practised among the surrounding peoples.

With a breaking heart, Abraham set off with his precious, dearly-loved son. As they journeyed to the place of sacrifice Isaac noticed that something was wrong.

The fire and the wood are here,' Isaac said, 'but where is the lamb for the burnt offering?' Abraham answered: 'God himself will provide the lamb for the burnt offering, my son.' (22:7–8)

As Abraham raised the knife to kill his son, God's angel stopped him:

Do not lay a hand on the boy,' he said. 'Do not do anything to him. Now I know that you fear God because you have not withheld from me your son, your only son.' (22:12)

Abraham found a ram in a thicket, caught by its horns. He offered it as a sacrifice to God instead. He knew now that his God did not want the human sacrifices that other gods required. But Abraham also discovered that he was prepared to trust God absolutely and to put him before everything.

The Jewish people regard Abraham as the father of their nation. Not only was he the physical ancestor of their tribes, but God's promise of a nation and a land to inherit were made to him. He is also the prime example of someone who trusts and obeys God wholeheartedly.

Jacob

In due course Isaac married and he had twin sons. Only one of the two would carry on the family line and God's covenant promises made to Abraham. Before the boys were born, their mother, Rebecca, was told by God that the younger son would be the chosen one. But Isaac favoured Esau, the elder — and Jacob tried to trick his older brother out of the right to succeed to God's promises and blessing.

In spite of his scheming and deception, Jacob really cared about God's promises, whereas his brother Esau, attractive and good-natured though he was, thought nothing of them. God used the many hard experiences of Jacob's subsequent life to bring him close and to change him from a wily deceiver to a man whose trust in God was firm.

On his way home after many years of exile, Jacob had a strange encounter. All night he wrestled with a mysterious stranger. At the end of the struggle Jacob exclaimed: 'I have seen God face to face!'

Jacob the schemer emerged as 'Israel', the one who struggles, or who perseveres with God. He passed this new name on to his descendants.

Jacob had six sons by his first wife, Leah, as well as a daughter, Dinah. He had two each by the slaves of his wives and, at length, two

When the Patriarchs Lived

Abraham, Isaac and Jacob are often called 'the Patriarchs', because they were the founding fathers of their nation. Although in the past some scholars questioned whether they actually existed, there are many good reasons for believing that they did. They probably lived in the Middle Bronze Age, between 2000 and 1500BC, though some put their dates between 3000 and 1000BC.

At that period many tribes in the area were migrating. The Patriarchs moved from one place to another in Palestine, where there were then a number of city-states which had strong ties with Egypt. The nomads may have been allowed to pasture their flocks in the fields once the crops had been harvested. They could also move to an oasis—Beersheba was one—to find grass and water.

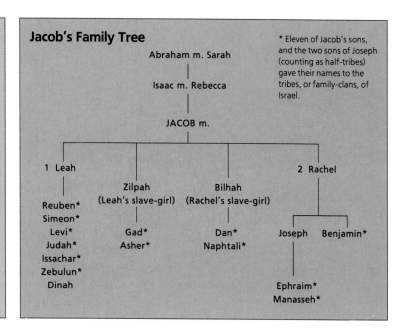

Jacob's Family Tree

Abraham m. Sarah

Isaac m. Rebecca

JACOB m.

1 Leah

Reuben*
Simeon*
Levi*
Judah*
Issachar*
Zebulun*
Dinah

Zilpah
(Leah's slave-girl)

Gad*
Asher*

Bilhah
(Rachel's slave-girl)

Dan*
Naphtali*

2 Rachel

Joseph   Benjamin*

Ephraim*
Manasseh*

* Eleven of Jacob's sons, and the two sons of Joseph (counting as half-tribes) gave their names to the tribes, or family-clans, of Israel.

The First Five Books of the Bible

The first five books of the Bible are often grouped together and are known as the *Pentateuch* or five books. The Jewish name for them is the Torah, which means instruction or teaching. These are the books of God's Law.

Nineteenth-century scholars evolved the theory that there were four distinct strands to the writings of the Pentateuch. Some of these strands were differentiated by the form of the name used for God. The writer who used the name *Yahweh* is known as J, the one using *Elohim* as E. A priestly group of writers is labelled P and the Deutero-nomical writers D—these are the ones who are believed to have put together and edited the book of Deuteronomy and other books with the same kind of message. The theory has become far more complex in recent years, with many further strands picked out. It is questioned today.

Some parts of the five books are clearly very ancient and would seem to go back to oral or written records of Moses himself. However, many different traditions were included and the final editors used their own skill and purposes in compiling the books. When those compilers lived is also uncertain.

Scholars continue the debate, sometimes forgetting that this way of looking at the text should not prevent us from seeing its primary meaning and its overall theme. What matters most is reading and understanding the text as it now stands.

sons by Rachel, his second wife, whom he adored. It was Jacob's eleven sons, and the two sons of his favourite, Joseph, who became the tribal leaders of the nation of Israel.

Joseph's story

Of all his sons, Jacob loved Joseph best. He was the first-born of his much-loved wife, Rachel. But the other brothers were jealous of Joseph especially when he told them about his dreams — dreams in which he lorded it over the rest of his family. One day, when he had been sent to visit his brothers who were away looking after the sheep, they found a way to get rid of him. They thrust him down an empty water cistern, then sold him to some merchants travelling to Egypt.

In Egypt Joseph's fortunes fluctuated violently. Bought as a slave by Potiphar, an important official of the king of Egypt — the Pharaoh — he showed himself capable and reliable. He was soon made steward of the household. But Potiphar's wife cast longing eyes at Joseph. When he refused her attempts to seduce him she cried rape, and Joseph was thrown into prison. But no matter what his circumstances, the writer tells us that 'the Lord was with Joseph'.

In prison Joseph soon won the jailer's trust. He excelled himself by explaining the dreams of two of Pharaoh's officials, imprisoned with him. The ancient Egyptians believed strongly in dreams as a key to future events. There were manuals on their interpretation. The butler, whose dream he interpreted, was released and he suddenly remembered Joseph when Pharaoh had a dream that no one could understand. Joseph was quickly taken from prison and made fit for the king's presence. He interpreted Pharaoh's dreams, readily acknowledging God as the source of his amazing insight: there would be seven years of plenty followed by seven years of terrible famine. Pharaoh, impressed, put Joseph in charge of all food storage and distribution.

So, by a quirk of fate — or, as Joseph believed, by God's plan — his unsuspecting brothers one day came to him to beg for food, for the famine had reached their land too. For some time Joseph kept his identity a secret, but at last he broke down and told them who he was, freely forgiving them and begging them to bring the elderly Jacob and their families to settle in Egypt, where there was food for them all.

There, in the land of Egypt, the book of Genesis ends. But God's promise was not forgotten. Before he died, Joseph gave instructions that when the extended family came to leave Egypt — as he was certain they would — they were to take his bones with them. He wanted to rest at last in the land of God's promise.

LAW AND LIBERTY

Exodus · Leviticus · Numbers · Deuteronomy

After the death of Joseph (with which Genesis ends) the people of Israel flourished and multiplied in Egypt. But the Egyptians soon forgot how Joseph had saved them from famine. Gratitude on the part of the rulers of Egypt turned to suspicion and hatred.

Exodus

At the end of some 300–400 years the sheer numbers of the Israelites posed a threat to the native Egyptians. The Pharaoh — Egypt's king — tried to suppress them by using the Israelites as slave labour for his ambitious building projects. But their numbers still grew, so he issued an edict that all Israelite boy babies were to be killed at birth.

One man and woman defied this command. For three months they hid their baby son, and when they could do so no longer his mother put him in a waterproof basket on the river, leaving Miriam, his sister, to keep watch. The baby in his basket was found by Pharoah's daughter, coming to bathe. Miriam came forward, suggesting her mother as a nurse for the baby. The princess, who named him Moses, gave the baby to her to be cared for until he was weaned. When Moses was older he was brought up and educated at the Egyptian court as the adopted son of the king's daughter.

Moses

Despite his royal upbringing, Moses' sympathies were all with his own downtrodden people, the Israelites. He tried to protect them from their slave-drivers and to settle their quarrels, hoping to champion their cause, but they rejected him. In the end, in his passion for justice, he killed an Egyptian foreman who was beating up an Israelite and had to flee the country.

For the next forty years Moses lived as a shepherd, spending long hours alone in the desert. One day, near Mount Sinai, he saw a bush on fire. What arrested his attention was the fact that the bush was not burned up. As he went to look more closely, a voice spoke to him from the burning bush.

'Do not come any closer,' God said. 'Take off your sandals, for the place where you are standing is holy ground.' Then he said, 'I am the God of your father, the God of Abraham, the God of Isaac and the God of Jacob.' (3:5–6)

God had heard the groans of his people. The time had come to deliver them from their slavery. He had chosen Moses to lead them out. Moses made one excuse after another. He was older and wiser than in his impetuous youth and not at all ambitious to take on the task.

'Suppose I go to the Israelites and say to them, "The God of your fathers has sent me to you" and they ask me "What is his name?" Then what shall I tell them?'

God replied:

'I AM WHO I AM . . . I AM has sent me to you.' (3:13–14)

At that time a person's name was believed to indicate their character. This mysterious name was a way of saying that God is known through his actions. It also tells us, in John Drane's words, that 'God is the Lord of time and he will do in the future what he has done in the past and is doing in the present.'

God's covenant name was revealed in a new way to Moses. One form of the name is Yahweh, often rendered Jehovah, but now indicated in most Bibles by LORD in capital letters.

God instructed Moses to tell the people of Israel that their God would deliver them. Many had forgotten what God was like, but they would soon have a demonstration of his

LIFE IN EGYPT

From the time of Joseph to the time of Moses (four centuries) the clans of Israel lived in Egypt—a kingdom whose history even then stretched back well over a thousand years. At the time of Moses, most of the inhabitants of Egypt were peasant farmers who farmed small strips of land. Their lives were regulated by the annual flooding of the Nile. It was the Nile which brought water to irrigate crops and produce the rich mud which made Egypt such a fertile land. During the flooding of the Nile, when no one could tend their land, many would be conscripted to work on state building projects.

The Pharaoh (Egypt's king and intermediary between the gods and humankind) was at the top of the social order and under him two viziers looked after the vast bureaucracy which oversaw and recorded every area of life.

Workmen and peasants lived in mud-brick homes but the nobles had more splendid houses and gardens. The wealth of information we possess about Egyptian life comes from tomb paintings and inscriptions, writing on temple walls and monuments, and artefacts found in tombs.

The Egyptians worshipped many gods, at local shrines and in the great temples, through the priests. Magic was an active part of religion. They believed in a life after death and every requirement for this new life was provided in the tomb of the dead person, where the carefully embalmed body was laid.

Model of a funerary boat, from the tombs of ancient Egypt.

The Nile has always been Egypt's great highway. It flows through the desert, sustaining a narrow band of cultivatible land on either bank.

Mediterranean Sea

LOWER EGYPT

● Tanis

Memphis ●

SINAI

River Nile

UPPER EGYPT

Red Sea

● Thebes

The Hebrew slaves were forced to make bricks for Pharaoh's great building projects. Scenes painted on the walls of tombs in Egypt show how the mixture of clay and straw was placed in wooden moulds, to be baked in the hot sun.

The image of Rameses II, most likely the Pharaoh of the exodus, dominates many of his great building works.

With the desert so close, a good harvest was vital. The grain was carefully stored and recorded.

These huge pillars are part of the great hall in the Temple of Amun at Karnak (dating from the thirteenth century BC). They stand as permanent testimony to the might of ancient Egypt, and the status of religion.

power, as Moses challenged the Egyptian king. When Moses objected that he was not a good speaker, God promised that his brother Aaron would go with him to do the talking. He would accept no excuses.

'Let my people go'

So Moses and Aaron confronted Pharaoh, the king of Egypt, with the demand that the people of Israel should be allowed to leave the country in order to worship their God. But he refused point blank. In order to demonstrate that God was stronger than Pharaoh and the gods of Egypt, and to change Pharaoh's attitude, a series of terrible disasters — the ten plagues — befell the Egyptians. First the life-giving waters of the Nile turned blood-red. Plagues of frogs, of flies and of lice followed. But Pharaoh hardened his heart and refused to allow the people to leave Egypt as God had commanded — and so his people suffered. After nine disasters Moses warned the king of a tenth and still more terrible one that was to come. The first-born son of every family in Egypt — even the first-born of the cattle — would die on a given night.

Unleavened bread (made without yeast and needing no time for rising) could be made quickly for the Passover meal, eaten as the people prepared to leave Egypt. Here a bedouin woman bakes bread in the traditional way, on an oven inside her tent.

The Passover

The people of Israel were learning about God's power and his mercy to them from these disasters too. Now, before the last plague struck, Moses told them to make special preparations. Every Israelite family was to kill a lamb and to sprinkle its blood on the doorposts and lintels of their house. It was a symbol: the life of the lamb was given on their behalf. Every family that sheltered in a house marked by the blood was safe from the destructive power of death.

The night of judgment for the Egyptians was to be a night of salvation and deliverance for the Israelites. Inside their homes they were to prepare a special meal of roast lamb and bitter herbs with unleavened bread. They were to eat their meal dressed ready for travel. As soon as that night was past, the Egyptians would be eager to speed the Israelites on their way.

Wailing and lamentation filled the land as death came to each Egyptian dwelling. Pharaoh told Moses to take the people and be gone. The Israelites were free at last to leave the land of their slavery and to set out for the land God had promised them since the time of Abraham.

The Red Sea

No sooner had the vast procession of Israelites with their flocks and herds left Egypt than Pharaoh regretted his decision to let his slaves escape. He sent an army to recapture them. It looked as if the Israelites were trapped. With the army at their heels, the way ahead was blocked by water.

The Red Sea, as the Bible calls it, is not likely to be the sea of that name today. A better translation is the Sea of Reeds — a stretch of water probably in the region of the present Suez Canal.

When the Israelites saw the approaching Egyptian horses and chariots they were panic-stricken. But Moses told them:

'Do not be afraid. Stand firm and you will see the deliverance the Lord will bring you today. The Egyptians you see today you will never see again.' (14:13)

As God commanded, Moses held his staff

over the sea, and a strong east wind blew back the water so that the people could cross on dry land. Only when they were safely over did the waters flow back, drowning the pursuing Egyptian army.

Moses and his sister Miriam broke into song and a dance of victory in which all the people joined:

'I will sing to the Lord, for he has triumphed
    gloriously,
    The horse and his rider he has thrown into
        the sea.
The Lord is my strength and my song,
    and he has become my salvation.' *(15:1–2)*

Throughout Israel's history this mighty deliverance at the Red Sea has been seen as God's supreme act of salvation for his people, with the Passover, his great act of redemption from slavery in Egypt.

Into the desert

Moses led the people away from the well-guarded coast road, south into the Sinai Desert, towards Mount Sinai. God had promised Moses that they would return to the very place of his calling. During all their long wanderings in the desert God is described as going in front of his people: a pillar of cloud by day and a pillar of fire by night were the signs that he was with them. Fire and cloud are often used as symbols of God's presence. The cloud here is described as bright and shining. Later, God's tent or tabernacle was to be another visible symbol of his presence.

The covenant

The covenant, or agreement, between God and his people Israel — made at Mount Sinai — is the core of the whole Old Testament. The covenant was based on God's free love and kindness to his people. He had chosen them to be his own in a special way. He would care for them and prosper them. Their side of the covenant was to obey God and keep the laws that he gave them through Moses.

The people were very enthusiastic about this agreement. They had no doubt that they could keep their side of the covenant —

although the rest of the Old Testament shows how far short they fell of being true to God and obeying him.

Moses went up the mountain to receive God's words and came down for the covenant ceremony. Awed by the cloud, the sound of a trumpet, and the thunder and lightning around them, the people willingly agreed to keep it. Moses sealed the covenant promises with the blood of animals.

The sign of the covenant relationship between God and Israel was the circumcision of all males, first required of Abraham. Circumcision was commonly practised among peoples in this part of the world as a rite of initiation into the adult world, but for the Israelites it marked their special relationship with God and in future would be carried out on the eighth day after birth. God gave them his special covenant name — the name which he had made known to Moses — to use from this point on.

The Ten Commandments

The central core of the many laws laid down in Exodus and Leviticus is the Ten Commandments or Decalogue. The first half sums up the people's relationship with God and the second half their relationship with others. These laws are far more than a passing set of rules for one group of people. They have been widely acknowledged as universal and permanent; the present-day laws of many countries in the West are based on them.

'I am the Lord your God, who brought you out of the land of Egypt, out of the house of bondage.
    You shall have no other gods before me.
    You shall not make for yourself a graven image . . . you shall not bow down to them or serve them . . .
    You shall not take the name of the Lord your God in vain . . .
    Remember the Sabbath day to keep it holy . . .
    Honour your father and your mother . . .
    You shall not kill.
    You shall not commit adultery.
    You shall not steal.
    You shall not bear false witness against your neighbour.
    You shall not covet . . . anything that is your neighbour's.' *(Exodus 20)*

Miriam (Moses' sister) led the singing and dancing after the escape from Egypt, playing the tambourine—like this small clay figure in the Rockefeller Museum, Jerusalem.

Mt Sinai, where God's code of laws was set down for his people as a basis of the covenant agreement between them.

Civil law

There are many other laws laid down in the Old Testament law books, some of them clearly relating to life as it was lived at that time.

Instructions are given as to how to act in particular situations. For example, if an owner's bull gored someone and he died, the bull had to be put to death. If the bull had a history of goring people then the owner had to pay the same penalty.

Other laws relate to family life and the treatment of slaves. One thing that they have in common is consideration for the weak and underprivileged, whom God is specially concerned to protect:

'When you reap the harvest of your land, do not reap up to the very edges of your field or gather the gleanings of your harvest. Do not go over your vineyard a second time or pick up the grapes that have fallen. Leave them for the poor and alien. I am the Lord your God . . .

Do not hold back the wages of a hired man overnight.

Do not curse the deaf or put a stumbling-block in front of the blind, but fear your God. I am the Lord.

Do not pervert justice; do not show partiality to the poor or favouritism to the great, but judge your neighbour fairly.

Do not go about spreading slander among your people.

Do not do anything that endangers your neighbour's life. I am the Lord . . .

Do not seek revenge or bear a grudge against one of your people, but love your neighbour as yourself. I am the Lord.' (Leviticus 19)

Ritual law

Another group of laws has to do with the worship and service of God. Some prescribe the way in which worship was to be offered to God. Others are food laws — laying down which foods could not be eaten. Pork and shellfish, amongst other things, were forbidden. These laws could well have been given to protect health in a hot climate. The separating of clean from unclean animals also symbolized Israel's separation from the nations.

There were many laws too which had to do with a person's ritual cleanness. These are rooted in hygiene but the over-riding reason was that Israel's God was a holy God. He was pure and untouched by sin. Physical uncleanness was a symbol of moral and spiritual defilement. If God was to live among his people they too must keep themselves holy and pure in every way.

The gold bull-calf

After the sealing of the covenant, Moses went up the mountain again and stayed for a long time in communion with God. The people grew tired of waiting for him to reappear. Breaking the promises they had just made, they begged Aaron to make a god for them that they could see and touch. He asked them for their gold jewellery and out of the gold he made a bull-calf. A loud and lusty celebration followed, an orgy of so-called worship with the bull-calf at its centre.

At last Moses and his aide, Joshua, came down the mountain. Moses carried the tablets of stone engraved by God with the Ten Commandments. Faintly at first but growing louder, they heard the uproar coming from the camp. Moses soon realized what was happening. He was furious. He flung down the stone tablets, breaking them in pieces, and stormed onto the scene of revelry, bringing the people quickly to their senses. He could not believe that so soon after vowing obedience to God's commands they could break the second commandment and bow down to a man-made image.

In fury Moses ground the bull-calf to powder, mixed it with the drinking water, and made the Israelites drink it. Yet a little while later it was Moses who trudged up the mountain again, seeking God's forgiveness and restoration for the people who had sinned so gravely. God revealed himself to Moses as

'the Lord, the compassionate and gracious God, slow to anger, abounding in love and faithfulness, maintaining love to thousands, and forgiving wickedness, rebellion and sin. Yet he does not leave the guilty unpunished.' (34:6–7)

Many times God forgave and restored his people. Sadly, idolatry was to mark Israel's conduct for many hundreds of years to come. Eventually it would lead to the break-up of the nation.

The tabernacle

God promised Moses that he would be with his people; his presence was made known in the pillars of cloud and fire. But God also chose to have a shrine made: a tent of his own in the midst of the Israelites' camp. Moses gave God's detailed instructions to the craftsmen who were to make this special tent or tabernacle. At the centre of a series of enclosures in the tabernacle was one called the 'most holy place'. There was no image of God there — as there would have been in other similar shrines of the period — that was forbidden. But there was a gold-covered box in which were placed the two tablets of the Law which Moses had brought down from the mountain.

A feature of this shrine was that every part of it was supplied with carrying-poles and rings. Because the people were on the move, the shrine must be moveable too. Israel's God was not like the gods of the people around, whose power was confined to the territory where their tribe lived. While his people journeyed as pilgrims, God promised to travel too, continuing to live among them.

But stringent guidelines were laid down, in case the people should think that they could treat God casually. Only appointed priests were allowed to serve in the tabernacle and when camp was pitched it was the priests' tents that surrounded God's tent. As well as signalling God's presence among his people, the tabernacle protected them from close contact with the awfulness and holiness of God's presence.

The Book of Exodus is full of God's glory and his holiness, but the writers also emphasize the fact that God was willing to live among his people, protecting and saving them. The people had many bitter lessons to learn during their wandering in the desert. Water supplies failed and often they grumbled and drove Moses to distraction with their complaints. But God is revealed as the one who constantly provides for their needs.

Exodus ends as the tabernacle is completed and the bright cloud of God's presence envelops it in all its glory. God is with his people.

The sacred bull-calf, modelled by Aaron for the people, belonged to the worship of Egypt as an emblem of fertility. This small bronze and silver statuette, unearthed in 1991 in a temple at Ashkelon, dates from the second century BC, indicating the survival of the cult for many centuries after Moses' day.

Leviticus

At first sight, Leviticus is little more than an account of how to offer sacrifices and carry out ceremonial laws. That is because it is concerned with the duties of the priests and Levites, as the title indicates.

Levites were members of the tribe of Levi. They were not priests because they were not descendants of Aaron — the first high priest. But they helped the priests in their duties. They needed detailed instructions if they were to carry out their services correctly.

The key word of Leviticus is 'holy'. The lifestyle of priests, Levites and people must be clean, pure and set apart for God. Because they are in covenant relationship with a holy God they must be holy too. They must be free from contamination, completely dedicated to God.

Right at the centre of the book we read about the religious festivals that marked the passage of the year for the Israelites. They celebrated God's past saving acts and his continuing care.

The Day of Atonement

If anything brought home to the people the holiness of God it was the annual observance of the Day of Atonement. On that day no one worked and everyone fasted. The people had to acknowledge and confess their failure to follow and obey God as they should. Then came a solemn ritual to take away their sins.

No one except the High Priest was allowed to go into the inner sanctuary of the tabernacle, where the golden box — the Ark of the Covenant or Covenant Box — was kept. Even he went in only once a year, on the Day of Atonement. He sprinkled blood on the lid of the Ark, known as the mercy seat, to

THE TABERNACLE
Israel's Tent of Worship

The instructions for making the tabernacle are set out in detail in the Book of Exodus. The Israelites were instructed to make a portable tent for God, to carry with them throughout their journey to the promised land. When they set up camp, God's tent would be erected at the centre. God was in the midst of his people: he was always present with them.

The tent had two rooms: the private inner room held the Covenant Box and the copy of God's laws. In the outer room was a lampstand with seven lamps, an altar for incense, and a table with twelve loaves of bread.

There was a large enclosure around God's tent: here people could come to the priests. An altar was provided for sacrifice. A large bronze basin held water for the priests to wash before going into God's tent.

The Tabernacle has been reconstructed by the Rev. L. Schouten at the Bible Museum, Amsterdam.

make atonement for the people's sins. The blood represented the life given.

'Atonement' is literally 'at-one-ment'; it carries the idea of reconciling God and the people, making them 'at one' by the removal of sin. The High Priest also offered animal sacrifices for the priests' and the people's sins. Then he selected two goats. One he killed as a sacrifice but over the other one he recited the sins of the people. Then he sent it out — a scapegoat for the people's sins — to take those sins away into the desert.

The Sabbath

The Sabbath — the principle of one day of rest after six days of work — has its roots in the creation story itself. The Genesis account says that God rested from his work of creation on the seventh day and that day became holy to the Lord. Keeping that day special was one of the Ten Commandments and marked out the Israelites as God's covenant people. The Sabbath seems to have been intended as a joyful celebration. It was a day on which the people could remember God's covenant and be free from everyday work. Even slaves and working animals were to enjoy the weekly holiday.

Passover

Passover was a key commemoration in Israel. It was the first of the annual festivals and once Israel reached the land of Canaan all Israelite men were commanded to come to God's sanctuary — later the temple — to celebrate it. On the first Passover night God delivered his people from slavery in Egypt, and for ever after those events were rehearsed during the Passover meal. God's redemption was recalled as the roast lamb was eaten, together with bitter herbs — a reminder of the bitterness of slavery in Egypt. They also ate bread made without yeast, for the feast of 'unleavened' bread was observed at the same time.

Some see Unleavened Bread as an agricultural festival because it was linked with the barley harvest, when a first-ripe sheaf of barley was offered to God. The Bible links the eating of unleavened bread with the first Passover, when the people were in such a hurry to leave Egypt that there was no time to wait for the dough they took with them to rise.

Festival of Weeks

This festival took place seven weeks after Passover and after the sheaf of barley had been offered to God. Its other name was Pentecost, as it occurred fifty days after the barley offering. It was a harvest of first-fruits. By this time the grain harvest was coming to an end and a special offering of grain was made to God. It was another occasion when all Israelite men were to go to God's sanctuary.

Festival of Tabernacles or Shelters

This was the third festival when Israelites were to present themselves to God at his sanctuary. It was a harvest thanksgiving and is sometimes called the Feast of Ingathering. It was a specially happy festival, loved by the children, when the people, once they were settled in Palestine, camped out in rough shelters made from branches. Some see this custom as stemming from the farmers' habit of living out in the fields while they harvested. Leviticus explains it as a reminder to the people that they lived in tents during their desert wandering.

Sacrifice

Sacrifice, especially when animals are involved, seems barbaric to many people today. But sacrifice was once practised worldwide as a means of bringing what can be seen and known in our world in touch with the spiritual world. In some religions, sacrifice is seen as a means of feeding and satisfying the gods. The Bible denies such a view but emphasizes the holiness — the absolute goodness — of God, which sets him apart from wrong and evil, and makes it necessary for some special way to be provided for sinful men and women to come close to him. Sacrifice was the appointed way.

Different offerings were prescribed for different occasions and situations, but in every case sacrifice recognized that the worshipper was unfit to approach God. A person's sin must be covered and atoned for if they are to come near to God. As time went by the need for forgiveness of sin became the main reason for sacrifice in Israel.

This was what happened:

The offerer approached the altar, which was in the open enclosure outside the tabernacle, bringing the specified animal. It had to be perfect, free from defects. He laid his hand on the animal's head, identifying himself with it. He then killed the animal himself, after which the priest put its blood on the horns and base of the altar. The body of the animal was burned on the altar. Sometimes part of the animal was cooked and shared in a meal.

There is no clear explanation of how sacrifice dealt with sin, but by identifying himself with the animal the offerer was clearly showing that because he had broken God's laws he deserved the fate the animal was to suffer. The animal died on his behalf. There were various types of sacrifice. In the 'fellowship offering', sharing and eating the cooked meat signified the sinner's renewed relationship with God and his fellow men and women.

The whole powerful ritual of sacrifice served as a strong visual aid, bringing home the individual's need to be put right with a holy God.

Ritual

Much of Leviticus and other parts of the Pentateuch are taken up with ritual. It is not possible to find explanations for the minute instructions that accompany the making of the tabernacle or the procedure in sacrifices. But it is important to give them due weight. Some social anthropologists hold the view that understanding a people's ritual is the key to knowing what makes them tick. It explains what their values are and what moves them most.

Every group within society has its own rituals, even though familiarity may make us unaware of our own. The Israelites' rituals were all intended to reinforce the holiness of the God they served — the fact that he was wholly good and untouched by sin. They reminded the people of the seriousness of

approaching God, of the need to obey God's laws and to observe the proper procedures in order to be holy too.

Leviticus 19 is a wonderful example of how Israel's holiness was to be lived out in everyday life. The laws cover many aspects of life, from honest scales to care for the underprivileged, as well as commands not to steal, lie or defraud. Love and reverence for God and for others lie behind all its teaching.

Leviticus also sets out God's provision for restoring his people and their inheritance, the land. Every seventh year was to be a 'Sabbath' year, when the land rested and lay fallow. Every fiftieth year was proclaimed a Jubilee year. Land was to be restored to its original owner and slaves set free.

Numbers

The book of Numbers lists the people of Israel in their clans — the title of the book comes from the census with which it begins. What may make dry and dusty reading to us was interesting and exciting to the people who were reading about their own ancestors. But the book of Numbers contains more than census figures. There are further laws mixed in with a recounting of some of Israel's experiences in their desert wanderings.

Kadesh-barnea

One key story tells how Moses sent twelve men — one from every tribe — to reconnoitre the land of Canaan from a place called Kadesh, before they prepared to enter it. The fruits they brought back were luscious but only two of the twelve spies believed that God could give them the land. The rest saw the inhabitants as giants who would easily repel them. The people sided with the ten, refusing to put their faith in God and his promise.

'That night all the people ... raised their voices and wept aloud.' (14:1)

In vain Caleb and Joshua, the two who trusted in God, entreated the people:

'If the Lord is pleased with us he will lead us into that land, a land flowing with milk and honey, and will give it to us ... The Lord is with us. Do not be afraid of them.' (14:8–9)

But the people would not listen to them, and because they failed to trust God the Israelites were condemned to wander in the desert for forty years — the time it took for that generation of unbelieving people to die out. Joshua and Caleb eventually led a new generation into the land.

Venomous snakes

Numbers says a great deal about the people's experiences in the desert and the lessons that God tried to teach them under Moses' guidance. On one occasion the Israelites had reverted to their frequent bouts of grumbling against Moses and God himself:

'Why did you bring us into this desert to die?'

In response, God allowed a plague of poisonous snakes to trouble them. The people came to Moses, full of remorse, asking him to pray to God to take the snakes away. In answer God told Moses to make a brass or

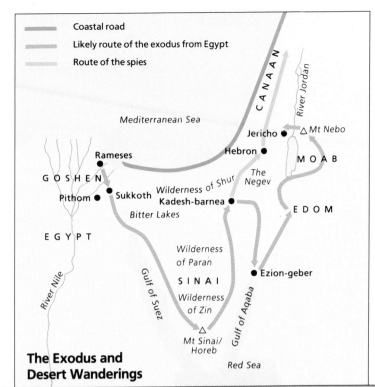

Coastal road
Likely route of the exodus from Egypt
Route of the spies

The Exodus and Desert Wanderings

Biography of Moses

Born in Egypt under Pharoah's death-threat; son of Amram, a Levite, and Jochebed   (Exodus 2, 6)

Hidden from Egyptian soldiers and put in a waterproof basket at the edge of the River Nile, he is found by Pharoah's daughter and brought up at court after initial care by his mother   (Exodus 2)

Championing his people, he kills an Egyptian foreman and is forced to flee the country   (Exodus 2)

In Midian he marries, and works as a shepherd for his father-in-law, Jethro, for 40 years   (Exodus 2–3)

Attracted by the bush burning in the desert, he is called by God to rescue his people   (Exodus 3)

Returns to Egypt; Pharaoh refuses to let the people go. Moses and Aaron announce a series of disasters—the Ten Plagues   (Exodus 7–12)

Death of the firstborn; the Passover; Moses leads the people out of Egypt   (Exodus 12–13)

The crossing of the Red Sea—and a song of triumph   (Exodus 13–15)

Receives God's Law for his people at Sinai and seals the covenant   (Exodus 20–24)

The golden calf. Moses breaks the tablets of the Law in anger, but later intercedes with God for the people   (Exodus 32)

Spies sent into Canaan from Kadesh; rebellion results in 40 years' desert wandering with Moses as leader, encouraging the people   (Numbers 13)

Water from the rock; Moses' anger   (Numbers 20)

Last great address to the people recalling them to the covenant; Moses hands over leadership to Joshua and views the Promised Land from Mount Pisgah   (Deuteronomy 34)

Death of Moses   (Deuteronomy 34)

Numbers describes Moses as 'a very humble man'. Perhaps this quality sums him up. He was brought up with all the advantages of a palace education. He was chosen by God to be his people's leader and, more than that, he enjoyed a close intimacy with God. Yet Moses never pushed himself forward or stood on his rights. Much of the time he bore the people's constant grumbling and disobedience with patience. It was usually when God's honour was at stake that he spoke strongly to them.

Not only did he lead the people out of slavery to the very boundaries of the Promised Land, but he also gave them the Law and ratified the covenant between them and God. He welded an unruly rabble into something like a unified people. He cared for their everyday needs—food and water—and dispensed justice for them. He also led them in military victories.

Deuteronomy sums up his greatness in these words:

'Since then, no prophet has risen in Israel like Moses, whom the Lord knew face to face, who did all those miraculous signs and wonders the Lord sent him to do in Egypt—to Pharaoh and to all his officials and to his whole land. For no-one has ever shown the mighty power or performed the awesome deeds that Moses did in the sight of all Israel.' (34:10–12)

When the people were bitten by poisonous snakes in the desert, many died—but God provided the means of healing. This is the venomous Fields horned viper.

copper snake and set it up high on a pole. Anyone who had been bitten could look at the brass snake and he would live. It was another simple visual aid to teach trust and obedience.

Food

When they were tired of their desert life, the Israelites would often talk longingly of the foods they used to enjoy in Egypt — fish, cucumbers, melons, leeks and garlic. There was no chance of finding these in the desert. Instead they had to satisfy their hunger with what they called 'miserable food'.

They were referring to the special food God provided for them throughout their desert wanderings. The writer in Exodus describes it as white, flake-like and sweet. It melted in the sun. The people called it *manna*, a word explained as meaning 'what is it?' since the people did not know what it was when they first saw it. It covered the ground every morning. It may in fact have been the Arabic *man*, a substance exuded by two types of insect living on tamarisk.

Prayers and blessings

Whenever the cloud of God's presence and the Ark of God came to rest, the Israelites pitched camp. This is the prayer that Moses would repeat:

*'Return, O Lord,
    to the countless thousands of Israel.'* (10:36)

When the cloud moved and the Ark set out again he would pray:

*'Rise up, O Lord!
    May your enemies be scattered;
    may your foes flee before you.'* (10:35)

Aaron and the priests pronounced this special blessing on the people:

*'The Lord bless you
    and keep you;
the Lord make his face shine upon you
    and be gracious to you;
the Lord turn his face towards you
    and give you peace.'* (6:24–26)

After the Israelites' years in the 'wilderness', the green and fruitful 'promised land' looked doubly inviting: a land 'flowing with milk and honey' in contrast to parched ground relieved only by the slender green thread of an occasional watercourse.

Deuteronomy

This book has been called the 'heartbeat of the Old Testament'. Its name means 'second law' because it describes the renewing of the covenant between God and Israel.

The book is in the form of a farewell discourse by Moses to the people of Israel as they reach the Promised Land at long last. Moses was not allowed to enter the land with them. He had once let his anger with the Israelites get the better of him and as a result, God said, he would see but not enter Canaan.

In Deuteronomy he reviews the past, reminding the people of all God's love and faithfulness through their years in the desert. He sets before them again the covenant promises — faithfully kept on God's side. They must be obedient for their part if they are to experience God's blessing in the new life that lies ahead.

The book ends with Moses' death, and the figure of Joshua, their new leader, emerging to lead them forward to the Promised Land.

Love and obedience

The theme of God's faithfulness runs through the book of Deuteronomy. Moses takes the Israelites back over their history of the past forty years, reminding them of God's constant care. Even the hardships that have come their way have been part of God's loving purpose:

'Remember the whole way by which the Lord your God has led you these forty years in the wilderness to humble and test you, and to discover whether or not it was in your heart to keep his commandments. So he afflicted you with hunger and then fed you on manna which neither you nor your fathers had known before, to teach you that people cannot live on bread alone, but that they live on every word that comes from the mouth of the Lord.' (8:2–3)

Date and Compiling of Deuteronomy

There are many different views as to when Deuteronomy was written, ranging from the time of Moses to after the exile (a difference of some 600 years). A number would agree that some of the content goes back to Moses himself but most believe that the book was written or compiled—or brought up to date in language—in the seventh century BC. Some think that it was compiled by Levites, others by scribes. But it may be the work of prophets from the northern kingdom of Israel, who had fled south to Judah after the fall of their capital, Samaria, and who wrote the book during the dark days of Manasseh's reign (see 2 Kings 21).

Many scholars believe that the compilers of Deuteronomy were also responsible for Joshua, Judges, and the books of Samuel and Kings. They recognize in all these books the same emphasis on God's covenant and the importance of obeying it. These compilers are known as 'Deuteronomists'.

The writers also emphasize how Israel should react to God's fatherly care. They should respond in loving obedience to him:

'Be careful to do what the Lord your God has commanded you; do not turn aside to the right or to the left. Walk in all the way that the Lord your God has commanded you, so that you may live and prosper and prolong your days in the land that you will possess.' (5:32–33)

Deuteronomy repeats the Law — the Decalogue and some of the laws that flow from it — then sums it all up in a single sentence:

'Hear, O Israel: the Lord our God is one Lord, and you shall love the Lord your God with all your heart, and with all your soul, and with all your might.' (6:4–5)

The Law is fulfilled by love.

3 HISTORY WITH A DIFFERENCE

Joshua · Judges · Ruth · Samuel · Kings · Chronicles

At first glance, the books of the Bible from Joshua to 2 Kings read very much like history books for the people of Israel. They recount the nation's experiences from the time they entered the Promised Land of Canaan until they were taken into exile to Babylon some 600 years later. But these books do more than recount events. In fact, in the Jewish arrangement of the Scriptures they are called, not history books but the books of the early prophets.

A prophet is one who speaks God's message, interpreting events from God's viewpoint and pronouncing his verdict. The writers of these books do just that. They are concerned not merely to detail the happenings of the years they chronicle but to explain the events as God sees them. They give God's perspective on human affairs. These books record history with a difference.

1 and 2 Chronicles are thought to have been written at a different time from the other books in this section, but they too use past events to point lessons for the readers of their own day. Written after the people's exile and return home, Chronicles was designed to encourage renewed faithfulness.

Joshua

There would never be another leader quite like Moses. He had led the people of Israel from slavery in Egypt to the very borders of the Promised Land of Canaan. But now Moses was dead: God would continue his saving work through a new leader. Joshua, who had been Moses' right-hand man, was God's choice to carry on where Moses left off. As Joshua faced the task God made him a special promise:

'As I was with Moses, so I will be with you; I will not fail you or forsake you. Be strong and of good courage; for you shall cause this people to inherit the land which I swore to their fathers to give them. Only be strong and very courageous, being careful to do according to all the law which Moses my servant commanded you.' (1:5–7)

These were strong words of encouragement — and Joshua needed them. Canaan, the land promised by God to Abraham's descendants, was not lying empty and waiting for the people of Israel. It was occupied by a collection of different tribes settled into city-states, built thick on the plains and along the route from Egypt to Syria and Mesopotamia (the land between the Tigris and the Euphrates rivers). At one time these city-states had been under Egyptian rule. Many of them were only about five kilometres apart but each had its own stronghold and ruler to support and protect its population. If the Israelites were to inhabit the land they must fight for their territory and displace people already there.

The first obstacle Joshua faced was the immensely strong border city of Jericho — one of the oldest cities in the world. He sent two men to reconnoitre while the Israelites were still on the far side of the River Jordan, Canaan's boundary.

The two spies must have been heartened when Rahab, the prostitute innkeeper of Jericho, hid them from the king's soldiers, assuring them that she had heard and believed the exploits of Israel's God on his people's behalf. News of Israel's successful battles had travelled ahead of them.

Crossing the Jordan

For three days the people camped before the seemingly impassable River Jordan. It was the final barrier to the Promised Land and stretched wide and deep in the spring flood, cutting them off from their goal. Then Joshua sent a message around the camp, telling everyone to be ready for God to act. The priests were to set out, carrying the Covenant Box, and the people were to follow — at a respectful distance.

As the priests with their precious burden waded into the river, its flow was arrested and the waters piled up further upstream. The people crossed on dry land, as their parents had crossed the Red Sea at the very beginning of the journey.

Joshua brought home to the people the lesson that this miracle taught. The God who could act in such power would certainly help them overcome the inhabitants of the land. The miracle of the crossing of the Jordan would be a guarantee of his help still to come:

'This is how you will know that the living God is among you and that he will certainly drive out before you the Canaanites.' (3:10)

Joshua ordered them to take twelve stones from the river to make a cairn to remind future generations of God's great act on their behalf.

their ram's-horn trumpets the soldiers were to shout with all their might.

Joshua put these extraordinary commands into action. On the seventh day, after the seventh circuit of the city, the soldiers shouted aloud and the city walls collapsed. The soldiers were able to walk straight in and capture the town and its people. Joshua and the people understood as never before that their victories in Canaan were God's concern and did not depend on their strength or skills alone.

Jericho, the 'city of palms', looked inviting to Joshua and his army. But the defences of this ancient city were formidable.

The commander of the Lord's army

Near Jericho, an armed man approached Joshua, who challenged him — friend or foe?

The newcomer replied:

'As commander of the army of the Lord I have now come.' (5:14)

Joshua fell down and worshipped. God was surely in control.

The fall of Jericho

Jericho was not to be conquered by siege or attack. Instead, a strange ritual was to be carried out. For six successive days, God told Joshua, his soldiers were to march around the embattled city. The advance guard would go first, with seven priests blowing their trumpets. Next would come the Covenant Box — or Ark — carried by priests, then the rearguard. The soldiers were not to speak or shout. On the seventh day the procession was to march seven times round the city. When the priests sounded one long note on

The people of Canaan

We naturally shrink from the bloody conquests that were carried out in the name of God. The writers of the Old Testament books saw these battles as God's judgment on the wickedness of the inhabitants of the land. Abraham had been told by God that his descendants would have to wait 400 years in Egypt before entering Canaan until 'the Amorites become so wicked that they must be punished'. Joshua's campaigns were seen as acts of cleansing and justice rather than of aggression and land-grabbing.

The religion of the land was certainly decadent. The Canaanite tribes had different gods, each of whom was thought to control their own land. The general name for a god was *baal*, which can be translated as lord, master or husband. Sometimes the baal would be represented by a bull or a snake image. The land was the baal's wife, and the people of the land his slaves.

Every village would have its shrine, on top of a hill or under a large tree, marked by an

The trumpet blast of the shofar heralded Jericho's fall.

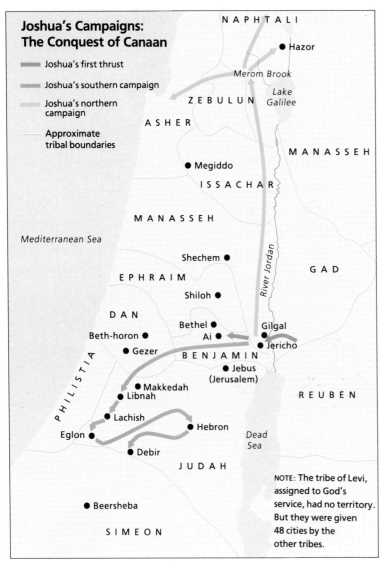

Joshua's Campaigns: The Conquest of Canaan

- ▬ Joshua's first thrust
- ▬ Joshua's southern campaign
- ▬ Joshua's northern campaign
- ▬ Approximate tribal boundaries

NAPHTALI
● Hazor
Merom Brook
ZEBULUN
Lake Galilee
ASHER
MANASSEH
● Megiddo
ISSACHAR
MANASSEH
Mediterranean Sea
Shechem ●
EPHRAIM
GAD
Shiloh ●
DAN
Bethel ● Gilgal
Beth-horon ● Ai ● ● Jericho
● Gezer BENJAMIN
● Jebus (Jerusalem)
● Makkedah
● Libnah
● Lachish REUBEN
PHILISTIA
Eglon ● ● Hebron
● Debir Dead Sea
JUDAH
River Jordan

NOTE: The tribe of Levi, assigned to God's service, had no territory. But they were given 48 cities by the other tribes.

● Beersheba
SIMEON

name, they used the baal shrines and adopted the rituals of baal worship, indulging in the same kind of immoral and cruel rites as their Canaanite neighbours.

Sharing out the land

Joshua embarked upon a campaign of battles, gaining victory over a number of city-states. Once the people of Israel had gained this foothold it was Joshua's task to apportion the territory among the tribes. Each tribe was then encouraged to kill or drive out the inhabitants of their section of land and to settle down there.

There are different views as to how this happened but the Israelites certainly did not annihilate the Canaanites all at once. They seem to have aimed first for the central hill areas rather than the fertile plains. But the real struggles came later than Joshua's time, when there were other contenders for the land — the Philistines, Ammonites and Moabites as well as the Canaanites themselves.

Joshua appointed special cities for the Levites throughout the land, as they were not granted any territory of their own. Their task was to help the priests in their service, paid for by the tithes that ordinary Israelites were bound by law to contribute.

Joshua the leader

Joshua had a long and eventful life. He had been Moses' right-hand man for many years before taking over the leadership of Israel. Towards the end of his life he made an impassioned plea to the people to remain faithful to God and to keep his laws:

'Now fear the Lord and serve him with all faithfulness... But if serving the Lord seems undesirable to you, then choose for yourselves this day whom you will serve... But as for me and my household, we will serve the Lord.' (24:14–15)

The people earnestly promised to serve God and be faithful to him and Joshua renewed the covenant promises between Israel and God.

upright stone or wooden post. Festivals were linked to sowing and harvest, and to new moons. Crops were offered to the gods, and animals were sacrificed. Baals were fertility gods, so worship involved ritual sex at the shrine. Drunkenness was common, especially at harvest festivals. Child sacrifice sometimes took place.

As the people of Israel settled in the land they began to feel — consciously or unconsciously — that it would be wiser and safer to incorporate the baal worship into their own. After all, these gods knew all about making crops grow — something that God had not done during their desert wandering. In time, although they worshipped in God's

The people known as the Canaanites had settled the land at the eastern end of the Mediterranean Sea by about 2000BC. By Joshua's time (about 1300BC) the land was divided up into small city-states, each with its own king. The cities were tiny by modern standards, but strongly walled and fortified.

The Canaanites were great traders, plying the Mediterranean Sea in their merchant ships—from Egypt to Crete and Greece. Tyre, Sidon, Berytus (Beirut) and Byblos were their main ports. Byblos—because of the trade in papyrus (the ancient form of paper)—gave the book its name: *biblia* (from which the word Bible also comes). Canaanites were also the first to develop an alphabet.

The fame of their craftsmen was widely known. Long after the Israelites had conquered Canaan, when they wanted the finest craftsmen to work on the temple, it was to Canaanite masons and carpenters that they turned.

A small jug for perfume.

Although there is much to admire about the Canaanites, their religion was brutal and debased. This figure is of a Canaanite 'Baal'—god of weather, fertility and war.

A Canaanite house from the period 2000 to 1550BC. The furniture, wooden vessels and baskets are reconstructed from Jericho; pottery is original Canaanite ware.

Judges

The title of the book of Judges conjures up the law and law courts. But the judges that we read about were not legal judges. They were exciting, charismatic figures who appeared in times of crisis and delivered the people from their enemies. Some of them also dispensed legal justice. Many fought battles as well as organizing the tribes to stand together and remain loyal to God. They were called judges because they were 'doing justice' — that is, putting right what was wrong, sometimes by battle.

The book of Judges follows a repeated pattern. The writers explain how Israel prospered all the time that the people were faithful to God. But when they deserted him for other gods, they were no longer able to resist their enemies and came under their domination. Then, in distress, they called out to God for help and he provided a judge, or deliverer, to meet the situation:

'Whenever the Lord gave Israel a leader, the Lord would help him and would save the people from their enemies as long as that leader lived ... But when that leader died, the people used to return to the old ways and behave worse than the previous generation.' (2:18,19)

The Israelite army, led by Deborah and Barak, assembled on the high ground of Mt Tabor, poised to attack Sisera and his Canaanites who were confined by their chariots to the plain.

Contenders for the land

Constant raids and pitched battles remind us that the time of the judges was a period of struggle to possess the land. Other groups wanted to expand their territory too. Different judges repulsed different enemies and usually only one or two tribes, not the whole of Israel, took part in the fray.

● A left-handed leader called Ehud led a battle against the Moabites.

● A woman judge — Deborah — with Barak, a soldier, fought against the Canaanites.

● Gideon attacked the Midianites.

● Jephthah attacked the Ammonites.

By the time of the judge called Samson, the Philistines were the enemy and continued to be for some long time to come.

Deborah and Barak

Deborah was a prophet and a judge who dispensed justice and wisdom from her regular place under a palm-tree between Ramah and Bethel. She gave a man named Barak a message from God that he was to fight against Sisera, a Canaanite army commander, who had superior power and all the military advantage of iron chariots. These Canaanites had been cruelly oppressing Israel for twenty years and the people had cried to God for help. Deborah promised Barak victory in God's name, but he was too frightened to go without her.

The order to attack came, and the armies of Sisera were thrown into confusion, seemingly by torrential rain and flooding which bogged down the chariots. Sisera made his escape on foot and suffered the ignominy of being killed by a woman while he slept in her tent. So Barak got no credit for the victory.

Gideon's story

For seven long years the Midianites, Bedouin tribesmen from the Arabian desert, made life unbearable for Israel. Hordes of them, riding camels, made forays into Israel, laid bare their crops and rustled cattle, sheep and

Reassured, Gideon mustered an army to meet the encamped Midianites but God told him that he had too many men. All who were afraid were told to go home but still God said there were too many. He told Gideon to take his men to the water to drink. Some got down on their knees to drink while others scooped the water into their hands and lapped it up. Those who lapped, God said, were to be Gideon's army — a bare three hundred men.

That night Gideon told his men: 'Get up! The Lord has given the Midianite camp into your hands.'

Each man was issued with a trumpet and an empty jar to conceal the flaming torch inside it. Then came Gideon's orders.

'Watch me,' he told them. 'Follow my lead. When I get to the edge of the camp, do exactly as I do.' (7:17)

They arrived at the camp just as the guard was being changed, which was causing temporary movement and unrest. At Gideon's lead, all three hundred blew their trumpets, shouting at the tops of their voices:

'A sword for the Lord and for Gideon!' (7:20)

Then they smashed their jars. Light from the torches blazed out, terrorizing the awakened sleepers. The battlecry of the trumpets and the brilliance of the torches put the Midianites into complete panic. They lashed out, often killing their own people, then fled into the darkness beyond the camp.

Gideon called for reinforcements to cut off their retreat at the fords over the River Jordan. Victory was complete.

Samson

Samson is probably the most famous of the judges. Before his birth his mother was told not to drink wine or beer or to eat any forbidden food because the boy was to be dedicated to God as a Nazirite. This Nazirite vow, usually taken by an adult (sometimes just for a short period), involved abstaining from alcohol and letting the hair grow long. It told everyone that this person was set apart in a special way for God's service. Samson was consecrated in this manner from birth.

donkeys. The Israelites were left with nothing to live on. So they cried out to God in their distress.

In answer, God sent his angel to a young man called Gideon, as he was threshing wheat in the hidden hollow of a winepress, safe from the eyes of marauding Midianites. He spoke to the timid young farmer:

'The Lord is with you, brave and mighty man!' (6:12)

He commissioned Gideon to rescue Israel from Midianite oppression, promising:

'I will be with you.' (6:16)

Gideon began by destroying his father's baal altar, and building instead an altar to God. Then he mustered an army to follow him. But still he had fears. Had God really called him, and would he give him victory? So he prayed:

'If you will save Israel by my hand as you have promised — look, I will place a wool fleece on the threshing-floor. If there is dew only on the fleece and all the ground is dry, then I will know that you will save Israel by my hand, as you said.' (6:36–37)

It happened as Gideon had asked, but still his doubts lingered. He prayed that God would repeat the miracle the other way round — that the fleece would be dry and the ground wet. Again God gave him his sign.

THE PHILISTINES

The Philistines were a sea people who came from Crete and settled in Canaan along the coastal strip in the thirteenth and twelfth centuries BC. They set up five city-states close to the coast: Gaza, Ashkelon, Ashdod, Ekron and Gath. They gave their name—Palestine—to the whole country. We do not know what gods they worshipped when they arrived in Canaan but they later adopted the Canaanite deities of Dagon, Ashtoreth and Beelzebub. They introduced iron into the area, and for some time had a monopoly over iron tools and weapons. This gave them a great advantage in war, since iron is much stronger than bronze or copper.

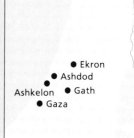

The land of the Philistines consisted of five coastal city-states.

This reconstruction of a Philistine house is on the site of the sea-port of Tell Qasile. The roof is made of mud over palm leaves and branches, supported by logs. There are two rooms plus an open area, roofed. The central courtyard has grinding stones and a wine and oil press.

Philistine pottery has its own distinctive decorative style.

This cast from Thebes (twelfth century BC) shows the head (and feathered headdress) of a Philistine soldier.

The Philistines swept down the east Mediterranean coast in warships like this one, terrorizing the people already settled there.

The Philistines (see feature), another immigrant people who lived along the coastal strip of Canaan, were the enemies that Samson was called to counter.

Samson was endowed with enormous physical strength. He killed a young lion with his bare hands and on another occasion he uprooted the city gates, doors, posts, lock and all. Yet his story is one of waywardness and missed opportunities. He married a Philistine girl, to his parents' chagrin, and revenged himself on her people's trickery by tying foxes — or jackals — together by their tails, setting fire to them, and letting them loose in standing corn and olive orchards.

Women were Samson's undoing. It was the beautiful Delilah, in the pay of Philistine spies, who at last wormed out of him the secret of his great strength:

'I have been a Nazirite set apart to God since birth. If my head were shaved, my strength would leave me, and I would become as weak as any other man.' (16:17)

As he slept with his head on her lap, Delilah called a man to shave off his hair. She woke Samson with the shout:

'The Philistines are upon you!' (16:20)

But his strength had gone with his broken vow, and the Philistines took him prisoner. His eyes were gouged out and he was put to grind corn in the treadmill of a Philistine prison.

At a feast to their god, Dagon, the Philistine rulers sent for Samson to provide entertainment. They mocked his weakness and blindness. But Samson's hair was beginning to grow again — and he felt the stirrings of his old strength and loyalty to God. He asked the boy who led him to guide his hands to the main pillars of the great hall. He prayed for God once more to give him strength, and he pulled on the pillars with all his might, bringing them crashing down. The building collapsed, killing the merrymakers and Samson with them.

'So the dead whom he killed at his death were more than those he had killed in his life.' (16:30)

Ruth

The book of Ruth tells the story of a family living in the time of the Judges. It includes many customs belonging to that period, though it may have been written much later. It is a story of much beauty and feeling. It recounts the plight of a widow and the love and loyalty of her daughter-in-law — born a stranger to the God of Israel — and of his loving care for them both.

Famine struck the town of Bethlehem, so the family of Elimelech left the land of Israel and went to live in the nearby country of Moab. But tragedy dogged them still, for not only did Elimelech die but some ten years later his two sons died too. Both young men had married Moabite wives. Naomi — widow and mother — longed for home and when she had news that there was once more food in Bethlehem she prepared for the journey back. Both her daughters-in-law offered to go with her. When she tried to dissuade them, one, Ruth, insisted:

'Entreat me not to leave you or to return from following you; for where you go I will go, and where you lodge I will lodge; your people shall be my people, and your God my God; where you die I will die, and there will I be buried. May the Lord do so to me and more also if even death parts me from you.' (1:16–17)

So Naomi and Ruth settled back in Bethlehem. Ruth provided food for them both by gleaning the remnants of corn from the fields at harvest time, as poor people were allowed by law to do. Unknowingly she chose a field belonging to Boaz, a relative of Naomi's husband. Naomi was certain that God's hand was in this seeming coincidence and she instructed Ruth how to act.

When harvest ended Ruth asked Boaz to fulfil the duty of a near relative, as laid down in law, and to buy back a field that had once belonged to Elimelech. His duty as a kinsman also meant that he should marry Ruth and this he gladly did. Their child brought comfort to the ageing Naomi.

The writer boldly lists the direct descendants of Ruth and Boaz, showing that they included the great King David himself. Ruth, who might have been despised as a foreigner, was his ancestor.

Some think that the story was written to highlight God's care for the non-Israelite as well as for his own people, and perhaps to redress the balance at a time when there was undue emphasis on racial purity.

1 and 2 Samuel

The two books of Samuel were originally one. They deal with another transition period in Israel's history, when the nation moved from rule by a judge, or charismatic leader, to the rule of a king. They are concerned with different patterns of leadership. They describe the days of the last two judges — Eli and Samuel — and the first two kings — Saul and David — thus making a link with Judges and with 1 and 2 Kings that follow.

The first book of Samuel, like Ruth, begins with the story of a family. Elkanah and his two wives were making their annual journey to the shrine at Shiloh to worship God. One wife, Penninah, had children, but the other, Hannah, had none. Hannah felt desperate about her childlessness, and when they were at the shrine she prayed to God:

'O Lord Almighty, if you will only look upon your servant's misery and remember me, and not forget your servant but give her a son, then I will give him to the Lord for all the days of his life.' (1 Samuel 1:11)

When her prayer was answered and Samuel was born, she was true to her word. She dedicated him to God and placed him in the care of Eli, priest at the shrine, when he was still a young child. Her prayer of thanksgiving to God was fervent and joyful:

'There is no-one holy like the Lord;
*   there is no-one besides you;*
*   there is no Rock like our God...*
The Lord sends poverty and wealth;
*   he humbles and he exalts.*
He raises the poor from the dust
*   and lifts the needy from the ash heap;*
he seats them with princes.' (1 Samuel 2:2, 7, 8)

As a boy, Samuel slept in the shrine where the Covenant Box was placed. One night he heard his name called — 'Samuel!' He hurried to where the old priest Eli lay, but Eli had not called him. Twice more the voice called

Samuel and twice more he ran to Eli. Then the old priest realized that God was speaking to the lad. He told him to go back to bed and when the call came again, to answer: 'Speak, Lord, for your servant is listening.'

Samuel did as he was told and God called again. He gave Samuel a message of doom for Eli's good-for-nothing sons.

After forty years of Eli's leadership Samuel succeeded him. He served the people well as a wise and upright leader, as priest at the shrine and also as a prophet and dispenser of justice.

The call for a king

Samuel grew old. His own sons were appointed judges, but they did him no credit. So the people of Israel asked Samuel to give them a king. By so doing they not only rejected him, they also rejected God. They were exchanging the rule of God, who had been king of his people, for that of an earthly ruler.

Samuel warned them about the kind of oppression they would suffer once power was centralized. Their kings would become petty dictators, exacting taxes and goods from them and making life hard. But the people persisted with their request and God instructed Samuel to do as they wanted. Samuel intended Israel's king to be God's regent — not above God's laws, but himself subject to God. As well as ruling justly and well he should encourage the people to keep their covenant with God and worship only him. He was not to be an autocratic despot, like the kings of the nations around.

Samuel was told to anoint a young man named Saul as the first king. He stood head and shoulders above the other men and looked every inch a leader. He began as a local military hero, then was proclaimed king of all Israel. But after a promising start Saul chose to go his own way and disobeyed God. At length Samuel told him: 'You have rejected the word of the Lord, and the Lord has rejected you as king over Israel.'

But Samuel still felt warmly towards Saul and was less than enthusiastic when God told him to go and appoint Saul's eventual successor.

David anointed

David, the youngest of eight sons, was looking after sheep when Samuel visited his family to choose one son as future king. David was hurriedly summoned when the seven others were rejected by Samuel. At God's prompting David's head was anointed with oil as a sign that he was appointed as the next king. This ceremony was discreetly kept private.

David and Goliath

After David had been anointed as future king of Israel, he continued to look after his father's sheep. But he was summoned to court to play the harp to relieve King Saul's violent attacks of depression, described as 'an evil spirit from the Lord'. At some stage he made the journey from his father's farm to the front lines of battle, where his three brothers were in King Saul's army.

The Philistine enemy was camped on one hill and the Israelites on the other, with a valley between. Goliath was the champion put forward by the Philistines to settle the battle against Israel in single combat. He strode out each day to issue his challenge, and the forces of Saul quailed at the sight of him.

When David arrived and heard the challenge he volunteered to confront Goliath, refusing the offer of the king's armour and choosing his shepherd's catapult and five smooth stones from the stream. Thus armed he went out, a slight figure against the might of the Philistine.

Goliath was incredulous:

'Come here,' he said, 'and I'll give your flesh to the birds of the air and the beasts of the field!'
(1 Samuel 17:44)

Biography of David

While still a shepherd boy, David is anointed king of Israel by the prophet Samuel   (1 Samuel 16)

Taken into the king's service, he plays the harp for Saul   (1 Samuel 16)

David kills the Philistine champion, Goliath (1 Samuel 17)

A deep friendship develops between David and King Saul's son Jonathan   (1 Samuel 18)

Saul grows jealous—David flees, his life in danger (1 Samuel 18–21)

David, outlawed and in hiding, eludes the king and twice spares Saul's life   (1 Samuel 22–24, 26)

David is crowned king, at the age of 30 (2 Samuel 5)

The Covenant Box is brought to the new capital city of Jerusalem   (2 Samuel 6)

David dreams of building a temple for God, who forbids it, but promises David a succession 'for ever' (2 Samuel 7)

David's military victories extend the frontiers of his kingdom   (2 Samuel 5, 8, 10)

David commits adultery with Bathsheba and murders her husband Uriah; the prophet Nathan is sent by God to David and rebukes him. David and Bathsheba's son dies, but a second son, Solomon, is born   (2 Samuel 11, 12)

Family troubles. Absalom, David's son, leads a rebellion and David flees him   (2 Samuel 15, 16)

Absalom is killed; David's sorrow. The king returns to Jerusalem   (2 Samuel 18, 19)

David names Solomon as the next king and gives him his last instructions. After a 40-year rule, he dies, leaving a strong and stable kingdom (1 Kings 1, 2)

A shepherd in the Judean hills watches over his flock as David did in the years of preparation for kingship. Here he learned to love God as the caring shepherd of his people.

David's answer held the secret to his success:

'You are coming against me with sword, spear and javelin, but I come against you in the name of the Lord Almighty, the God of the Israelite armies, which you have defied.' (1 Samuel 17:45)

Then he put a stone in his sling and hurled it at Goliath's forehead. Goliath fell to the ground, stunned, and David ran over, took the huge man's own sword and struck off his head. The terrifed Philistine troops fled in disorder, pursued by the Israelite army.

David and Jonathan

After the slaying of Goliath David took up residence at Saul's court and became a successful officer in his army. A deep friendship sprang up between David and Jonathan, Saul's son. They trusted each other wholly and were deeply loyal to one another.

Saul soon grew furiously jealous of David and his prowess in battle. Jonathan tried to shield him from his father's anger, finally warning David that he must leave court and go into hiding or Saul would murder him.

From then on David led a cat-and-mouse existence, often eluding Saul only by the skin of his teeth. Yet when he had Saul in his power, on two occasions, David refused to kill him because he was God's anointed king.

Saul and Jonathan were tragically killed in battle against the Philistines and David mourned them deeply. He wrote a lament:

'Saul and Jonathan —
in life they were loved and gracious,
and in death they were not parted.
They were swifter than eagles,
they were stronger than lions.

I grieve for you, Jonathan my brother;
you were very dear to me.
Your love for me was wonderful,
more wonderful than that of women.

How the mighty have fallen!
The weapons of war have perished!'
(2 Samuel 1:23–27)

David the king

After a power struggle with another son of Saul, David became king over the whole kingdom of Israel.

David represented the model of what an Israelite king should be, in spite of his failures. He is described as a man 'after God's own heart'. His rule was later looked upon as the golden age of Israel.

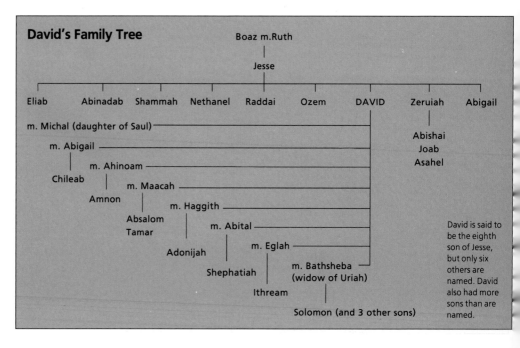

David's Family Tree

Boaz m.Ruth
Jesse

Eliab　Abinadab　Shammah　Nethanel　Raddai　Ozem　DAVID　Zeruiah　Abigail

m. Michal (daughter of Saul)
　　m. Abigail
Chileab　　m. Ahinoam
　　Amnon
　　　　m. Maacah
　　Absalom
　　Tamar
　　　　　m. Haggith
　　　　Adonijah
　　　　　　m. Abital
　　　　Shephatiah
　　　　　　　m. Eglah
　　　　　Ithream
　　　　　　　m. Bathsheba
　　　　　　　(widow of Uriah)
　　　　Solomon (and 3 other sons)

Abishai
Joab
Asahel

David is said to be the eighth son of Jesse, but only six others are named. David also had more sons than are named.

David's failures

One spring day David looked out of his palace window and saw a beautiful woman bathing. She was Bathsheba, wife of one of his loyal army officers, who at that very time was away fighting for David. The king gave orders for Bathsheba to be brought to the palace. Soon after, Bathsheba sent him word that she was pregnant.

David sent for her husband, talked with him of army matters, then suggested that he should go home to his wife. But Uriah did not swallow the bait. He steadfastly refused to enjoy the comforts of home while his fellow soldiers were at battle.

In desperation, David plotted Uriah's death. He sent a note to his army commander, by Uriah's hand, ordering him to put Uriah in the front line. The order was obeyed and Uriah died in battle. David then married Bathsheba.

God sent the prophet Nathan to David to tell him that he had broken God's laws. Nathan made his point through a story.

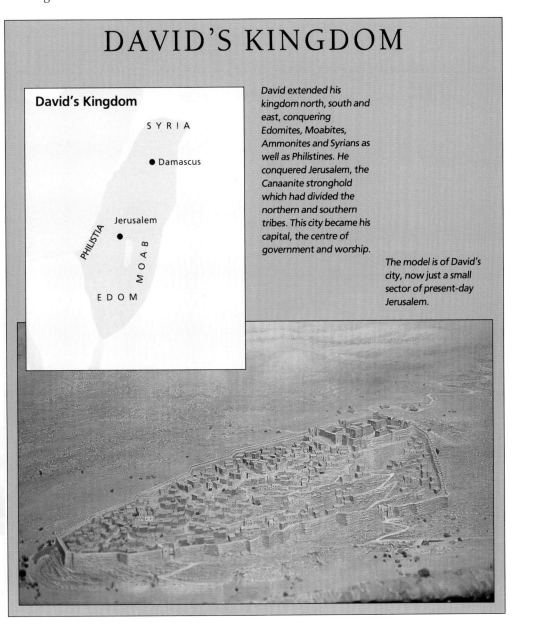

DAVID'S KINGDOM

David's Kingdom

SYRIA

● Damascus

PHILISTIA

Jerusalem ●

MOAB

EDOM

David extended his kingdom north, south and east, conquering Edomites, Moabites, Ammonites and Syrians as well as Philistines. He conquered Jerusalem, the Canaanite stronghold which had divided the northern and southern tribes. This city became his capital, the centre of government and worship.

The model is of David's city, now just a small sector of present-day Jerusalem.

'Two men lived in a town — one very rich and the other poor. The rich man had flocks in abundance but the poor man had one ewe lamb which he and his family loved and kept as a pet. When the rich man was entertaining a traveller he ordered the poor man's lamb to be taken and killed for the meal.'

When David heard the story he burned with anger and declared that the rich man deserved to die for his inhumanity.

Then Nathan said to the king: 'You are the man!'

David was humble enough to accept the rebuke, to recognize his guilt and to confess his sin to God. He was forgiven, but Bath-sheba's child died. Another son, Solomon, was born to them and when David was old and dying he chose this son to be king after him.

God's covenant with David

David's great dream was to build a wonderful temple for God, fit to contain the Covenant Box. At first the prophet Nathan went along with his plans but later he brought word from God that David was not to build a house for God. But God would build the 'house' of David: he promised to establish David's family line.

'Your house and your kingdom shall endure for ever before me; your throne shall be established for ever.' (2 Samuel 7:16)

This is an important chapter as the basis for the Messianic strand of promises. The coming king, whose kingdom would never end, was to be a descendent of David.

David was full of praise and thanksgiving to God for his covenant promise. And he contented himself with preparing materials for the temple that, in time, his own son Solomon would build.

1 and 2 Kings

As the title suggests, the two books of 1 and 2 Kings, that were originally one, tell the story of the kings of Israel. They record the rise, decline and fall of the Hebrew monarchy. These events are not presented as dull facts and figures but in vivid, living stories of men and women.

The voice of the writer comes through clearly, giving God's verdict on each successive ruler. The comment is, 'He did what was right in the eyes of the Lord,' or, sadly, more often, 'He did what was evil in the sight of the Lord.' Prosperity or calamity followed.

Sometimes prophets appeared. They spoke for God, telling king and people what God's verdict was. They were particularly outspoken in their defence of the underdog and emphasized the need for justice and righteousness. If Israel was to maintain the covenant relationship with God, king and people must obey God and show kindness and mercy to fellow members of the covenant. The prophets were prepared to tell the king to his face when he was usurping the rule of God or corrupting justice.

Solomon's wisdom

Soon after he had been crowned king in place of his father, David, Solomon went to God's shrine at Gibeon to offer sacrifices. While he was there God spoke to him in a dream: 'Ask for whatever you want me to give you.'

Solomon prayed:

'O Lord my God, you have made your servant king in place of my father David. But I am only a little child and do not know how to carry out my duties ... So give your servant a discerning heart to govern your people and to distinguish between right and wrong.' (1 Kings 3:7–9)

God was pleased that Solomon had asked for wisdom and promised to give it to him, and to add the things that Solomon had not asked for — riches and honour.

Solomon became famous in many lands for his wisdom. One story is told of two prostitutes who came to him for judgment. Both had a baby but one child had died and now each was claiming the living child as her own. Solomon gave the order that the child should be cut in half and one half given to each woman. At once the true mother protested. She would give the child to the other woman, if only his life could be spared. Solomon had arrived at the truth by his wise counsel.

SOLOMON'S TEMPLE

Solomon's temple was built according to Phoenician design. It was noted not for its size but for its beauty. The expensive cedar panelling which lined the stone building was covered with gold. The inside of the building was 27 metres long and 9 metres wide. There were two main rooms. The inner one—the Most Holy Place or Holy of Holies—was a cube, measuring 9 metres in length, width and height. It contained the Covenant Box, in which were Moses' tablets of the Law. Two cherubim spread their wings to meet over the top of it. These carved figures were made from olive wood covered with gold leaf.

In the outer room was a gold-covered altar on which the priests burned incense. The altar for animal sacrifices stood in the courtyard outside.

Solomon builds the temple

Solomon began to build the temple after four years as king. He renewed the friendship David had had with Hiram, King of Tyre. Hiram could supply him with skilled craftsmen and with cedar wood from the mountains of Lebanon. Tree-trunks were floated down the coast from Tyre, then dragged overland to Jerusalem. The temple was probably built entirely of stone, lined with cedar. No sound of hammer or other tool was heard at the sacred site. Stone was brought ready dressed from the quarry beneath the city.

The completed temple was not large. It closely followed the pattern of the tabernacle, with two inner rooms and extensive outer courts. But it was superbly decorated and took seven years to complete.

At the dedication of the temple Solomon acknowledged that no building, however splendid, could house almighty God:

'But will God really dwell on earth? The heavens, even the highest heaven, cannot contain you. How much less this temple I have built!' (1 Kings 8:27)

When Solomon had finished praying, the writers tell us that the glory of the Lord filled the temple.

Solomon's reign

Solomon's reign was outwardly one of huge prosperity. He did not fight to extend his boundaries, as David had done, but safeguarded his empire by trade and marriages that were politically useful. He built splendid palaces for himself and his wives, and the crowning splendour of the

KINGS AND PROPHETS

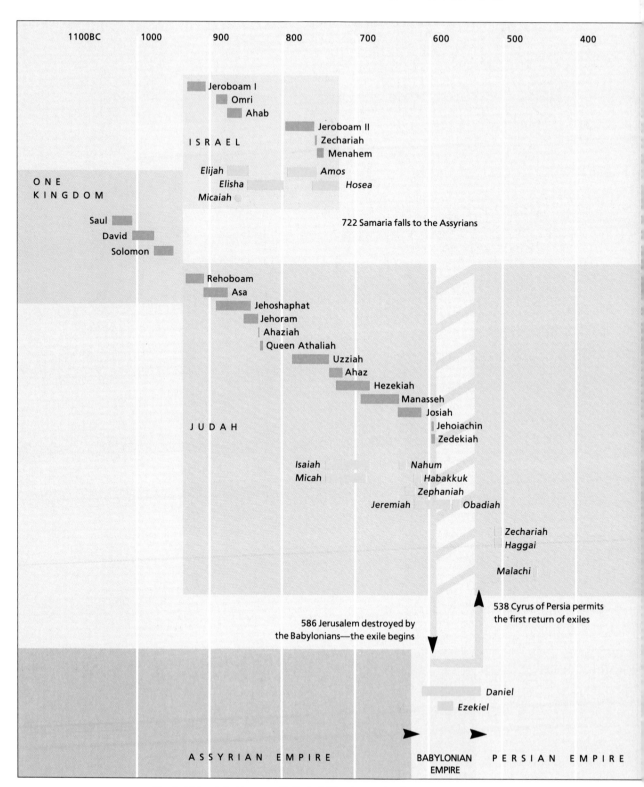

1100BC   1000   900   800   700   600   500   400

Jeroboam I
Omri
Ahab

Jeroboam II
Zechariah
Menahem

I S R A E L

Elijah   Amos
Elisha   Hosea
Micaiah

O N E
K I N G D O M

Saul
David
Solomon

722 Samaria falls to the Assyrians

Rehoboam
Asa
Jehoshaphat
Jehoram
Ahaziah
Queen Athaliah
Uzziah
Ahaz
Hezekiah
Manasseh
Josiah
Jehoiachin
Zedekiah

J U D A H

Nahum
Isaiah   Habakkuk
Micah   Zephaniah
Jeremiah   Obadiah

Zechariah
Haggai

Malachi

538 Cyrus of Persia permits
the first return of exiles

586 Jerusalem destroyed by
the Babylonians—the exile begins

Daniel
Ezekiel

A S S Y R I A N   E M P I R E   BABYLONIAN   P E R S I A N   E M P I R E
EMPIRE

The chart lists only the kings named in the text: it is not a complete list
Some reigns overlap because of co-regencies
We have no date for the prophet Joel

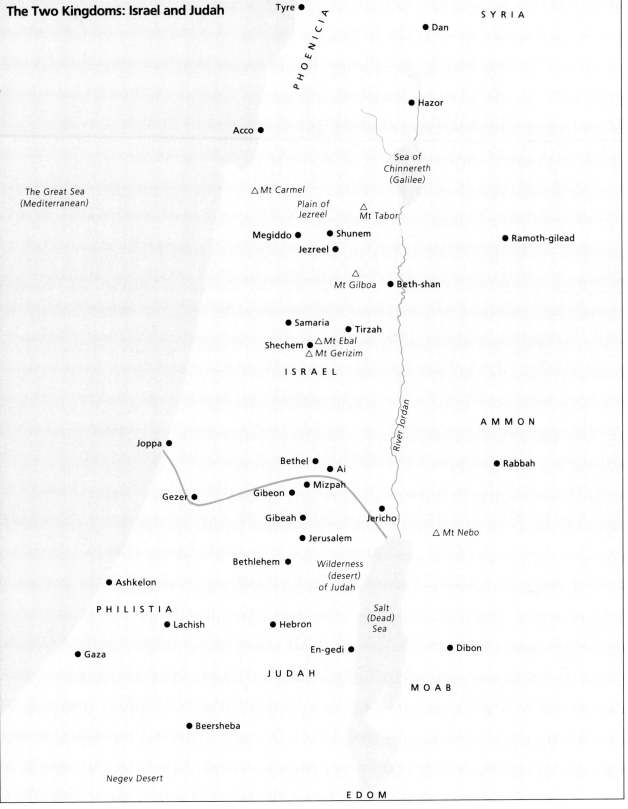

The Two Kingdoms: Israel and Judah

● Tyre

S Y R I A

● Dan

P H O E N I C I A

● Hazor

Acco ●

*Sea of
Chinnereth
(Galilee)*

*The Great Sea
(Mediterranean)*

△ Mt Carmel

*Plain of
Jezreel*

△
Mt Tabor

Megiddo ●　● Shunem

Jezreel ●

● Ramoth-gilead

△
Mt Gilboa　● Beth-shan

● Samaria

● Tirzah

Shechem ● △ Mt Ebal
△ Mt Gerizim

I S R A E L

River Jordan

A M M O N

Joppa ●

Bethel ●
● Ai

● Mizpah

Gibeon ●

Gezer ●

● Rabbah

Gibeah ●

Jericho ●

● Jerusalem

△ Mt Nebo

Bethlehem ●

*Wilderness
(desert)
of Judah*

● Ashkelon

P H I L I S T I A

● Lachish

● Hebron

*Salt
(Dead)
Sea*

● Gaza

En-gedi ●

● Dibon

J U D A H

M O A B

● Beersheba

Negev Desert

E D O M

temple. He built a fleet of trading ships at Ezion-geber, at the tip of the Gulf of Aqabah. Near here, too, were his copper mines and his smelting industry. He also bred and exported horses.

Solomon divided up the country into administrative districts — each with a governor — for taxation. He also used forced labour for his vast building projects.

There are brilliant and flamboyant descriptions in Kings and Chronicles of his fabulous wealth. Silver was thought nothing of in a kingdom where gold was so plentiful. Solomon's exotic imports included peacocks and apes, gold, silver and ivory.

His fame spread and the Queen of Sheba arrived after a long journey — perhaps from the Yemen — to visit this far-famed king. The writer tells us that she came to test him with hard questions, although her visit may also have been a trade mission. He answered all that she asked him; his wealth and wisdom exceeded her dreams:

'The report I heard in my own country about your achievements and wisdom is true. But I did not believe these things until I came and saw them with my own eyes. Indeed, not even half was told me; in wisdom and wealth you have far exceeded the report I heard . . . Praise be to the Lord your God who has delighted in you and placed you on the throne of Israel.' (1 Kings 10:6–9)

The queen showered him with gold, precious stones and spices and he gave her lavish gifts in return.

Everything about Solomon was larger than life and, sadly for the common people, this applied also to his taxes and slave labour. In consequence, when Solomon died he left an embittered people smouldering with rebellion. His wisdom had not saved him from making some basic mistakes, both in his relationship with God and with his people. He had even begun to worship the gods his foreign wives had brought with them. The writers comment:

'The Lord became angry with Solomon because his heart had turned away from the Lord, the God of Israel.' (1 Kings 11:9)

The division of the kingdom

After Solomon's death a delegation arrived to ask his son, Rehoboam, if he intended to lighten the people's burdens. The older court advisers counselled him to accede to these requests but Rehoboam followed the advice of his young courtiers and threatened even tougher measures:

'My father made your yoke heavy; I will make it even heavier. My father scourged you with whips; I will scourge you with scorpions.' (1 Kings 12:14)

The southern tribes, who had been more leniently treated by Solomon, remained loyal to Rehoboam. But the king's threats were too much for the northern tribes, who broke away and set up a separate kingdom under the rule of Jeroboam, a court official under Solomon. The northern kingdom kept the name Israel; the southern kingdom is Judah from here on.

From this point the writers follow the fortunes of both Israel and Judah, keeping the accounts more or less chronologically parallel. Israel had more territory and wealth than Judah but was less politically secure. Judah was further away from the main trade routes so was less important strategically to would-be invaders and safer from attack.

Jeroboam I of Israel

Jeroboam was characterized by the writers as the king who led Israel into sin. He did this by setting up shrines at two sites, Dan in the north and Bethel in the south. These shrines had religious significance for both Israel and the Canaanites. Jeroboam was determined to prevent his people from trekking back to Jerusalem, the old centre of kingship and worship, so he installed a golden bull-calf in each of these shrines. These may have been meant to depict the bearers of God's throne, but they soon became objects of worship in their own right. The bull-calf had long been a fertility symbol in Canaanite worship. In the writers' view, this profaning of the true worship of God sowed the seeds of Israel's ultimate downfall, two hundred years later.

Omri and Ahab of Israel

In the reigns of Omri and his son, Ahab, Israel grew strong. Omri built a new capital for Israel at Samaria. Ahab married the Sidonian princess Jezebel, cementing an alliance with Phoenicia. She brought with her the baal worship of her people, and tried to foist it onto Israel. The writers comment about Ahab:

'He did more to provoke the Lord, the God of Israel, to anger than did all the kings of Israel before him.' (1 Kings 16:33)

But a fearless prophet called Elijah suddenly appeared on the scene. He boldly tried to recall Israel to covenant faith. (See chapter 4 for the stories of Elijah and his successor, Elisha.)

Reaction to the baal worship, and the injustices of Omri's and Ahab's reigns, led Jehu, an army officer, to bring off a successful coup. But he turned his righteous campaign into a cruel bloodbath, even killing Ahaziah, king of Judah, who was visiting his Israelite ally.

Judah

Judah was blessed with more good kings than Israel. King Asa, grandson of Rehoboam, was a good and godly king for most of his life and so was his son Jehoshaphat. But *his* son, Jehoram, made an arranged marriage with Athaliah, daughter of Ahab and Jezebel, who was as wicked as her mother.

When their son, Ahaziah, was killed by Jehu, Athaliah became a powerful queen mother in Judah. She slaughtered all the heirs to the throne, seizing power herself and imposing baal worship on the land for six years. But, unknown to her, one of the king's sons was rescued and hidden by his aunt and her husband, a priest in Jerusalem. After six years of secrecy this young boy was publicly crowned king. Athaliah's shriek of 'Treason!' served only to attract the attention of the guards, who quickly put her to death.

Israel and Judah

Jeroboam II in Israel overlapped with Uzziah in Judah and both enjoyed prosperous reigns of over forty years. Between them they increased the boundaries of their lands almost to its extent in Solomon's reign. Yet the writers' comment on Uzziah is only partly favourable and Jeroboam is said to have sinned against the Lord. The writers judged these kings less by their political achievement and prosperity than by their obedience or disobedience to the covenant laws.

The Assyrian 'Black Obelisk', from the time of Shalmaneser, shows subject Israelites bringing tribute from King Jehu.

Israel

Although outwardly prosperous, Israel was morally impoverished. There was political and social breakdown. The prophet Amos had denounced the sins of Israel in Jeroboam II's reign. He had accused the rich of living a life of ease and entertainment, exploiting the poor and disregarding their rights. There was no justice in the courts or pure religion at the shrines.

When Jeroboam died his son Zechariah became king. After six months he was assassinated and Shallum reigned for a month before being assassinated in his turn. Menahem succeeded him but his ten-year reign was marked by failure to obey God's covenant law. He also made large concessions to Assyria. Further coups followed until finally Assyria, strong under a ruler called Tiglath-Pileser III, laid siege to Samaria. After two terrible years the starving people of Israel surrendered. In accordance with Assyrian

ASSYRIA

For most of the Old Testament period the Assyrians occupied the land between the Tigris and Euphrates rivers—present-day Iraq. Assyria had become a major power by 1100BC, but it was from about 900BC that the Assyrian Empire was established.

Tiglath-pileser III—known in the Bible as Pul—increased the bounds of his empire in all directions.

The Assyrians were cruel and merciless in war. The king would sit enthroned at the city gate while the chief men of the captured people were paraded before him in cages or chains. Then they would be tortured, blinded and burnt to death.

One king boasted that he had erected a human column of writhing agony. Meanwhile scribes counted the heads of the common people who were dead, before heaping them in a pyramid.

Ashurbanipal (669–636) ruled in Nineveh, the Assyrian capital, and made his palace a centre of literature and the visual arts. He had a library of 20,000 clay 'books'. The history and traditions of Mesopotamia were all written down at his command.

This was done by indenting wet mud blocks with a wedge-shaped stick in cuneiform (or wedge) writing (see *Writing* feature). The mud bricks were

then baked hard in the sun. Much of what we know of ancient Mesopotamian civilization comes from this collection of clay tablets.

Assyrian carvings show Ashurbanipal at his favourite sport of hunting. He is depicted travelling in a light, two-wheeled chariot, armed with javelin or bow and arrow. On one expedition he boasted of bagging thirty elephants, 370 lions and 250 other wild beasts.

This carving from Nineveh shows the Assyrian King Ashurbanipal hunting onagers.

This Assyrian carving shows an Assyrian soldier with two Israelite captives. In the eighth century BC Assyrian kings conquered Israel and laid siege to Jerusalem.

The Assyrian Empire

This great winged bull once decorated the palace of King Sargon of Assyria.

These black basalt lions formed the base of a column at the entrance to the temple of Tainat, eighth century BC. Lions feature a great deal in Assyrian carvings and sculpture.

policy, they were deported and other conquered peoples brought in to settle their land. The history of the ten tribes was at an end.

Judah

With Israel gone, Judah was more vulnerable to Assyria, the border of whose empire was now less than twenty miles away. Ahaz, king of Judah, had refused to heed the wise advice of Isaiah, God's prophet and an adviser to the king and court. Ahaz was forced to pay heavy tribute to Assyria, and to please them he encouraged worship of the Assyrian gods.

'Sennacherib's Prism', an Assyrian document in stone, describes the emperor's siege of Jerusalem. He speaks of shutting up King Hezekiah 'like a bird in a cage'.

But his son, Hezekiah, was prepared to listen to Isaiah, and moved shrewdly to assert his independence. He strengthened Jerusalem's fortifications, reorganized the army and made a tunnel to ensure the water supply to the city. He was later forced to send tribute to Assyria, but escaped an Assyrian attack. This is how the writers describe a disaster that befell the Assyrians in their camp outside Jerusalem:

'That night an angel of the Lord went to the Assyrian camp and killed 185,000 soldiers. At dawn the next day, there they lay, all dead! Then the Assyrian Emperor Sennacherib withdrew and returned to Nineveh.' (2 Kings 19:35, 36)

It seems that a deadly plague ravaged the Assyrian force.

Manasseh, Hezekiah's son, reigned for fifty-five years and was a disaster. He reintroduced baal worship, even in the temple itself. It was left to his grandson, Josiah, to set about reform and to clean up the temple. During the repair work, the Book of the Law (most likely Deuteronomy) was discovered. When the king heard its message he was dismayed. He summoned the nation's leaders to renew their covenant promises at a public meeting at the temple. But God's message to Judah was that punishment would fall: in spite of Josiah's attempts to put things right, the people's disobedience was deep and widespread.

The kings that followed Josiah were weak and foolish. The Babylonians, who by now had conquered Assyria, besieged Jerusalem, then carried off its treasures, with King Jehoiachin and the leading citizens. A puppet king, Zedekiah, was put on the throne in 597BC but he attempted to rebel and after a further eighteen-month siege, Jerusalem fell to Nebuchadnezzar of Babylon.

The city was sacked, the sacred temple torn down, and most of the people deported to Babylon. Only the true prophets, who had warned of the coming doom, saw any ray of hope beyond this exile. (See chapter 6 for the story of the nation in exile and after.)

1 and 2 Chronicles

It would be easy to respond to Chronicles by saying 'We've heard it all before!' — for these books repeat many of the stories already recounted in Samuel and Kings. Chronicles begins with tribal lists establishing the nation's provenance, then focuses on the history of Judah from the time of David to the fall of Jerusalem. It adds to the material in Samuel and Kings, particularly emphasizing the preparations for the temple, its building and its dedication. And it concentrates on the kings of Judah — David's family line.

Chronicles was probably written much later than Joshua to Kings — the group of books thought to have been written or edited by the same people who compiled Deuteronomy. But, like them, Chronicles is history with a purpose.

Many think that Chronicles was written for the Jews of the fourth century who were living in the Persian Empire (see chapter 6). The stories of the nation before the exile were as much past history to them as they are to us. But the writers used the stories of Judah's kings and priests to illustrate their themes — of God's grace and his judgment.

It is important to notice what the Chroniclers leave out, as well as what they include. The reigns of David and Solomon are held up as the golden times. There is no mention of David's adultery with Bathsheba and his part in Uriah's death, nor of Solomon's worship of false gods. And from the point when the kingdom is divided there is scarcely any mention of the northern kingdom of Israel. It may be that the Chroniclers see it as too corrupt from its very beginning. They are certainly more concerned to follow the kings of David's line and trace how God's covenant promise of an everlasting kingdom was carried out.

The Chroniclers select and describe past events vividly in order to bring out the lessons of history: how God deals with his people. Where there is wilful disobedience God must judge and punish, but afterwards he restores and his merciful goodness is seen in action. These are the principles by which God acts in every age: his forgiveness and kindness in restoring and blessing are far greater than his people deserve. God's care for his people is well expressed in the words of King Asa, who went out against the enemy acknowledging:

'Lord, there is no-one like you to help the powerless against the mighty. Help us, O Lord our God, for we rely on you, and in your name we have come against this vast army.' (2 Chronicles 14:11)

The Chroniclers see God's people in their own day following in the path of his people in days gone by.

THE EARLY PROPHETS

Elijah · Elisha · Micaiah · Amos · Hosea · Isaiah Micah

It takes a brave person to stand up in public and say, 'This is what God says,' but that is what the prophets were prepared to do. God did not remain silent during Israel's long history and the prophets were his mouthpieces.

Sometimes they had a warning message for the king, or more often for the whole nation. Always it was a message recalling Israel to their covenant agreement with God. When the nation tried to control their own affairs by alliances with foreign powers; when they ill-treated the poor and underprivileged; when they mixed worship of God with the cruel and evil practices of baal worship, the prophets told them just what God thought about their behaviour.

Very often they warned the people what God would do if they did not change their ways. But the threat of defeat or exile was always relieved by the promise of blessing if they repented. The voice of the prophet, like the voice of conscience, stirred them to return to the faithful God who still loved and cared for them.

Prophets of different kinds

The Jewish faith was not the only one to have its prophets, although the role of prophet in other religions was rather different. Their job was to forecast the future for the king or for someone who paid them for their services. Often they went into trances or some kind of ecstatic state before delivering their oracle.

Prophets in Israel sometimes foretold the future but more often than not it was conditional, depending on the way in which the people received God's message. If they repented and turned back to God they would be rescued, but if they continued to forsake God and act unjustly they would suffer at the hands of their enemies.

Sometimes bands or schools of prophets would live together in communities or at the sanctuaries. Others were employed at the king's court. Not all of these were genuine prophets. Some simply told the king what he wanted to hear, promising him victory and success. The prophet Jeremiah made scathing comments about the false prophets of his own day who pretended that all was well, refusing to look facts in the face:

*'Do not listen to what the prophets are
        prophesying to you;
    they fill you with false hopes.
They speak visions from their own minds,
    not from the mouth of the Lord.'* (23:16)

The prophets of Israel who made their mark were lone figures. Elijah and Elisha appear in 1 and 2 Kings, and the writers tell us a good deal about their actions and miracles as well as the kind of message they preached. But the Bible books which are named after a prophet — Isaiah, Jeremiah and the rest — usually give us the prophet's messages more fully and tell us less about his life. These are the 'writing prophets': they (or a scribe or disciple) wrote down their spoken messages at the time or soon after. The first of these, chronologically, is Amos, who appeared forty years after Elisha's death, around 760 to 750BC.

In the Bible, the books of the prophets come after Psalms and the Wisdom literature. The longer prophets — Isaiah, Jeremiah, Ezekiel — come first, followed by the minor, or shorter, prophets, so the order is not strictly chronological.

Oracles and actions

The 'writing prophets' usually spoke God's message in oracles — short poetic utterances, often beginning or ending with

Miracle in the Old Testament

Many scholars regard miracle in the Old Testament—in the stories of Elijah, Elisha and others—as folklore. They explain that such wonders were gradually added to stories told by word of mouth, becoming greater in the telling. That is one way of dealing with what is a problem to most modern readers.

Others note that miracle does not occur throughout the Old Testament but at certain periods of Israel's history. There were miracles associated with the freeing of the Israelite slaves in Egypt (the Ten Plagues) and the desert wanderings. There was also a spate of miracles around the time of Elijah and Elisha.

The Egyptians, at the time of Moses, had to recognize the overriding claims of Israel's God. It was important, too, for the people of Israel to learn that they were to return to the true God.

In the time of Elijah, baal worship had cut at the roots of Israelite faith. The people had to be recalled to a God whose power was greater than that of any idol.

At these periods miracle was used to bring Israel back to covenant faith in God.

The Bible does not distinguish as sharply as we do between miracle and natural happenings. God is believed to be present in all events, whether natural or miraculous. He is the God of every storm and of the annual harvest as well as the God who sent down fire on Mount Carmel.

Sometimes a natural cause is given for a miracle—for example, the wind which blew back the waters of the Red Sea. God is seen to be at work, whether through normal or extraordinary means, to bring his purposes to pass.

The prophet's role and message

The prophet had certain important functions. First, it was his task to discipline the king. Israel was God's people — God was their king — and the nation's earthly kings served only as his representatives. They were not above God's laws and were not to be tyrants: Nathan took King David to task over the Bathsheba/Uriah episode; Elijah rebuked King Ahab for exploiting one of his subjects (see below).

It was also the prophet's role to stand up for justice — whether in the courts or in everyday dealings between Israelites. God cared about scales being accurate and wages promptly paid. He defended the cause of the poor and the underprivileged particularly.

Above all it was the prophet's task to remind Israel of their covenant relationship with God and all that that entailed. Israel was to obey God's laws, to give their love first to God and then to fellow-members of the covenant.

The prophets had much to say about formal worship too. Sacrifice and offerings meant nothing to God unless the offerer obeyed God's laws and was just and kind to others. Samuel told Israel's first king, Saul:

'To obey is better than sacrifice,
*   and to heed is better than the fat of rams.'*
(1 Samuel 15:22)

Elijah and Elisha

The great prophet Elijah strides onto the stage with no introduction, to confront the morally weak King Ahab of Israel and his baal-worshipping wife Jezebel. He pronounced a drought:

'As the Lord, the God of Israel, lives, whom I serve, there will be neither dew nor rain in the next few years except at my word.' (1 Kings 17:1)

Elijah himself did not escape the effects of the drought. He also had to keep clear of Ahab and Jezebel. So God directed him to a brook in the Kerith Ravine, east of Jordan. The brook supplied him with water and ravens brought him bread and meat, night

During a great drought the Bible tells of ravens bringing food to the prophet Elijah.

the words, 'The Lord said'. As well as containing these oracles, their books sometimes tell us the circumstances in which the prophet spoke and give some relevant information about him.

The prophets often gained their insight from visions, which laid bare God's purposes. They sometimes dramatized their message with symbolic actions. For example, Jeremiah hurled a clay pot to the ground to signify how Judah would be broken in pieces as a nation. A dramatic action like that would have far more effect than words alone.

and morning. But in time the brook dried up and God told Elijah to go north, out of the land of Israel into Sidon, where a widow would feed him.

When he arrived at the town of Zarephath he saw a woman collecting sticks. He asked her for water and something to eat and she told him that she was about to go and cook a last meal for herself and her son. Famine was severe here too. Elijah told her first to make him a small cake. He promised:

'This is what the Lord, the God of Israel says: "The jar of flour will not be used up and the jug of oil will not run dry until the day the Lord gives rain on the land."' (1 Kings 17:14)

Elijah's great contest with the prophets of Baal was staged on Mt Carmel.

Contest on Carmel

In the third year of the drought, Elijah received the command to return to King Ahab. He told the king to summon the people of Israel to witness a decisive contest on Mount Carmel between the God of Israel and the 450 prophets of Baal, who were supported by Jezebel. Both sides were to prepare an altar. The god who could call down fire to burn the waiting sacrifice would prove himself the true God.

The prophets of Baal had first turn. They prayed to Baal for fire and danced all day around his altar, gashing themselves in their frenzy as they tried to wring an answer from their god. Their efforts were all in vain.

Then it was Elijah's turn. He repaired the altar to God which had been torn down, and doused it with water to make a miracle more difficult. Then he prayed that God would indeed answer by fire in order to vindicate himself as the true God and bring the people back to him.

In response to his prayer, fire came down and burned up the sacrifice. The people, in amazement, acknowledged the God of Israel as the true God. Baal, god of thunder and rain, had been unable to break the drought or send lightning to consume the sacrifice. At a time of widespread departure from God, Elijah had powerfully drawn the people back to their covenant relationship.

Elijah hears God's voice

Elijah's courageous stand was followed by a period of weakness and depression in the face of Jezebel's murderous threats. He journeyed despondently to Mount Sinai where God spoke to him:

'A great and powerful wind tore the mountains apart and shattered the rocks before the Lord, but the Lord was not in the wind. After the wind there was an earthquake, but the Lord was not in the earthquake. After the earthquake came a fire, but the Lord was not in the fire. And after the fire came a gentle whisper.' (1 Kings 19:11, 12)

God spoke to Elijah in a gentle whisper or a 'still, small voice'. He reassured Elijah that he was not alone in his loyalty to God. There were 7,000 in Israel who had not worshipped

Baal. God gave Elijah fresh work to do and the promise of help from Elisha, a young man who would be his disciple and succeed him as prophet in Israel.

Naboth's vineyard

Elijah had the courage to stand up for God's laws of justice, in spite of Queen Jezebel's opposition. King Ahab coveted a vineyard adjoining his palace which he wanted to turn into a kitchen garden. The owner, Naboth, refused to sell it to him because it was his family inheritance.

Jezebel believed that the king's desires should override the ordinary citizen's rights. So she arranged for Naboth to be arrested on trumped-up charges and stoned to death. His land could then revert to the king.

All went according to plan, but as Ahab walked with satisfaction in his newly acquired garden, Elijah met him and warned him that because of this evil his royal house would end in disaster. Events proved him right.

Elijah's departure

As Elijah's life neared its end, the prophet gently tried to persuade his disciple Elisha to leave him. But, as they went from one place to another, Elisha refused. He must have felt in his bones that the time of parting was close.

When they reached the River Jordan Elijah struck the water with his rolled-up cloak and the water divided for them to cross on dry ground. Elijah asked Elisha:

'Tell me, what can I do for you before I am taken from you?' (2 Kings 2:9)

Elisha's request was for a 'double portion' of Elijah's spirit — to inherit Elijah's spiritual power and authority. His master promised that if Elisha saw him go, it would be his.

'As they were walking along and talking together, suddenly a chariot of fire and horses of fire appeared and separated the two of them, and Elijah went up to heaven in a whirlwind.' (2 Kings 2:11)

When the grieving Elisha made his way back, he took the cloak of Elijah, which had fallen from him, and struck the waters of Jordan as his master had done, asking:

'Where now is the Lord, the God of Elijah?' (2 Kings 2:14)

The waters parted for him as they had for Elijah. Elisha had inherited the prophet's God-given power.

Elisha demonstrated this through miracles. He moved in high circles, advising the king, and foretold the lifting of the Syrian siege of the capital, Samaria. He also performed 'small' miracles of kindness and help for the poor. It was he who authorized the anointing of Jehu as king, though a later prophet, Hosea, condemned Jehu's bloody actions.

False and true prophets

The story of the prophet Micaiah demonstrates the difference between a true prophet of God and those who prophesied to curry favour.

King Ahab asked King Jehoshaphat of Judah to join him in attacking Ramoth-gilead, a city then belonging to Syria. First

The prophet Amos denounced the luxury-loving people of Samaria: they decorated their houses with ivory carvings while oppressing the poor.

keeping sheep in Judah. Perhaps he first visited the northern kingdom of Israel when he was selling his wool, for he prophesied there during the prosperous reign of King Jeroboam II.

He was shocked by the complete disregard for justice in cities like Bethel which claimed to be very religious. He spoke out with great feeling and vehemence. Israel, he insisted, was specially privileged as God's chosen nation. Therefore her people were doubly guilty for neglecting justice. The people had kept up their religious routine of sacrifice but it was sheer hypocrisy, since they utterly failed to act justly in the courts or in their everyday dealings with the underprivileged. Amos denounced the luxury-loving women and the wealthy merchants who ground the faces of the poor. He told the people what God required:

'Let justice roll on like a river, righteousness like a never-failing stream!' (5:24)

they decided to ask God's advice, through the 400 prophets who lived at court. With one accord the prophets advised the king to attack, assuring him of victory.

Jehoshaphat felt that this answer was too good to be true and persuaded Ahab to consult one other prophet, Micaiah, who was not a favourite of the king because he invariably prophesied ill. Sure enough, Micaiah warned the king that all Israel would be scattered on the mountains like sheep without a shepherd.

Angrily Ahab ordered his men to throw Micaiah into prison and keep him there on a diet of bread and water until the king's victorious return. Micaiah declared:

'If you do return in safety, the Lord has not spoken by me.' (1 Kings 22:28)

It was in this disastrous battle that Ahab lost his life. He had refused to listen to the true voice of God.

Amos

The prophet Amos was careful to point out that he was not a professional prophet: he earned a living not from prophecy but by

Hosea

Hosea prophesied to the northern kingdom of Israel, to which he belonged. It was after the time of Amos, when some of the disasters Amos had predicted were coming to pass. Hosea's message did not come from visions but from the experiences of his own life.

Hosea suffered the pain of marriage to a wife who was unfaithful to him. At God's instruction he did not divorce her, as most husbands would have done at that time, but set out to find her and to buy her back from the slavery into which she had sunk.

God showed Hosea that Israel had behaved towards God as Hosea's wife had done towards the prophet. Just as Hosea's love for Gomer, his wife, was stronger than his anger, so God's covenant love for his people would never fail.

Hosea described the ways in which Israel had broken their covenant relationship with God. They had been unfaithful in seeking political alliances with one nation after another. Then they had committed spiritual adultery by forsaking the true worship of God for the practices associated with baal worship. They had also broken God's laws for living. Those who belonged in covenant relationship to God should behave with covenant love and justice to one another.

In all these ways Israel had forsaken God. Hosea appealed to them to return to God in genuine repentance, so that he could restore the covenant relationship.

There is no place in the Old Testament where the depth and poignancy of God's great love for his people Israel is so clearly described:

' "How can I give you up, Israel?
  How can I abandon you? . . .
My heart will not let me do it!
  My love for you is too strong.
I will not punish you in my anger;
  I will not destroy Israel again.
For I am God and not man.
  I, the Holy One, am with you,
I will not come to you in anger." ' (11:8, 9)

Isaiah

The book of Isaiah is a high point in the Old Testament. The prophet has profound spiritual insights and his oracles are rich in poetry.

Isaiah was an aristocrat, the friend of kings, and a cultured statesman who lived and prophesied in the southern kingdom of Judah during the reigns of King Jotham, King Ahaz and King Hezekiah. He advised Ahaz not to be afraid of the enemies of Israel and he supported Hezekiah when the threat of Assyria loomed large. He made God's purposes known to kings, as well as bringing God's word to the people.

Isaiah's call to be a prophet, described in Isaiah 6, came through a startling and brilliant vision in the year that King Uzziah died. Isaiah saw the Lord exalted, filling the temple with his presence and surrounded by winged creatures whose constant refrain was 'Holy, holy, holy!'

Isaiah's response was a deep sense of his own sinfulness and that of his people:

' "Woe to me!" I cried. "I am ruined! For I am a man of unclean lips, and I live among a people of unclean lips, and my eyes have seen the King, the Lord Almighty."

'Then one of the seraphs flew to me with a live coal in his hand, which he had taken with tongs from the altar. With it he touched my mouth and said, "See, this has touched your lips; your guilt is taken away and your sin atoned for." '

Then God asked:
'Whom shall I send? And who will go for us?'

The prophet responded:
'Here am I. Send me!'

And God said
'Go . . .' (6:5–9)

Isaiah, like the prophets before him, was scathing about outward observance of worship which had no root in right living. He pictures God as weary of religious celebrations when the people 'trample' his temple courts. Instead, he wants them to 'cease to do evil and learn to do good'.

Isaiah repeatedly refers to God as 'the Holy One'. His own vision, stamped indelibly on his mind, must have brought this characteristic of God home to him. To be holy means to be dedicated and set apart. In this sense of the word the heathen deities were holy too. It was necessary to go through certain rituals in order to approach them. But Isaiah's concept of God's holiness goes much deeper. God is different, set apart by his utter

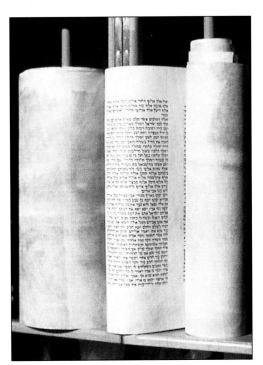

Before books took their present form, documents were written on papyrus or parchment scrolls. The prophecies of Isaiah and Jeremiah were recorded on scrolls like this.

goodness and purity. Beside him even the best of human beings is sinful and unclean. Just as Isaiah himself needed to be cleansed by the coal from the temple altar, so the people must repent and be cleansed and forgiven by God if they were to approach him.

Alongside this description of God's separateness is the reassurance of God's presence with his people. Isaiah speaks of the coming of one called Immanuel, which means 'God with us'. These two striking and seemingly opposite concepts are summed up in the words:

'I am the high and holy God, who lives for ever. I live in a high and holy place, but I also live with people who are humble and repentant, so that I can restore their confidence and hope.' (57:15)

In the first thirty-nine chapters Isaiah prophesies to the people of Judah in the reigns of Ahaz (736–716BC) and Hezekiah. He supported Hezekiah during the tense period of Assyrian aggression (Isaiah 37). Isaiah recognized that not everyone would repent or be rescued from the troubles that were to come. He talked about the faithful 'remnant' or few, who would return to God and survive his judgment on the land.

Later prophecies of Isaiah

From chapter 40 onwards Isaiah's prophecies range far beyond the time of King Hezekiah. They tell of the return of the few from the land of Babylon following years of captivity, and of King Cyrus, who would order their release from exile (538BC).

There is no reason why Isaiah should not have foretold events so far ahead, but they would scarcely have been relevant to those living at the time. Most scholars therefore think that from chapter 40 onwards we are reading the work of another prophet who lived in Babylon during the time of the exile. He is often referred to as Second — or Deutero — Isaiah. It is suggested that his writings were added to those of First Isaiah to use up the available space on the scroll. ('Books' in Bible times were long rolls of papyrus or parchment, written on the inside — and sometimes on the back too — and rolled up from either end. Naturally there

The Hope of a Coming Messiah

God had made a covenant with King David, promising him that there would always be a king descended from him on the throne. Some of the prophets recognized in this promise the hope of a great king, like David, who would inherit the kingdom in a coming age. The word 'Messiah' was used to refer to this coming king.

'Messiah' means 'anointed one'. All kings were anointed with oil as a sign that they were appointed by God for their high office. But this coming king was to be God's anointed in a very special sense. Some of the prophetic oracles were understood by Jewish teachers to refer to the coming Messiah, even though they had a contemporary fulfilment too.

Isaiah seems to have been speaking specifically about the coming Messiah in some of his oracles:

'A child is born to us!
* A son is given to us!*
* And he will be our ruler.*
He will be called, "Wonderful Counsellor",
* "Mighty God", "Eternal Father",*
* "Prince of Peace."*
His royal power will continue to grow;
* his kingdom will always be at peace.*
He will rule as King David's successor,
* basing his power on right and justice,*
* from now until the end of time.'* (9:6, 7)

was a limit to the length of a scroll — it must be manageable for the reader to handle.) In many ways the different parts form a unity.

Some of the most beautiful oracles from this section of Isaiah are a series of poems known as the Servant Songs (42:1–4; 49:1–6; 50:4–9; 52:13 — 53:12). They describe the perfect servant of God — very different from the disobedient servant Israel — who is gentle and humble and finally suffers on behalf of his people:

'He was despised and rejected by men;
* a man of sorrows, and acquainted with*
*   grief...*
Surely he has borne our griefs
* and carried our sorrows...*
But he was wounded for our transgressions,
* he was bruised for our iniquities;*
upon him was the chastisement that made us
*   whole,*
* and with his stripes we are healed.*

All we like sheep have gone astray;
    we have turned every one to his own way;
and the Lord has laid on him
    the iniquity of us all.' (53:3–6)

Isaiah proclaimed the uniqueness of God in an age of many gods. He stressed, too, the ultimate salvation of 'the ends of the earth'.

Micah

Micah, who was contemporary with Isaiah, was a very different kind of person. He was a rough, outspoken peasant who declared his oracles both to Israel in the north and Judah in the south. He spoke fiercely of God's desire for justice and of the destruction that would come upon Jerusalem if its rulers, priests and false prophets did not repent. In Jeremiah we read that Micah's prophecy was heeded and that king and people repented. So it has been suggested that Micah may have been responsible for Hezekiah's reforms.

Micah summed up God's requirements in these memorable words:

'The Lord has told us what is good. What he requires of us is this: to do what is just, to show constant love, and to live in humble fellowship with our God.' (6:8)

Isaiah and Micah have one famous oracle in common. Some think that they are both quoting from an earlier unknown author. The oracle describes Jerusalem and the

The prophets stood for justice. Those who cheated by using false weights and scales would incur God's judgment.

nations in an ideal future:

'It shall come to pass in the latter days that . . .
    many people shall come, and say:
"Come, let us go up to the mountain of the Lord,
    to the house of the God of Jacob;
that he may teach us his ways
    and that we may walk in his paths" . . .
and they shall beat their swords into
        ploughshares,
    and their spears into pruning hooks;
nation shall not lift up sword against nation,
    neither shall they learn war any more.'
        (Isaiah 2:2–4; Micah 4:1–3)

THE PROPHETS AND THE NATIONS

Jeremiah · Nahum · Zephaniah · Habakkuk · Joel Obadiah · Jonah

God had chosen Israel to be his special people and had entered into a covenant relationship with them. It might seem as if the nations around did not matter or were not the concern of God. But the prophets thought quite differently. They believed that their God was God of the whole world. He was not like the local deities who were thought to hold power only in their own limited territory. His power extended far beyond the boundaries of little Israel. As Isaiah put it:

'He brings princes to naught and reduces the rulers of this world to nothing.' (40:23)

In the first place the prophets saw the surrounding nations as responsible to God for their actions. Amos denounced the peoples that bordered on Israel for their inhumane behaviour. They might not understand God's laws as Israel did, but they were still held guilty for such unnatural acts as ripping open pregnant women. All the nations are answerable to God.

Secondly, the nations around, as well as Israel, were subject to God's control. They might think that their actions were part of their own policy, but God's sovereign will was behind all that happened in the international arena. Isaiah pictures God whistling for Assyria to come and act as his agent in punishing Israel. Isaiah also refers to Cyrus, the Persian king, as God's servant. When Cyrus lets the captives go free (see chapter 6) he is fulfilling God's will, whether he is conscious of it or not.

Isaiah — and others — speak of a future time when all the nations will be gathered into the people of God (Isaiah 9, for example).

Jeremiah

Some of the prophets were specially concerned with the affairs of other nations. When God called Jeremiah he told him: 'I appoint you over nations and kingdoms to uproot and tear down...to build and to plant.'

Jeremiah's authority from God went beyond the confines of Israel. One of his first visions was of a simmering, seething cooking-pot in the north, ready to boil over and discharge its scalding contents on the land. The meaning was that, 'Destruction will boil over from the north on all who live in this land.'

Jeremiah's long years of prophesying were overshadowed by this vision of trouble from the north. His was not a popular message. The Babylonians, whom he came to recognize as that northern aggressor, would overrun the land and take the people into exile. For years Jeremiah declared his message of doom, while all around other prophets were foretelling prosperity. There was no cloud on the horizon to indicate the coming trouble, and Jeremiah was ill-treated and misunderstood. Even today his name is a byword for miserable pessimists.

Sometimes Jeremiah felt that he could not bear the burden that he had been given. When skies looked blue he sometimes thought that he had been mistaken in his message, or even that God had deliberately misled him. 'I have been your dupe,' he tells God bitterly, 'everyone ridicules me.'

But Jeremiah recognized that although things might look good on the surface, at a fundamental level the nation had moved away from God. King Josiah's reforms had only gone skin-deep. There was a rottenness in the nation that would lead at last to its downfall.

Jeremiah made many enemies. His attitude to the temple made him deeply resented and hated. Most people regarded the temple with awe and superstitious reverence. They were sure that, as God's dwelling, it was utterly safe from attack. But Jeremiah derided such ill-founded trust.

'It's no good repeating "the temple of the Lord" in pious tones,' he told them. Mere words, repeated out of superstition, would not save them. God wanted them to love and obey him.

Jeremiah had a scribe called Baruch, who wrote down his oracles. But when the scroll was read to King Jehoiakim he slashed it section by section with his knife and burned it. At God's direction Jeremiah and Baruch began again and painstakingly wrote the oracles on a new scroll. God's word could not be so easily destroyed.

Jeremiah and the potter

Jeremiah saw images of God at work in the everyday world as well as in visions. One day he watched a potter at his wheel. When the pot that he was making was spoiled, the potter began all over again, sometimes remaking it, sometimes making something different.

'God can do the same with you,' Jeremiah told the people. 'What he wanted to make of you has been spoiled, but if you repent he is able to make something new.'

Jeremiah and the new covenant

Like every other prophet, Jeremiah tried to bring Israel back to keeping their covenant promises to God. But he went further than the rest. He recognized that men and women were incapable of keeping those laws and promises as they should. He foretold a day when God would make a new covenant which had a different basis. It would be rooted in God's forgiveness and his help.

'The new covenant that I will make ... will be this: I will put my law within them and write it on their hearts. I will be their God and they will be my people ... I will forgive their sins and I will no longer remember their wrongs.' (31:33–34)

Nahum

Nahum lived and prophesied near the end of the seventh century BC — the time of Assyria's supremacy. His oracle is a poem of rejoicing at the defeat of the Assyrian capital, Nineveh. It may seem wrong to exult in the downfall of others, but the Assyrians had behaved so cruelly towards the peoples they captured that their doom was seen as justice.

'The Lord does not easily become angry,
but he is powerful
and never lets the guilty go unpunished.' (1:3)

Even though God had used Assyria to punish Israel, the Assyrians too were subject to God's control, and accountable to him.

Nahum provides a highly dramatic

The potter moulding the clay provided Jeremiah with a powerful image of God and his people: what is spoiled can be remade.

picture of Assyria's last struggle. Some have suggested that only an eyewitness could capture the scene so exactly. In the days before television or film, word pictures gave a graphic presentation of exciting events:

'Chariots dash wildly through the streets,
rushing to and fro through the city squares.
They flash like torches
and dart about like lightning ...
The gates by the river burst open;
the palace is filled with terror.
The queen is taken captive ...
Like water from a broken dam
the people rush from Nineveh!
"Stop! Stop!" the cry rings out —
but no one turns back.' (2:3, 4, 6, 8)

64

Zephaniah

Zephaniah lived and prophesied in the time of King Josiah (who reigned from 640 to 609BC). Perhaps he spoke out in the decade before Josiah's reforms (621BC), because the prophet gives a black picture of Judah's sin and threatens terrible judgment from God against Jerusalem and the nation. The general attitude is that 'The Lord never does anything, one way or the other.'

But God *will* act. Zephaniah calls for Judah to repent. Then he turns to other nations on whom God's judgment will also fall. Even so, like many of the prophets, he sees beyond the doom and gloom. He ends by painting a happy picture of Israel in the future, restored and once more blessed by God.

Zephaniah and the Day of the Lord

Zephaniah touches on that favourite theme of the prophets — the 'Day of the Lord'. 'The great day of the Lord is near — very near and coming fast!' he warns. But, he goes on:

'that will be a bitter day . . . a day of fury, a day of trouble and distress, a day of ruin and destruction, a day of darkness and gloom.'
(1:14–15)

He pleads with the people to come to their senses and repent. If only they will do what is right, and humble themselves before God, they may escape the punishment that will come on that day.

Habakkuk

By Habakkuk's time (at the end of the seventh century) the Babylonians had come to power. God revealed to him that he would use Babylon as a weapon of judgment on the nations. Habakkuk realized that Judah would be attacked too, and this for him posed an unanswerable question. How could God, who is pure and righteous, use such a wicked nation as the Babylonians to punish a people more righteous and God-fearing than they were? He complained bitterly to God about the injustice of this — then waited for God to reply.

God's answer was that all evil will be punished in the end. Meanwhile, 'those who are righteous will live because they are faithful to God'.

God will act in his own time, meanwhile Habakkuk is to trust God completely and keep his commands. The conclusion of his prayer is a classic example of one person's

'I will climb my watch-tower,' said the prophet Habakkuk, 'and wait to see what the Lord will tell me to say.' Watch-towers like this enabled farmers to keep watch against thieves (human or animal) as their crops ripened.

steadfast trust in God:

'Even though the fig-trees have no fruit
*   and no grapes grow on the vines,*
even though the olive-crop fails
*   and the fields produce no corn,*
even though the sheep all die
*   and the cattle-stalls are empty,*
I will still be joyful and glad,
because the Lord God is my saviour.
The Sovereign Lord gives me strength.' (3:17–19)

Joel

We know very little about Joel or when he
lived. Some place his prophecy in the early
days of King Joash, about 835 to 825BC.
Others think he lived during the time of the
Persian Empire, after the exile. (The exile
began in 586BC and was the period of about
70 years in which Judah was captive in
Babylon — see chapter 6.) Joel may in fact
have lived between those times, during the
exile. He speaks of a terrible plague of
locusts, but this cannot be linked with any
known event. In its utter destruction this
attack symbolizes for him the coming Day of
the Lord — 'a dark and gloomy day'.

But Joel brings a message of hope. If only
Israel will repent and turn back to God, he is
able to 'restore the years that the locust has
eaten'.

Joel also paints a wonderful picture of a
coming day of God's blessing, when his Spirit
will be abroad in the world:

'It shall come to pass afterward,
*   that I will pour out my spirit on all flesh;*
your sons and your daughters shall prophesy,
*   your old men shall dream dreams,*
*   and your young men shall see visions . . .*

And it shall come to pass that all who call upon
the name of the Lord shall be delivered.' (2:28, 32)

Obadiah

Obadiah is the shortest book in the Old
Testament. Obadiah's message was for Edom
— Israel's south-eastern neighbour — in the
bitter days following the fall of Jerusalem in
586BC. The people of Edom are the
descendants of Esau, the brother of Jacob.

Obadiah, as a descendant of Jacob, therefore
sees Edom as a 'brother'. Yet the Edomites
had taken advantage of Jerusalem's fall —
looting the captured city and helping the
invaders. Obadiah condemns their heartless
attitude:

'You should not look down on your brother
*   in the day of his misfortune,*
nor rejoice over the people of Judah
*   in the day of their destruction,*
nor boast so much
*   in the day of their trouble.'* (1:12)

He prophesies retribution for Edom in
their mountain fastnesses:

' "The pride of your heart has deceived you,
*   you who live in the clefts of the rocks*
*   and make your home on the heights,*
you who say to yourself,
*   'Who can bring me down to the ground?'*
Though you soar like the eagle
*   and make your nest among the stars,*
*   from there I will bring you down,"*
*   declares the Lord.'* (1:3–4)

Obadiah sees ahead to the day when Israel
will again possess the land and 'the kingdom
will be the Lord's'.

*Joel describes an army of
locusts attacking the
land—a sign of the coming
day of God's judgment.*

*To the east of the great
Aravah rift valley are the
hills of ancient Edom, the
nation against whom
Obadiah prophesied.*

Jonah

The book of the prophet Jonah is different in kind from any of the other prophetic books. It tells of the dramatic events in the prophet's life but does not record his messages. It is a superbly written book with many strands of meaning — and it is one of the best-known stories in the Bible.

We know nothing about Jonah or the incidents described from any other records. There is a reference to a prophet called Jonah in 2 Kings. He is said to have lived during the reign of King Jeroboam II in the eighth century BC. But we do not know if this is the same Jonah. Many scholars believe that the book of Jonah was written late, in the period after the exile.

Jonah's story

God called Jonah to go to the hated Assyrians, and warn them that judgment would fall on the city of Nineveh because of their wickedness. But Jonah was so horrified by the assignment that he set off in the opposite direction, taking a boat bound for Spain.

He was asleep below decks when a violent storm arose. The sailors first prayed to their gods, then cast lots to discover the troublemaker who had caused this ill luck. The lot fell on Jonah who admitted that he was running away from 'the Lord, the God of heaven, who made land and sea'.

The sailors were deeply shocked but unwilling to throw Jonah over the side as he advised them to do. Eventually they did so

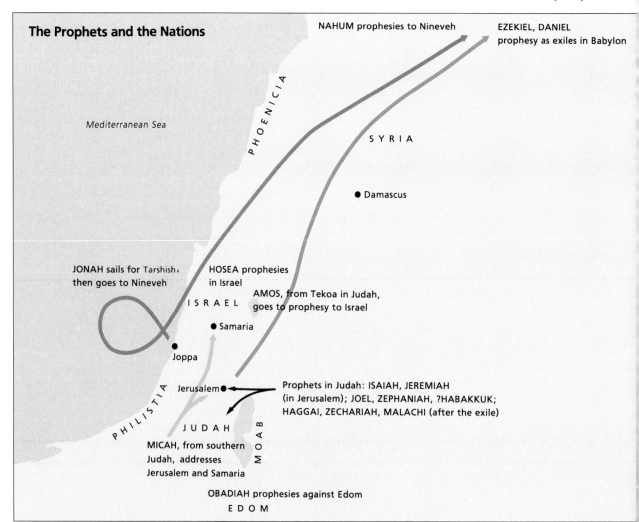

The Prophets and the Nations

NAHUM prophesies to Nineveh

EZEKIEL, DANIEL prophesy as exiles in Babylon

Mediterranean Sea

PHOENICIA

SYRIA

● Damascus

JONAH sails for Tarshish, then goes to Nineveh

HOSEA prophesies in Israel

AMOS, from Tekoa in Judah, goes to prophesy to Israel

ISRAEL

● Samaria

● Joppa

Jerusalem ●

Prophets in Judah: ISAIAH, JEREMIAH (in Jerusalem); JOEL, ZEPHANIAH, ?HABAKKUK; HAGGAI, ZECHARIAH, MALACHI (after the exile)

PHILISTIA

JUDAH

MOAB

MICAH, from southern Judah, addresses Jerusalem and Samaria

OBADIAH prophesies against Edom

EDOM

but, instead of drowning, Jonah was swallowed by an enormous fish. Within the fish he thanked God for his deliverance. At the end of three days, at God's order, the fish vomited Jonah onto dry land.

God once again told Jonah to go to Nineveh — and this time he obeyed. His warning was so successful that king and people genuinely repented, and God decided to exercise mercy. Jonah was mortified, but it was no more than he had expected. His word as a prophet had been undermined and his desire for vengeance on the Assyrians thwarted. He sat in the blazing sun to watch the city, perhaps still hoping for delayed judgment to fall on it.

God caused a plant to grow up which gave him welcome shade and relief from the heat. But the next day God sent a worm to attack the plant so that it withered and died. A burning east wind beat down and Jonah, exposed to the heat, was furious. God asked him if he had any right to be angry and he replied: 'I have every right to be angry — angry enough to die!'

God gently drives the lesson home. If Jonah feels so strongly about a mere plant over whose growth he had no control, how much more is God entitled to feel compassion for all those men, women and children in Nineveh who 'cannot tell their right hand from their left, and many cattle as well'.

The message of Jonah

The book of Jonah is a small masterpiece. Not only is it narrated with economy, sophistication and wit but it has many layers of meaning.

Some believe that it was written at a time — like that following the exile of the Jews in Babylon — when there was great emphasis on racial purity and a contempt for Gentiles. The story aimed to neutralize such an attitude with subtle wit. Almost every group of non-Jews shows up well: the sailors are

God-fearing and compassionate; the people of Nineveh repent at Jonah's preaching. Jonah, meanwhile, is a sorry picture of rebellion and uncharitableness.

Some see the book as portraying repentance. Jonah repents after his first act of disobedience and so do the people of Nineveh. At the close of the book we are left wondering if Jonah will repent again.

The book certainly portrays God's sovereignty. It is he who is in control both of the whole Assyrian people and of his disobedient servant Jonah. He 'prepares' a storm, a fish, a plant, a worm and a wind to fulfil his purposes and teach Jonah the lessons he needs to learn.

The story of Jonah also depicts God's mercy. God is not legalistic and judgmental. He shows mercy to the Ninevites. He gives Jonah a second chance. He not only shows Jonah mercy but tries to teach his servant to reflect his own attitude towards others. God is just, and must punish evil and disobedience on the part of his own people and that of other nations. But he is also a God who has compassion on the frailty and ignorance of men, women — and cattle too.

Jonah was sent to Nineveh, capital of Assyria, whose armies had caused God's people such suffering. Scenes from the fall of Lachish were vividly depicted by Assyrian stone-carvers commissioned to record the victory.

6

CAPTIVITY AND RETURN HOME

Ezekiel · Ezra and Nehemiah · Haggai · Zechariah
Malachi · Esther · Daniel

When Judah's good King Josiah died in the battle of Carchemish in 605BC it marked the end of settled rule. Although Babylon defeated the great southern power of Egypt in the battle, Egypt controlled Judah and Syria for a little longer. Necho of Egypt deported the new king, Jehoahaz (or Shallum), to Egypt, putting a puppet king, whom he named Jehoiakim, on the throne and exacting heavy tribute from him. Jehoiakim was utterly weak. He allowed all the pagan cults that Josiah had banned.

Because Babylon had crushed Egypt, Jehoiakim soon had to transfer allegiance — and tribute — to the Babylonian king Nebuchadnezzar. Foolishly he tried to rebel, and in 598 Nebuchadnezzar came in force to Jerusalem. Jehoiakim's eighteen-year-old son, Jehoiachin (or Coniah), was now king and after a three-month siege he surrendered in 597. He and the leading citizens were taken to Babylon, where he seems to have ended his days in peace.

A puppet king, Zedekiah, was put on the throne of Judah by Babylon. Zedekiah asked Jeremiah's advice, then refused to take his counsel to remain loyal to Babylon. Instead, he plotted with Egypt and called down the wrath of Nebuchadnezzar. Jerusalem was again besieged and in 587 the walls were breached.

Zedekiah fled from the palace but was captured near Jericho. He was forced to watch his sons being put to death, before his eyes were gouged out and he was taken to Babylon in chains. A month later Jerusalem was burned to the ground, the citizens were deported and some were executed.

What was left of Judah was made a Babylonian province and put under the governorship of a good man, Gedaliah. But a band of men, under the leadership of one of the king's family, assassinated him. Those who remained fled to Egypt, taking a reluctant Jeremiah with them. Things could not have been more hopeless.

Israel in exile

'By the waters of Babylon,
there we sat down and wept,
when we remembered Zion.'

Psalm 137 describes the deep grief of the Jewish captives as they mourned their terrible fate. The beautiful city of Jerusalem had been razed to the ground and the sacred temple destroyed. After living through the horrors of siege and capture they now found themselves many hundreds of miles from home, in a strange land. It seemed to be the end of all their hopes. Yet when they had reached rock bottom the very prophets who had pronounced their doom had a message of hope.

Jeremiah, the most pessimistic of them all, at the moment when the enemy was hammering at the city gates, had actually bought back a piece of land that once belonged to his family. He certainly believed that there was a future and a hope for the people of Israel in their own land.

Jeremiah made it clear, too, that hope for the future lay with the people who had been taken captive. Those who were left behind in Jerusalem thought they must be the ones who were acceptable to God. But Jeremiah described his vision of two baskets of figs. One contained good, sound fruit but the other was full of rotten figs. The good figs are the captives, he explained, the rotten ones are those left in the land — the ones that Jeremiah himself chose to stay with.

Ezekiel

Ezekiel was a young priest who went to Babylon with the first group of captives in 597BC. Under normal circumstances he would have looked forward to carrying out the duties of a priest at the temple in Jerusalem. Instead God called him to the work of a prophet in Babylon. Like Jeremiah, he foretold further trouble for Jerusalem and its people and this came to pass in 587 to 586BC when Jerusalem was sacked.

Ezekiel, more than most prophets, illustrated his message with startling actions. He must have drawn fascinated audiences as he enacted the coming siege of Jerusalem for passers-by, weighing out rations for his meals. He shaved off his hair and beard and dug a way out from his mud-brick house by night as if escaping from the enemy. By such bizarre and dramatic acts he startled people into listening to his message.

But when Nebuchadnezzar successfully attacked Jerusalem for the second time in 587 and things were at their very worst, Ezekiel, like Jeremiah, began to bring a message of hope to the people. God will restore and rebuild, he assured them.

Ezekiel's vision of God

Ezekiel had a burning sense of the otherness of God, from the time of the first vision he received as an exile in Babylon. It was probably in his thirtieth year — the age at which he would have begun his duties as a priest in the temple. Out of the fireball at the heart of a windstorm on the plains of Babylon he saw a moving, living machine, a vehicle to uphold God's throne.

It was composed of four creatures, each with four faces, connected to intersecting wheels like casters that could move in any direction. Above their wings was a sparkling expanse and above that a throne of sapphire on which was the 'likeness of the glory of the Lord'.

Like Isaiah before him, Ezekiel never forgot the awe and majesty of the vision of God that he received at the time of his calling.

The valley of dry bones

Ezekiel's most telling vision was of a valley full of dry human bones. 'Can these bones live?' God asked him. Then, at God's command, Ezekiel spoke to the bones:

'As I was prophesying, there was a noise, a rattling sound, and the bones came together, bone to bone. I looked, and tendons and flesh appeared on them and skin covered them, but there was no breath in them.' (37:7–8)

God commanded Ezekiel to prophesy to the wind — a word which can also mean breath or spirit:

'I prophesied as he commanded me, and breath entered them; they came to life and stood up on their feet — a vast army.' (37:10)

God assured Ezekiel that he could — and would — just as miraculously restore and renew the life of his people Israel.

Ezekiel also described how God would give his people loving, obedient hearts:

'I will give you a new heart and put a new spirit in you; I will remove from you your heart of stone and give you a heart of flesh. And I will put my Spirit in you and move you to follow my decrees and be careful to keep my laws.' (36:26, 27)

The new temple

At the end of his book Ezekiel describes his vision of a new, ideal temple for the renewed

The Captives in Babylon

Ezekiel describes himself as living among the Jewish exiles by the Chebar river. The Chebar has been identified as a large irrigation canal, which looped round from the River Euphrates in Babylon back to the main river. The captives may have been allowed to build dwellings there, on the site of previous cities. Ezekiel's house was probably of mud-bricks.

It was not a prison-camp existence, for the captives were free to come and go. They were allowed civil liberties, they could communicate with Jerusalem and they were free to travel in Babylon and see all the wonders of that city.

THE BABYLONIANS

Babylonia (in southern Iraq) was one of the earliest centres of civilization in the Middle East. The Babylonians had a long history. The oldest known writing was found in Babylonia. A thousand years before Abraham, Babylonia was a centre of civilization. Around 1850BC King Hammurabi of Babylon was formulating his famous law-code.

In the eighth century BC, however, the Assyrians were supreme. Then the Assyrian Empire fell, swiftly and suddenly: in 612BC Nineveh fell to the Medes and Babylonians, and the new Babylonian Empire began.

The best-known Babylonian king is Nebuchadnezzar II. He was responsible for the famous buildings of Babylon, and the 'hanging gardens' which were one of the wonders of the ancient world.

In 586BC Nebuchadnezzar's army destroyed Jerusalem and took many of the people captive to Babylon. Ezekiel and Daniel were prophets-in-exile.

The Babylonians were skilled mathematicians who made astronomical tables and listed and classified plants, animals, birds, fish and stones. Their religion was based on magic and astrology. Although the rise of Babylon meant political change, the religious and cultural changes were small because Assyria and Babylonia had a common culture.

A lion in glazed brick, from Nebuchadnezzar's Babylon.

← Nebuchadnezzar made Babylon a magnificent city. The Ishtar Gate (reconstructed here) and processional way led to the great temples. The gateway was built of blue glazed brick decorated with animal figures. (One of the brick-kilns outside the city may have been Daniel's 'fiery furnace'.)

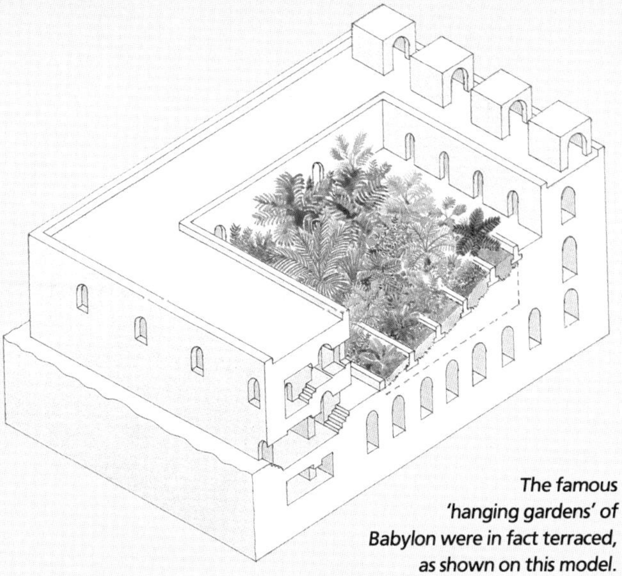

The famous 'hanging gardens' of Babylon were in fact terraced, as shown on this model.

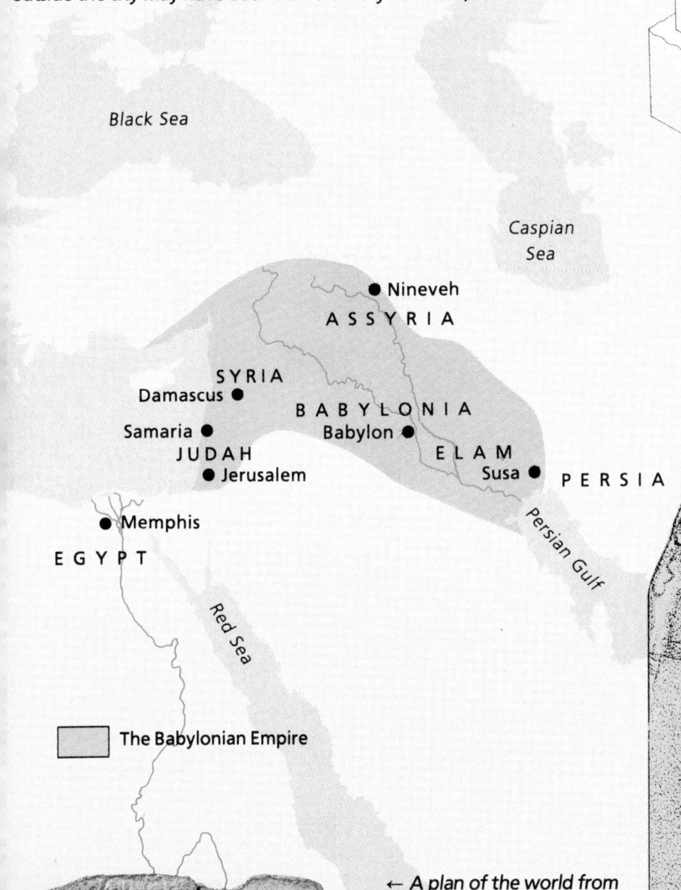

Black Sea

Caspian Sea

● Nineveh
A S S Y R I A

S Y R I A
Damascus ●
B A B Y L O N I A
Samaria ●   Babylon ●   E L A M
J U D A H   Susa ●   P E R S I A
● Jerusalem

● Memphis
E G Y P T

Persian Gulf

Red Sea

☐ The Babylonian Empire

← A plan of the world from seventh-century Babylonia.

→ Babylonian King Merodach-baladan grants land to an official. Above the figures are emblems of four gods: Nabu, Ninhursag, Ea and Marduk.

Ezekiel, exiled in Babylonia, had a vision of a new Temple in Jerusalem. From the sanctuary flowed streams of water, bringing life wherever they flowed. The Dead Sea, no longer salt and barren (as here) teemed with fish.

worship of God. He describes too a restored creation. A river of fresh, life-giving water was flowing from under the threshold of the temple. Ezekiel's guide

'measured off a thousand cubits and then led me through water that was ankle-deep. He measured off another thousand cubits and led me through water that was knee-deep. He measured off another thousand and led me through water that was up to the waist. He measured off another thousand, but now it was a river that I could not cross, because the water had risen and was deep enough to swim in — a river that no-one could cross.' (47:3–5)

The river abounded in fish. It flowed at last into the Dead Sea, sweetening its saltness. Trees grew along the banks — their fruit providing food and their leaves healing. Ezekiel envisages a land where foreigners as well as Israelites will be welcomed. The name of its city will be — THE LORD IS THERE.

God and the individual

Jeremiah and Ezekiel both quoted a familiar proverb of the day — 'The fathers have eaten sour grapes and the children's teeth are set on edge.' However, Ezekiel makes it clear in chapter 18 that God does not act in this way. The generation that had been guilty was the one that suffered judgment.

The prophets usually emphasized the responsibility of the people as a whole. In the West today, the individual is emphasized rather than the community. But Ezekiel spoke, too, of God's dealings with the individual person: God would hold people guilty or innocent according to their own personal response to him.

The return home

Jeremiah had told the people that God had promised to look after the 'good figs' — the captives who had been taken to Babylon — and, in time, to bring them back again to their own land. After some seventy years that promise came true. The psalmist painted a jubilant picture of the people returning from exile:

'When the Lord brought back those who returned to Zion,
    we were like those who dream.
Then our mouth was filled with laughter,
    and our tongue with shouts of joy.' (Psalm 126)

But the little groups of exiles who returned in several waves to their own land were straggling and small. Only a remnant — to use Isaiah's words — had returned. Isaiah had written about the Emperor Cyrus. God said:

'He is my shepherd
    and will accomplish all that I please;

he will say of Jerusalem, "Let it be rebuilt,"
and of the temple, "Let its foundations be
laid."' (44:28)

Cyrus was the Persian king who had taken over the Babylonian Empire by conquest. He did exactly as Isaiah had said. He issued an edict saying that the Lord of heaven had appointed him to build a temple for him in Jerusalem. He gave all the people from Judah the chance to go back to their land for that purpose. But many of the exiles were not enthusiastic to return. Josephus, who wrote a history of the Jews much later, in Roman times, says that they were too comfortable where they had settled in Babylon.

But it suited Cyrus for the peoples to be repatriated, so he appointed Sheshbazzar as governor of Judah and sent him off with the first little group of exiles to return to Judah and make a start on the temple. They took with them the gold and silver vessels belonging to the temple which Nebuchadnezzar had taken and Cyrus gave back.

A bit later Zerubbabel, a grandson of King Jehoiachin, led another group back.

The next main wave returned with Ezra, the priest, in 458, and in 444BC Nehemiah, who became governor, returned with others. Altogether these events, described in the books of Ezra and Nehemiah, span just over one hundred years.

Order of Events in Ezra/Nehemiah

It is not easy to get a clear picture of the order of events in Ezra and Nehemiah. As we have it described in those two books, there were three main movements under three personalities.

First, Zerubbabel returned in 538–516BC to rebuild the Temple. Joshua was high priest and Haggai and Zechariah prophesied during this period. At last the Temple was rebuilt.

Secondly, in 458BC Ezra the priest came back, with the purpose of teaching the law of Moses to the people.

Thirdly, in 444BC Nehemiah arrived as governor to rebuild the city walls, repopulate Jerusalem and rout their enemies. Nehemiah tells his own story in the book of his name.

Ezra and Nehemiah

Ezra and Nehemiah are lively and exciting books which in many places read more like notes and material jotted down for a future book than the finished thing. There are extracts from temple records, from the decree of Cyrus and from various official letters. Some of the writing is in Hebrew, some in Aramaic. Aramaic was the language commonly used in the Persian Empire and spoken by Jews back home in Palestine as well as those still in exile. There are extracts too from Ezra's and Nehemiah's diaries. Nehemiah is written in the first person and gives the fuller story of the period.

Nehemiah was an important official, cup-bearer to King Artaxerxes of Persia. He was shocked when he received news, many years after the first return of exiles, that the city walls of Jerusalem were still broken down and matters generally little improved. After prayer and careful preparation he got permission from the Emperor to return.

Once there he inspected the ruins and decided on a plan to rebuild the wall. When that was done, the people's morale would improve and they would see themselves as a nation once again. With excellent organizing ability, Nehemiah called together a workforce and the wall was completed in fifty-two days. But not without opposition. There were those already living in the land who wanted to fraternize with the returning Jews. Nehemiah would have none of it, so there was trouble and constant harassment. It seems harsh, but what mattered to Nehemiah was to maintain the purity of his people and of their faith. Chapter 5 of the book gives an example of Nehemiah's practical, economic justice.

After a governorship of twelve years Nehemiah went to report back to the Emperor in Susa. When he returned to Jerusalem he was horrified to find that the people had reverted to the ways of those around them. The Sabbath was no longer observed although, from the giving of the Law, keeping the Sabbath holy had been a sign of the covenant relationship with God. Foreigners were living in Jerusalem, even in the temple buildings. With all his accustomed zeal, Nehemiah set

Nehemiah was wine steward (cup-bearer) to the Persian king Artaxerxes. This stone carving shows a cup-bearer at the Assyrian court. The position was important: the king trusted his cup-bearer with his life.

about putting things right.

Ezra's role was to instruct the people in the Law. The Law was written in Hebrew and the people spoke Aramaic, so it was necessary for the writings to be interpreted as well as explained. Ezra stood on a raised platform at a huge outdoor assembly, with Levites to help him in his task. For days the people once more celebrated the Feast of Booths while they received steady instruction in the Law.

Both Ezra and Nehemiah were very angry when they learned that Israelite men had been marrying non-Jewish wives. Ezra insisted that they divorce them. Both men felt that it was imperative to maintain the purity of the people of God, keeping the Jewish race separate and distinctive. They also taught the importance of keeping the Law. Both these principles preserved the Jewish nationality and faith. Both also encouraged a narrow nationalistic outlook and legalistic behaviour in the centuries ahead.

The early chapters of Ezra describe how the returned exiles first turned their hand to rebuilding the temple. This was some time before Nehemiah organized the rebuilding of the city walls. There was great celebration when the foundations of the temple were laid. A mighty shout of praise went up and the choir and orchestra played and sang:

'The Lord is good, and his love for Israel is eternal.' (3:11)

Yet some of the older people present were sad because of the great contrast between the rebuilt temple and the glories of Solomon's great temple as they remembered it. They wept out loud while the younger ones shouted for joy.

The powerful feelings and enthusiasm did not last. Soon the neighbours living around, whose offers of help had been refused, began to make the building project as difficult as possible. The people lost heart. At the same time Cambyses, Cyrus's son, who had inherited his empire, seems to have plundered Judah for food supplies. So the people were poor and dispirited.

The Elephantine Papyri

A number of documents in Aramaic have been discovered at Elephantine, an island near Aswan on the River Nile. They date from about the time of Ezra and Nehemiah and tell us about life among a group of Jews who lived there. They seem to have constituted a military outpost, perhaps sent by the Persians to guard this frontier position.

A letter called the Passover Papyrus dates from 419BC and is said to be from the Emperor Darius. It lays down the correct practice for the keeping of Passover. The Persians were insistent that their subject people carried out their own religious rites correctly.

Haggai and Zechariah

It was two prophets, Haggai and Zechariah, who jolted the people into action again. Haggai reminded them that it was no time for them to relax in their own well-built houses instead of getting on with the building of the Lord's house. God must come first. He encouraged the people too by reminding them that God was with them.

Zerubbabel the governor and all the people took heart and set to work on the temple once again. Both prophets had special words of encouragement for Zerubbabel and Joshua, the High Priest, assuring them that God had chosen them for his purposes. Zechariah used the title 'the Branch' or 'Shoot' to refer both to Zerubbabel and Joshua. Later Jewish scholars saw this title as referring to the Messiah, who would be both king and priest.

Chapters 9 to 14 of Zechariah are so different from the early chapters that some think they are by a different writer. They are not concerned with the present but with the end of time. Some of this section is apocalyptic (see notes under *Apocrypha* and *Revelation*).

Malachi

Malachi, whose book is the last in the Old Testament, was another prophet who belonged to this period. He was horrified at the easy, careless way in which the people thought about God, with worship as a chore and any cheap and second-rate offering good enough to sacrifice. They thought it made little difference whether people served God or disobeyed him. They seemed quite unaware of God's strong love and fatherly care of them.

Malachi determined to shake them into recognizing God's holiness *and* his loving justice. The prophet's style is dramatic and direct, as if we have the very words he spoke. He asked the kind of questions that the people would ask if they put their feelings about God into words: 'How have you shown your love for us?'

They cannot see that they have failed to respond to God's initiative, and ask: 'How have we despised you?'

Malachi answered these questions in a clear and challenging way. He also reproved the men for divorcing the wives they had married when they were younger, in order to find more attractive partners. Breaking faith with one another in this way was very close to breaking covenant faith with God. So Malachi warns of God's coming in judgment like a refiner's fire that will separate dross from pure metal. Who could stand up to such an ordeal?

'The Lord Almighty says, "The day is coming when all proud and evil people will burn like straw. On that day they will burn up and there will be nothing left of them. But for you who obey me, my saving power will rise on you like the sun and bring healing like the sun's rays."'
(4:1–2)

Esther

'Chance comes to us from the hand of God' — that could be one way of summing up the message of the book of Esther, even though it never mentions the name of God.

The book of Esther is above all a first-rate story, superbly told. It is set in Persia in the reign of Ahasuerus or Xerxes and tells of the Jewish community passing through persecution. Mordecai, a Jew who has become a court official, enters his cousin and ward — the beautiful young Esther — for the

The day of God's judgment proclaimed by Malachi was, for those who obeyed God, the day when his 'saving power will rise on you like the sun and bring healing like its rays'.

beauty competition which is arranged in order for the king to select the next queen. Esther is the chosen bride and becomes queen, but her nationality is not divulged.

Meanwhile, Mordecai falls foul of the king's favourite, Haman, whom Mordecai, as a good Jew, refuses to bow down to. In revenge, Haman plans the wholesale massacre of the Jewish community, for which he gains the unsuspecting king's consent. Mordecai warns Esther, telling her that this is her chance to save her people.

After fasting she bravely approaches the king, even though she has not lately been called to his presence and so could have incurred his anger. But he accepts her invitation to attend a banquet she will give, accompanied by Haman. At the banquet she still withholds her real request, inviting both of them to a further feast at which she promises to ask the king directly for what she wants.

CYRUS AND THE PERSIAN EMPIRE

The Persian Empire was founded by Cyrus the Great in 549BC. In time he conquered Babylon too. He began to repatriate the peoples who had been deported there. It was in his own interests to have loyal subjects scattered throughout his empire. Cyrus also adopted a very tolerant attitude to the religions of those he had conquered. He encouraged their beliefs and even embraced some of them himself.

The Persian Empire

In 530 Cyrus died while fighting in the eastern region, and was succeeded by his son, Cambyses, who was a very different kind of man. He murdered his brother to keep the throne secure. In 525 Cambyses added Egypt to his empire. In 522, when Cambyses committed suicide, there was confusion over his heir, several claiming to be the murdered brother.

Darius, an army general, seized control of the army and took the throne. He reigned from 521 to 486 and was one of the most powerful of the Persian emperors. By 520 Darius had restored order and it was in this year that Haggai and Zechariah began to prophesy and the work on the Temple was resumed (Ezra 5 and 6).

486–465 Xerxes I reigned. That is his Greek name; the Hebrew is Ahasuerus, the name by which he is known in the book of Esther.

464–423 Artaxerxes I reigned. The events of Ezra 7 to the end of Nehemiah took place in his reign.

423–404 Darius II. The letters known as the Elephantine Papyri belong to this period.

404–359 Artaxerxes II

359–338 Artaxerxes III

The two centuries of the Persian Empire were very important for the Jewish people. The Persians encouraged and subsidized the expeditions back home to Judah. Their religious policy gave freedom to all their peoples, even though they were integrated into one administrative group.

Figures of Persian guards decorated the glazed brick walls of King Darius' palace at Susa (500BC).

Even in ruins the palace of King Darius at Persepolis conveys something of its original scale and splendour.

The Cyrus Cylinder

A cylinder recovered from the foundations of a building in Babylon records Cyrus' exploits. He describes how he had returned the inhabitants to their lands, along with sacred objects and images, overseeing the building of sanctuaries. He exclaims, 'May all the gods whom I have resettled in their sacred cities ask daily . . . for a long life for me.'

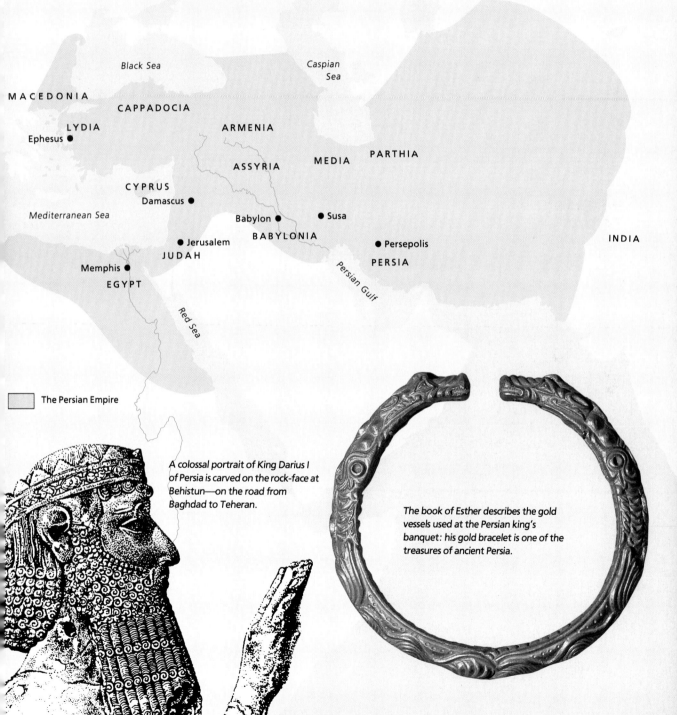

Black Sea

Caspian Sea

MACEDONIA

CAPPADOCIA

LYDIA

Ephesus ●

ARMENIA

ASSYRIA

MEDIA

PARTHIA

CYPRUS

Damascus ●

Mediterranean Sea

Babylon ●

● Susa

BABYLONIA

● Jerusalem

JUDAH

● Persepolis

PERSIA

Persian Gulf

INDIA

Memphis ●

EGYPT

Red Sea

▢ The Persian Empire

A colossal portrait of King Darius I of Persia is carved on the rock-face at Behistun—on the road from Baghdad to Teheran.

The book of Esther describes the gold vessels used at the Persian king's banquet: his gold bracelet is one of the treasures of ancient Persia.

Then, at the centre of the story, comes the king's sleepless night. To fill the wakeful hours he calls for royal records to be brought and reads in them about a successful attempt by Mordecai, some time earlier, to prevent the king's assassination. He discovers that Mordecai has never been rewarded, so asks Haman, who has come early to court to ask for Mordecai's execution, to give him the honours he has deserved.

At the second banquet Esther exposes Haman's wicked plot against her people. The king, unable to break his first edict, issues a secondary one which will allow the Jews to defend themselves when they are attacked, and Haman is hanged on the gallows he had prepared for Mordecai.

Even without the mention of God's name, the book wonderfully depicts the two contrasting lifestyles of Haman, the man who trusts in chance and luck, and of Mordecai, who believes in the God who can control chance to bring about his purposes for his people.

The book of Esther is read at the annual Jewish festival of Purim, which, according to the book of Esther, was inaugurated by Mordecai to celebrate the Jews' deliverance. The word *purim* is linked to the word for lots, reminding them that their enemy Haman cast lots to determine the date of his expected vengeance. Instead, the day became one of victory for the Jewish people.

The book of Esther begins with a description of the sumptuous riches of the Persian court. This beaten gold bowl is one of the 'Oxus treasures' from Persia, dated about 500BC.

Daniel

The first six chapters of the book of Daniel tell the exciting and dramatic story of a little group of young Jews. They were taken to Babylon with the first contingent of captives. After a period of training in the wisdom of Babylon they became leaders and advisers at the Babylonian court.

The leading figure is Daniel. Right from the start, he took a stand for his Jewish principles by refusing to eat the food prepared for the young students at the king's court. To the surprise of the official in charge, he and his three friends were soon seen to prosper on a vegetarian diet.

Later, Daniel, alone among the wisdom teachers and astrologers at court, was able, with God's help, to narrate and interpret the king's dream of a giant statue. Daniel sees in it a vision of four kingdoms and another, God's kingdom, which, like the stone in the dream which crashes into the statue, will crush the others completely. The king confessed:

'Your God is the greatest of all gods, the Lord over kings, and the one who reveals mysteries.' (2:47)

The next adventure concerns Daniel's three friends. Nebuchadnezzar built a statue of himself and put it on display. When the orchestra struck up, everyone was commanded, on pain of death, to fall down and worship it. Shadrach, Meshech and Abednego refused point-blank to worship any but God. They bravely told the king:

'O Nebuchadnezzar, we do not need to defend ourselves before you in this matter. If we are thrown into the blazing furnace, the God we serve is able to save us from it, and he will rescue us from your hand, O king. But even if he does not, we want you to know, O king, that we will not serve your gods or worship the image of gold you have set up.' (3:16–18)

At the king's command they were thrown headlong into the huge, fierce furnace. But there, in the flames, the king saw the three men walking unscathed, with a fourth, godlike figure beside them. Trembling with fear he called for them to be taken out of the fire. They came out unharmed, and Nebuchadnezzar praised the God of Shadrach, Meshech and Abednego.

In Daniel 4 we read how Nebuchadnezzar had a second dream of a great tree which an angel ordered to be felled. Daniel, one of the king's civil servants, dared to challenge him to repent and do justice. He again interpreted the dream for him, warning the king that he was that tree — due to be cut down to size for a period because of his great pride and self-satisfaction. Sure enough, for a time the king suffered a form of madness before being restored to his throne. Then, his sanity restored, Nebuchadnezzar praised God, exclaiming:

'Now I, Nebuchadnezzar, praise and exalt and glorify the King of heaven, because everything he does is right and all his ways are just. And those who walk in pride he is able to humble.' (4:37)

The next story takes place at the very end of the Babylonian Empire, on the night when it fell. The prince and his court were enjoying an orgy of feasting and drinking, using the sacred cups taken from the temple at Jerusalem, when a hand began to write on the plaster of the wall. Belshazzar, the terrified king, summoned Daniel, who interpreted the mysterious symbols, warning the king that he had been judged and found wanting and that his kingdom was coming to an end. The time was indeed at hand — and Darius the Mede seized power.

In the last of these stories, Daniel, now an old man, was a leading official in the reign of Darius. His fellow officials were jealous of him and used his constant habit of prayer as a weapon for his downfall. They persuaded the king to throw to the royal lions any who made request to god or man other than the king. Then they reported Daniel for praying at his window. The reluctant king was forced to keep his word and carry out the punishment. Next morning he hurried to the lion pit and found Daniel unharmed. His God had 'shut the mouths of the lions'.

When was Daniel written?

Many scholars believe that the book of Daniel was written very much later than the

A number of stone carvings show Assyrian kings hunting lions. In Babylon, King Darius ordered Daniel to be thrown into his lion-pit.

events it is supposed to portray, perhaps in the second century BC. They do not think the stories have anything to do with the captives in Babylon: they were meant to encourage the Jews who were undergoing persecution at the hands of the Greek king, Antiochus Epiphanes. Many of the challenges met by Daniel and his friends have a strong bearing on those facing the Jews at that time.

The rest of the book is apocalyptic, a form of writing belonging mainly to the two centuries before Christ (see notes under *Apocrypha* and *Revelation*). It takes the form of mysterious visions involving strange beasts and cosmic powers. This type of writing was a form of code, intended to be understood only by the readers, who were suffering persecution from a dangerous enemy.

POEMS AND HYMNS

Psalms · Song of Solomon · Lamentations

Someone who is happy wants to sing, and a person in love or desperately miserable often finds comfort in poetry. The language of poetry and song finds an echo in moments of great joy and great sorrow. It speaks for us all at the deepest level.

The Bible is full of poetry. Little bits of it burst out all over the place. But there are also particular books of the Bible written in poetry which are the songs and poems of the Hebrew people.

Hebrew poetry

One feature of all poetry is that, like dance, it forms patterns. But how the patterns are made varies from one language and culture to another. Often they are formed by sounds. Words may rhyme. Or the patterns may be those of rhythm, depending on the number of beats in a line, or else in the matching sounds of words put alongside each other. Of course, there is more to making poetry than patterns like these. Words are chosen with great precision and imagery is used to enhance the meaning.

The pattern of Hebrew poetry does not depend on rhyme, or on the number of 'feet' (beats) in a line but on what has been called 'thought rhyme'. This way of making poetry is called 'parallelism'. The matching together of ideas forms the pattern. The statement made in the first line is repeated in other words in the next. Here is an example:

*'The heavens declare the glory of God;
    the skies proclaim the work of his hands.'*
        (19:1)

Sometimes a variation on the first idea appears in the second. The next verse of Psalm 19 says:

*'Day after day they pour forth speech;
    night after night they display knowledge.'*

The thought may continue into a third line or even more, as it does later in this psalm.

There is another form of parallelism in which the second line contrasts with the first. For example:

*'Those the Lord blesses will inherit the land,
    but those he curses will be cut off.'* (37:22)

At other times the second line goes a stage further and makes a climax to the first:

*'Surely goodness and love will follow me all the
        days of my life,
    and I will dwell in the house of the Lord for
        ever.'* (23:6)

In fact there are many ways in which parallelism can form a pattern. Hebrew poetry is not tied down to a fixed number of feet in a line, but usually the number of stresses in one line will be matched by the same number in the next.

There are two great advantages with this kind of poetry. First, because it is less rigid than rhyme or metre it can be composed more spontaneously. Perhaps that is why there are so many outbursts of poetry throughout the Bible, occurring as proverbs, snatches of thanksgiving and prayers.

The other advantage of Hebrew poetry is that it loses less in translation than poetry in most other languages. When poetry depends on rhyme or the sound of words, it may lose much of its richness in another language. But thought rhymes are retained.

The Book of Psalms

Men and women down the ages have found comfort and exhilaration in the book of Psalms, and still do today. Whatever the mood — whether the reader is full of joy or sunk in deepest misery and suffering — there is a psalm to match and voice it. The whole range of human emotion is present in these

MUSIC

The Bible often mentions music, musicians and musical instruments. It contains a whole book of religious songs — the Psalms.

The trumpet announced festivals and summoned the people. The ram's-horn *shofar* called people to war. Victories were celebrated with singing and dancing.

King David was a skilled musician. As a boy he charmed King Saul with his skill on the harp (*kinnor*). And as king he organized the music for the Temple his son Solomon was to build.

Coins, lamps, carvings and mosaics showing musical instruments from early times are amongst the finds of archaeologists.

Musicians from Zinjirli, eighth century BC, are shown playing lyres and hand-drums.

This clay figurine depicts a woman playing a double flute.

Reconstructed from discoveries in the royal graves at Ur (about 2,500BC) is this lyre.

Bridging the centuries, a group of boys today dance to their leader's pipe beside the Dead Sea.

An ivory carving from Megiddo shows a musician playing the kinnor, King David's harp.

poems drawn from the depths of experience. But the writers of the psalms were not recording their joys and sorrows for the world in general. They were pouring out their hearts to God. So many of the psalms are also prayers.

There are psalms to voice the emotion of happiness, expressed in praise to God, like Psalm 103:

'*Praise the Lord, O my soul;*
*   all my inmost being, praise his holy name.*
Praise the Lord, O my soul,
*   and forget not all his benefits —*
who forgives all your sins,
*   and heals all your diseases...*' *(103:1–3)*

But the psalms can express deep despair too, like these words from the previous psalm, 102:

'*Hear my prayer, O Lord;*
*   let my cry for help come to you.*
Do not hide your face from me
*   when I am in distress.*' *(102:1–2)*

The writer goes on to outline his utter misery and sense of forsakenness. Quite often, by the end of such a psalm a note of hope in God has crept in. But there is no pretence. The writers are not afraid to tell God exactly how they are feeling.

In some psalms the writer is very aware of guilt before God. The poem is a prayer for pardon. Psalm 51 is one such, with its plea:

'*According to your great compassion*
*   blot out my transgressions.*
Wash away all my iniquity
*   and cleanse me from my sin.*' *(51:1–2)*

Sometimes the mood is calmer. The best-loved psalm of all, Psalm 23, is full of quiet trust in a loving shepherd — God who can provide for his flock and keep them safe, even through the terrors of life and death.

'*The Lord is my shepherd; I shall not want.*
He maketh me to lie down in green pastures: he
*   leadeth me beside the still waters.*
He restoreth my soul: he leadeth me in the paths
*   of righteousness for his name's sake.*
Yea, though I walk through the valley of the
*   shadow of death, I will fear no evil for*
*   thou art with me; thy rod and thy staff*
*   they comfort me.*

Thou preparest a table before me in the presence
*   of mine enemies: thou anointest my head*
*   with oil; my cup runneth over.*
Surely goodness and mercy shall follow me all
*   the days of my life; and I will dwell in the*
*   house of the Lord for ever.*' *(23)*

The shortest psalm in the book overflows with gladness and praise:

'*Praise the Lord, all you nations;*
*   extol him, all you peoples.*
For great is his love towards us,
*   and the faithfulness of the Lord endures for*
*   ever.*
Praise the Lord.' *(117)*

The longest psalm is 119. It is also an acrostic, which means that every stanza begins with a different letter of the Hebrew alphabet, in the correct order. The whole psalm is about God's word and laws, which are the psalmist's delight:

'*Your word is a lamp to my feet*
*   and a light for my path.*
I have taken an oath and confirmed it,
*   that I will follow your righteous laws...*
Accept, O Lord, the willing praise of my mouth,
*   and teach me your laws.*' *(119:105–108)*

Some of the psalms were clearly written for the king and for court occasions. Psalm 45 is a brilliant wedding poem for a royal bridegroom. Another royal psalm is 72, with its prayers for the reigning king:

'*Endow the king with your justice, O God,*
*   the royal son with your righteousness.*

Psalm 23 is known as the 'shepherd psalm': God, the good shepherd, provides 'green pastures' for his people.

worship in Solomon's temple and perhaps at other local shrines too. We have one reference to a psalm being sung when David brought the Covenant Box into Jerusalem (2 Samuel 6:5).

Many of the themes in the psalms have their roots in the temple worship. Psalm 118, for example, describes a sacrifice being prepared. Other psalms have a question and answer pattern as if they were used in liturgy, with the people singing the responses. Psalm 24 is a good example of this kind of psalm with its question:

'Who is this King of glory?'

and the response:

'The Lord strong and mighty
    the Lord mighty in battle . . .
    he is the King of glory.' (24:8, 10)

David and the psalms

The titles and notes that appear at the beginning of a psalm were later additions, perhaps inserted when the psalms were made into collections. Many of the psalms bear David's name. At the top is written 'A psalm of David'. This could also be translated as 'a psalm for David', to indicate that the psalm was written for King David or one of his descendants. The psalm would then have been part of a collection belonging to the royal house, written for the king of the time. But although some scholars doubt David's authorship, it is likely that at least some of the psalms that bear his name were written by David himself. We know that he was a consummate musician and that he organized the music and singing for the future temple.

There are a number of psalms with headings linking them to specific events in David's life. Some scholars do not put any faith in these biographical notes but others believe that, even though a later hand may have made the connection, the tradition is a valid one. David's experience of life was rich and varied and ran the whole gamut of human emotions. It would not be surprising if such experiences found expression in many of the psalms.

Psalm 119 is a joyful celebration of God's Law. The psalmist expresses delight in obeying God's commands. At a Bar Mitzvah celebration in Jerusalem today, the scrolls of the Law are carried high in the same spirit of joy and devotion.

He will judge your people in righteousness,
    your afflicted ones with justice.' (72:1–2)

Not all psalms, by any means, are individual outpourings of emotion. Often, as with Psalm 66, they are quite clearly written, or adapted, for the community of God's people to experience and sing together:

'Praise our God, O peoples,
    let the sound of his praise be heard.
He has preserved our lives
    and kept our feet from slipping.' (66:8–9)

The Psalms as hymn book

Many people believe that the psalms were brought together in their present form to serve as the hymn book of the restored temple, after the return from captivity in Babylon in 520BC. It is now thought that prophets worked alongside priests in the worship of the temple, and that some of the psalms could be their work.

But many of the psalms were probably used by Israel in the worship of God from as early as 1000BC. Some scholars conclude that most of the psalms stem from the

The psalms in use

The book of Psalms is the biggest collection of poems in the Bible. Although we speak of them as one book, they are actually divided into five separate books, the sections beginning at Psalm 1, Psalm 42, Psalm 73, Psalm 90 and Psalm 107. Each book ends with a doxology, or short song of blessing to God. These divisions of the book go back to at least the second or third century BC.

Probably these five collections were used separately at one time, though the original groups seem to have been added to. For example, Book Two ends with the words, 'The prayers of David, the son of Jesse, are ended' — yet other psalms of his appear in later sections.

There are blocks of psalms bearing the same heading — for example, 'A Psalm of the sons of Korah'. These men belonged to one of the Levite families, some of whom became singers and musicians in the temple choir which David founded.

Another group of psalms, 120–134, is headed 'A Song of Ascents'. The most popular theory is that these psalms were sung by pilgrims as they made the journey up to the temple at festival time.

There are all kinds of directions given at the beginning of many of the psalms which seem to be instructions to a choirmaster or to the instrumentalists and singers. Some probably indicate which tune the psalm was to be sung to; others may give directions about the musical instruments to be used. The word that occurs most is 'selah'. No one now knows what it meant. Perhaps it signalled a change of musical accompaniment, a pause in the music, or an instruction to the singers to sing more loudly.

As well as joyful singing and dancing and choral work, a variety of musical instruments accompanied worship. Psalm 150 tells the worshippers to:

'Praise him [God] with the sounding of the
        trumpet,
    praise him with the harp and lyre,
praise him with tambourine and dancing,
    praise him with the strings and flute,
praise him with the clash of cymbals.' (150:3–5)

Cursing psalms

These psalms are a problem to many because they quite plainly call down vengeance and cursing on the psalmist's enemies. Psalm 137 is one example, with its desire for vengeance on the countries of Edom and Babylon.

The teaching of Jesus to forgive enemies plainly contradicts such an attitude and it may seem inappropriate to echo such words today. But before condemning the writers, it is important to recognize in these curses a cry for justice. It is right to want to see the innocent vindicated and justice done. The very strength of the language used shakes the readers out of their complacency and makes crystal clear what wickedness really is. It is still justifiable to burn with anger against cruelty and evil, and be moved to call out on behalf of those who have been wronged.

Messianic themes

Jewish interpreters saw references to the Messiah — the King who was to come — in some of the passages in the psalms. One example might be Psalm 110:

'The Lord says to my lord:
    "Sit at my right hand
till I make your enemies
    your footstool."'

Some scholars believe that the king in Israel held a very special place as mediator between God and his people and they see these lofty ascriptions as referring to the king of the time. No doubt in the first place some allusion to the reigning king was intended, but it is reasonable to believe that they had Messianic significance too, looking forward to God's anointed one.

The Song of Solomon

The Song of Solomon expresses the joy of human love between man and woman. The poems are frank and passionate expressions of sexual love and its satisfaction.

Jewish and Christian readers alike have not always been able to accept such unashamed hymns to human love. So the poems have often been interpreted as celebrating the relationship of God to Israel, or, in Christian times, of Christ to his bride, the church. But there are no real grounds for treating the book in such a way. It would seem better to accept it at face value — a book in the Bible which recognizes human sexuality and the faithful love of man and woman as part of God's good creation.

The church is often accused of being negative about sex and frowning on human sexuality. But the Bible does no such thing. The relationship between man and woman, including the physical one, came before the fall (see chapter 1). Sexuality is God's good gift and the Song of Solomon is a reminder of the fact.

The poems themselves are full of rich eastern imagery. Both lovers express their feelings for each other freely. In spite of the culture of that time there is no hint of male aggression or of the woman being the victim. Love is shared equally; he exclaims:

'Like a lily among thorns
is my darling among the maidens'

and she responds:

'Like an apple tree among the trees of the forest
is my lover among the young men.
I delight to sit in his shade
and his fruit is sweet to my taste.
He has taken me to the banquet hall
and his banner over me is love.' (2:2–4)

Although Solomon's name is mentioned several times in the poems he is probably not the author. Solomon had a huge harem and a reputation as a lover, so it is not surprising to find his name used in the context of love. No one can be sure when the book was written. Perhaps different poems come from different periods.

Many people have tried to decipher a story-line in the book and to allocate the speeches to different speakers. One theory suggests that Solomon wanted to bring a simple country girl into his harem, when she was in love with one of her own people. But it is almost impossible to make a convincing drama or sequence of events out of the book. It is far easier to accept it as an anthology of love poems.

Winter is over, the almond blossoms, 'the song of doves is heard in the fields': this is the setting for the love-poems of the Song of Solomon.

Lamentations

The title of this book, which follows Jeremiah in our Bibles, speaks for itself. This is a book of laments. The writer pours out his heart in deep anguish and pain because of the terrible fate of Jerusalem at the hand of her Babylonian captors in 587BC. It is a harrowing experience to read the five poems which make up this book. Yet thousands of refugees today have endured some of the terrible sights and sounds that the writer witnessed at first hand. Babies die from hunger in their mothers' arms, while children fall starving in streets where young and old lie dead.

It is a fearful picture too of cruelty endured at the hands of a ruthless enemy. The gates of the city lie buried in rubble and the temple, the nation's pride and joy, is torn down.

The writer's grief is more intense because he realizes the cause of the tragedy. He recognizes that it is the guilt of the nation that has brought about their ruin. False prophets had reassured them that all was well, and they had failed to acknowledge and repent of their sins. Yet, even in the midst of so much misery and despair, the writer sees a ray of hope. Because God is a covenant God, who always keeps his promises, there is hope for a repentant Israel. The writer affirms with incredible faith and courage:

'The Lord is good to those whose hope is in him,
*   to the one who seeks him;*
it is good to wait quietly
*   for the salvation of the Lord . . .*
*   there may yet be hope.'* (3:25, 26, 29)

Lamentations and the Writings

Lamentations belongs to the section of the Old Testament which Jewish rabbis called the Writings. It was part of the five scrolls or *Megilloth* which were collected together because each was read at one or other of the Jewish festivals. Lamentations, not surprisingly, was read when the destruction of Jerusalem was commemorated.

The book consists of five poems (five chapters in the Bible). The first four are in acrostic form. It is a very complicated

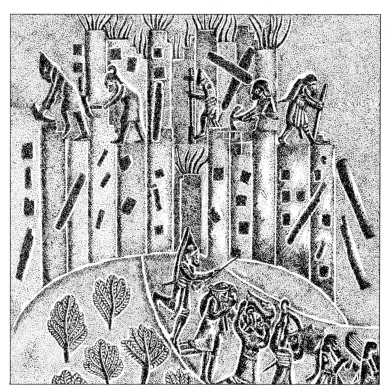

pattern, but deep emotion is often best harnessed to a strict discipline of style. The poems are written in the form of dirges or mourning songs.

No one knows who the author is, though tradition has suggested Jeremiah. But Jeremiah was certainly not led astray by the false prophets who had foretold prosperity. He was a true prophet who had foreseen and warned the people about the coming Babylonian capture of Jerusalem. The writer, whoever he was, must clearly have been an eyewitness.

The five laments of the Book of Lamentations express all the pain of Jerusalem's destruction. 'No one comes to the Temple now to worship . . . The girls who sang there suffer.' The city is in ruins, the survivors taken captive. A palace carving from Nineveh, a century before, showing Assyrian soldiers sacking a city, evokes the scene.

8

STORIES AND WISE SAYINGS

Proverbs · Job · Ecclesiastes

Wisdom in the Old Testament sense had to do with the skills of everyday living, whether at the court, in the market-place or in the home. To be wise was to know how to handle relationships with other people, how to manage business shrewdly, how to do your daily work well. To be wise meant knowing the ropes, having discernment and good judgment.

To sum it all up, wisdom meant knowing how to cope in your own province — as a parent, a child, a courtier, a working person — and to succeed. Wisdom might also include intellectual attainment. 1 Kings 4 says that Solomon 'described plant life, from the cedar of Lebanon to the hyssop that grows out of the walls. He also taught about animals and birds, reptiles and fish.'

Wisdom in the Bible also has to do with making right moral decisions. A key thought of the book of Proverbs is that reverence for God is the first step in wisdom and that true wisdom is a gift from God. The fool, the opposite of the wise, is not someone who has very little brain, but someone who makes wrong moral choices, as well as lacking discernment and good judgment.

Wisdom literature

The theme of wisdom runs through the whole of the Old Testament, but some books are specifically labelled as Wisdom literature. They are Proverbs, Job and Ecclesiastes, together with Wisdom of Solomon and Ecclesiasticus among the Deuterocanonical books (see the Apocrypha in *The Old Testament Books*). Wisdom literature is written as poetry and abounds in pithy sayings and wise proverbs. The books aim to furnish answers to the questions about life that men and women always ask.

The Book of Proverbs — everyday wisdom

Someone has described the Book of Proverbs as godliness put into working clothes. It may seem at first sight to be more concerned with giving shrewd advice than teaching religion. Its subject matter is as varied as everyday life itself. It tells the reader how to treat parents' advice, how to behave at a rich man's banquet, how to value your wife and avoid getting involved with loose women, how to be a good friend — and how to treat enemies too.

There is a wealth of instruction on life at home, life at court, life in the market-place, life among friends and among neighbours — in fact in every area of living. At the lowest level it deals with good manners but it also teaches about tactical dealing and right practice. Beneath all the good advice is the overriding maxim:

'Trust in the Lord with all your heart. Never rely on what you think you know. Remember the

---

Where was Wisdom Learned?

Those who were going to serve at court needed advanced instruction in wisdom compared with the requirements of the ordinary person. They needed skill in international diplomacy as well as home affairs. No doubt there were wisdom teachers and schools attached to the royal court where such training was given. But, in the main, instruction in wisdom was given and received within the family. Parents, grandparents and village elders passed on their received and acquired wisdom to the next generation. So the writer of Proverbs urges:

'Listen, my son, to your father's instruction
    and do not forsake your mother's teaching.
They will be a garland to grace your head
    and a chain to adorn your neck.' (1:8–9)

Lord in everything you do, and he will show you the right way. Never let yourself think that you are wiser than you are; simply obey the Lord and refuse to do wrong.' (3:5–7)

It is difficult to give a coherent picture of Proverbs, because much of it consists of short pithy sayings which switch from one subject to another with bewildering speed. But it is full of lively interest and colourful descriptions. The miniatures that it paints are priceless.

There is the lazy man, turning on his bed like a door on its hinge. 'There is a lion in the road, a fierce lion roaming the streets!' is his excuse for not getting up.

There is the nagging wife who is like 'water going drip-drip-drip on a rainy day'.

There are longer pen portraits — such as the one of the loose woman, with her bold looks, her perfumed sheets and her tale of a husband who has gone on a long journey. She tempts the unwary traveller, who accompanies her like an ox to the slaughter.

There is the realistic picture of someone who has had too much to drink, with bloodshot eyes and the sensation of being 'out on the ocean, sea-sick, swinging high up in the rigging of a tossing ship', only able to gasp 'I need another drink!'

Proverbs has a good bit to say about neighbours and friends and recognizes the priceless gift of friendship:

'A man of many companions may come to ruin,
    but there is a friend who sticks closer than a
        brother.' (18:24)

'Wounds from a friend can be trusted.' (27:6)

'People learn from one another, just as iron sharpens iron.' (27:17)

'You might as well curse your friend
    as wake him up early in the morning with a
        loud greeting.' (27:14)

In Proverbs 31 there is a pen picture of the perfect wife, listing her accomplishments which include catering for her household, shopping wisely and making good business deals:

'Her children arise and call her blessed;
    her husband also, and he praises her:
"Many women do noble things
    but you surpass them all."

Charm is deceptive, and beauty is fleeting;
    but a woman who fears the Lord is to be
        praised.
Give her the reward she has earned,
    and let her works bring her praise at the city
        gate.' (31:28–31)

An important central portion of the book of Proverbs personifies wisdom as a woman inviting all who will to come to her feast and share in it. In a passage of lyric beauty in Proverbs 8 wisdom describes her origins:

'I was made in the very beginning
    at the first, before the world began . . .
I was his daily source of joy,
    always happy in his presence —
happy with the world
    and pleased with the human race.' (8:23, 30–31)

Wisdom is the virtue equally at home with God and with people and the one who brings both together.

Much of the advice in Proverbs is good common sense, the voice of experience addressing the inexperienced. The proverbs prescribe the choices that will pay dividends. But underlying all is the moral framework of trust and obedience to Israel's God. Although none of the great events in Israel's history is mentioned, it is significant that eighty-eight times out of a hundred, the name used for God is the covenant name Yahweh, the LORD — the 'I AM' by which God revealed himself to Moses and his people Israel.

Who wrote Proverbs?

Several different authors are named in the text — Solomon, Agur and Lemuel as well as others referred to as 'wise men'. The book ends with the acrostic poem about the ideal wife which is anonymous. Nothing is known of Agur or Lemuel, although they seem to have been non-Jews. Solomon was a byword for wisdom. The book begins with the words: 'The proverbs of Solomon', which is picked up again in 10:1: 'These are Solomon's proverbs,' and again in 25:1: 'Here are more of Solomon's proverbs.'

No doubt there are many different sources, including non-Israelite ones, for the numerous wise sayings, some of which may be much earlier than Solomon. But it seems

The 'ideal wife' of Proverbs 31 is a multi-talented woman, capable not only of clothing her family but of selling her wares to the merchants, and buying land. Her secret is the wisdom that comes from trusting God and following his instructions.

Proverbs is a book of practical wisdom, providing instructions for life at home and in the market-place.

Wisdom Literature and Other Cultures

Wisdom literature similar in form to the Bible's Wisdom books has survived from other cultures—Egyptian and Assyrian in particular. Maxims and proverbs made good material for copybooks, so many of the sayings have been preserved in this form from the exercises of trainee scribes. Some of this wisdom concerns age-old questions to do with suffering and the meaning of life. It dates from the period when David was king in Israel (from 1000BC) and even earlier.

There are good reasons to think that Israel borrowed from some of these early writings. One Egyptian manual, called *The Teaching of Amenemope*, has certain passages so similar to some in Proverbs that there must have been borrowing. It is likely that Proverbs was the borrower, since the Egyptian material goes back well before the time of Solomon and may even be as early as the twelfth century BC.

1 Kings tells us that 'kings all over the world heard of [Solomon's] wisdom and sent people to listen to him'. That piece of information implies there was a good exchange of thought among the courts and schools of wisdom of different countries at that time.

his touch can be recognized among them. The book of Kings tells us:

'Solomon's wisdom was greater than the wisdom of all the men of the East, and greater than all the wisdom of Egypt. He was wiser than any other man . . . He spoke three thousand proverbs and his songs numbered a thousand and five.' (1 Kings 4:30, 32)

When was Proverbs written?

There is one key to its date in Proverbs itself: 25:1 says that these further proverbs of Solomon were 'copied by men at the court of King Hezekiah of Judah'. So we know that the book in its present form could not have been earlier than the sixth century BC. It used to be thought that the wise men or sages came on the scene late, and a date of the fifth to the third century was suggested. But it is now recognized that Wisdom literature was written early in other cultures. It is possible that all the material in Proverbs was in existence by the time of Solomon himself, even if it was edited later and the first nine chapters and the last chapter added then.

Job — and the issue of suffering

Proverbs answers the question 'What?' It tells us what a wise person is, what a fool is, what a husband or parent should do and what is the right behaviour in many situations. It also seems a bit like a 'how to succeed' manual: obeying God and doing what is right will bring rewards. But Hebrew wisdom dug deeper than that. While accepting that honest, upright behaviour *usually* brings rewards, it was not afraid to face squarely the problem of the innocent sufferer. Good is not always rewarded with health and long life, and those who least deserve it sometimes seem to suffer most. The book of Job is concerned with why the innocent suffer, although it does not actually give an answer to this unanswerable question.

The story of Job is probably a very ancient one. It tells of a wealthy and well-regarded man with a thriving farm and family. In a series of terrible accidents he loses one after another of his possessions, and even his children. Finally his own health breaks down and he is left wretched and stripped of everything. In this situation he still insists on trusting in God. His friends come to visit him as he sits on an ash heap, covered in boils. After sitting silently with him for some while they begin to offer reasons for his suffering. They are only too ready to tell him where he has gone wrong and what he should do if he wants his fortunes restored.

Their ideas are expressed in a series of poetic speeches, to each of which Job gives his answer. Rather than comforting him, this reasoning of his friends (unlike their silence) exacerbates Job's misery. They insist Job must have done something wrong to be suffering such misfortunes. The best thing he can do is to acknowledge the fact and repent before God, then all will be well again. The three friends — later joined by a fourth — plead their case in fine poetry and rhetoric.

Job is ready to admit he is not perfect: 'How can a mortal be righteous before God?'

Yet he knows that his life has been good and honest, he has done nothing blameworthy nor been guilty of rebellion against God. He is sickened by the trite response of his 'friends' to his tragic situation. 'Doubtless you are the people, and wisdom will die with you!' he exclaims, 'but I have a mind as well as you; I am not inferior to you.'

Job sees little hope if there is to be no reversal of his fortunes in this life. With great sadness he concludes:

'At least there is hope for a tree:
    If it is cut down it will sprout again,
    and its new shoots wil not fail.
Its roots may grow old in the ground
    and its stump die in the soil,
yet at the scent of water it will bud
    and put forth shoots like a plant.
But man dies and is laid low;
he breathes his last and is no more.' (14:7–10)

Yet like others in the Old Testament, Job does glimpse some kind of vindication beyond the grave. In a cryptic verse in chapter 19, where the original text is unclear, Job says:

'I know that my Redeemer lives,
    and that in the end he will stand upon the
        earth.
And though this body has been destroyed,
    yet apart from my flesh I will see God.'
        (19:25–26)

But still Job longs for the chance to confront God now:

'If only I knew where to find him;
    if only I could go to his dwelling!
I would state my case before him.' (23:3–4)

Finally, when the friends have had their say and Job has poured out his bitterness and self-justification, he has an encounter with God. But, instead of answering Job's questions, in chapters 38 and 39 God confronts Job with unanswerable challenges.

The Problem of Suffering

Although the problem of suffering is the most difficult anyone can face, it is especially difficult for those who believe in an all-powerful and all-loving God, as the Hebrews did. Either God does not love—and so does not care enough to intervene—or else he is unable to help—and therefore his power is not absolute. But the prologue to the book of Job gives a clue to the problem which is never actually disclosed to Job.

Satan, the adversary of God and humanity, taunts God with the suggestion that Job trusts God only for what he can get out of it. He argues that Job serves God because it pays him to do so. Job would soon turn round and curse God if he lost his possessions, his family or his health. Because God has implicit confidence in Job's faith, he gives Satan limited power to bring troubles on Job.

But in spite of this hint that suffering comes from God's adversary, not as a direct result of God's will, the book gives no real answer to the problem of suffering. What is made clear is that although blessing and prosperity can normally be expected to follow upright living, life is much more than a system of rewards and punishments. There is a mystery at the heart of suffering which cannot be understood. But the God who stands behind it all is infinitely worthy of awe, trust and obedience. A whole new dimension would be added later by the suffering of God himself, in the person of Christ.

Job's suffering leads him to question God. The response is a fresh vision of God's greatness, the power of the Creator.

'Where were you when I laid the earth's
    foundation? . . .
Have you ever given orders to the morning,
    or shown the dawn its place? . . .
Have you comprehended the vast expanses of
    the earth? . . .
Have you entered the storehouses of the
    snow? . . .
Can you bring forth the constellations in their
    seasons? . . .
Do you know when the mountain goats give
    birth? . . .
Do you give the horse his strength?' (38:4, 12, 18, 22,
    32, 39: 1, 19)

These are not bullying questions: God is bringing Job to a realization of the immense power of the Creator. There is no comparison — no room for argument — between one as great and powerful as God and one as limited and puny as Job. Job is sobered and overpowered by this revelation of God's greatness and knowledge. He responds:

'My ears had heard of you
    but now my eyes have seen you.
Therefore I despise myself
    and repent in dust and ashes.' (42:5–6)

In the epilogue, God does not tax Job with arrogance or lack of reverence. It is the friends, with their smug and inadequate answers, that God reproves. But Job's prayers on their behalf will be answered. Job, meanwhile, is restored to his former state of health and wealth.

When was Job written?

It is not easy to say who wrote the book of Job or when it was written. It is subtly constructed and full of beautiful poetry. It may have been the work of a professional

Wisdom teacher, either at court or at one of the shrines where there were books — and those who could read. A wide range of dates has been suggested, from the time of Moses to the time of Greek supremacy after the exile. The time of Solomon is probably the earliest possible date. It may be that the story is a very old one which was written up in this form at a much later time.

Ecclesiastes: the search for meaning

Ecclesiastes belongs in the real world where people question the meaning of life.

What is it all for?
Where is it all leading?
What is the point of anything?

Ecclesiastes contains many sayings similar to those in Proverbs, but the main burden of the book is the writer's search for meaning. He investigates every way of knowing and experiencing life in order to discover if there is any purpose or pattern in it. He tries study, pleasure, creative projects, hard work and wealth. He pictures himself as Solomon because here was a man who had an abundance of wisdom as well as every earthly possession. He concludes, at the end of his search, that everything is mere 'vanity' (a puff of wind or a wisp of vapour — nothingness, utter futility).

The Jewish rabbis did not feel happy about including Ecclesiastes among the officially recognized books of Scripture (see article on *The Old Testament Books*), because in the writer's reckoning God seems to be absent from his world. Yet the author is not an atheist. He recognizes God's creation and control in the constant round of seasons and cyclic events. What he cannot see is any meaning in it for men and women, who are caught up in the apparently futile repetition of life. He does see a natural pattern or rhythm:

'There is a time for everything
    and a season for every activity under heaven:
a time to be born and a time to die,
a time to plant and a time to uproot . . .
a time to weep and a time to laugh,
a time to mourn and a time to dance.' (3:1, 2, 4)

But the endless repeating of the pattern makes no sense, because one destiny — death — awaits all, rich and poor, good and bad alike. But his advice to the young is:

'Remember your Creator
    in the days of your youth,
before the days of trouble come
    and the years approach when you will say,
    "I find no pleasure in them." ' (12:1)

Then, in a beautiful and poetic series of pictures, he describes the onset of old age:

'When the keepers of the house tremble,
    and the strong men stoop,
when the grinders cease because they are few,
    and those looking through the windows grow
        dim . . .
when men are afraid of heights
    and of danger in the streets;

The writer of Ecclesiastes sees a pattern to life, a 'season' for everything, sowing and planting, birth and death, joy and sorrow.

Ecclesiastes paints a vivid picture of old age. For young and old alike, the same advice is given: 'Remember your Creator...'

*when the almond tree blossoms
    and the grasshopper drags himself along
    and desire no longer is stirred.
Then man goes to his eternal home
    and mourners go about the streets.
Remember him — before the silver cord is
        severed,
    or the golden bowl is broken;
before the pitcher is shattered at the spring,
    or the wheel broken at the well,
and the dust returns to the ground it came from,
    and the spirit returns to God who gave it.'*
    (12:3–7)

Perhaps in the end there is some resolution. The writer concludes that, although life may seem meaningless, there is a God who holds us accountable for the way in which we live our lives. So:

*'Fear God and keep his commandments,
    for this is the whole duty of man.
For God will bring every deed into judgment,
    including every hidden thing,
    whether it is good or evil.'* (12:13–14)

On a more optimistic note too:

'This is what I have found out: the best thing anyone can do is eat and drink and enjoy what he has worked for during the short life that God has given.' (5:18)

In spite of the doom and gloom, Ecclesiastes has a right to its place in the Bible. Everyone at times has felt the way the writer feels, and what he has to say gives space for doubt. It is reassuring to discover that it is natural and normal to question life. It pushes back the boundaries of faith to their furthest limit and encourages the reader to be honest about misgivings, rather than to mouth second-hand beliefs. Once doubt has reached its limit, the ground is cleared to begin to build a personal and more stable faith. There are those who have found their starting-point in Ecclesiastes.

Who is the author of Ecclesiastes?

The book begins: 'These are the words of Qoheleth' — a word which is not easily translated from the Hebrew. It can mean philosopher, preacher, teacher, speaker or president. It may be an academic or ecclesiastical title. The writer speaks as if he is Solomon, but he may be taking on the mantle of the wisest and wealthiest man that his readers know of in order to prove his point.

Some see the book as a critique of secularism. The writer is showing what life without faith in God is like. According to this suggestion he repeatedly uses the expression 'under the sun' to define life lived in a secular world.

When was Ecclesiastes written?

Hebrew tradition placed the book in the time of King Hezekiah (sixth century BC) but a date in the third or second century BC seems more likely.

A great many books that had to do with the Jewish faith were written in Old Testament times. Many of these were stored alongside the scriptures in boxes reserved for written scrolls. But that does not mean that they were all considered worthy to be included in the body of books that made up the Jewish sacred writings. The problem was to know which of the books should be included.

Sacred writings were regarded as special in a unique way. They were believed to be God's words to his people. The books that make up the Old Testament were recognized as having this authority and set apart from the rest as Scripture. Appointed councils and official bodies put their seal of approval on what had already been accepted.

The word used to describe these chosen books is 'canon'. The canon of Scripture is the body of books that makes up the Bible. 'Canon' comes from a word meaning a reed or measuring-rod. The canon contains the books by which people measure or size up their faith and its practice. The word canon can also mean a list or index, from the marks made on the measuring-rod. So canon also means the list of books chosen.

The Law
The first five books of the Bible, known as the Law or Torah, were recognized as sacred writings from very early on. By the time of Ezra the scribe, in about 400BC, they were in their present form and recognized as holy writing.

The Prophets
The books of the prophets, written down in the lifetimes of the prophets or a little later, were all accepted as scripture soon after 200BC.

The Writings
The third division of the Jewish scriptures, the mixture of books known as the Writings or Hagiographa, presented more of a problem. They were the last to be 'canonized'. Some were accepted without doubt. The Psalms had already gained a special place in everyone's affections because of their use in the liturgy and worship of the Temple. But other books were less convincing.

How about Esther and Ecclesiastes, which do not mention the name of God, and the Song of Solomon, which is unashamedly a love poem? People were not quite sure whether they should be included in the body of Scripture. Then there were the many other books—stories, history and wisdom literature—which had sprung out of the same tradition. Were they to be included in the canon or not?

Some people think that the Hellenized Jews living in Alexandria in Egypt in the first and second centuries BC were more accepting of these extra books and included them, whereas the Jews living in Palestine were not.

The Jewish canon of Scripture
As late as the beginning of the Christian era a few lingering doubts about some books still remained. By the time of the fall of Jerusalem to Rome in AD70 Jewish scholars were concerned to resolve these doubts and confirm the list. The Temple had been destroyed. The old centre of the Jewish faith had gone. It was therefore all the more necessary for Jews scattered everywhere to have a properly agreed list of Scripture.

The school at Jamnia
At this time there was an academy on the coast of Palestine at Yavneh (Jamnia). It had been founded by a rabbi who had escaped from the siege of Jerusalem. Some of the best Jewish scholars of the day flocked to it and it became a great centre of Jewish learning. Discussions about the canon took place here in AD90 and the final ruling is dated from that time. No official or binding decision was made. But their ruling was universally accepted, partly because of the high regard in which the school at Jamnia was held and partly because the decision tallied with general opinion.

The Old Testament books in Jewish Bible order:

THE LAW OR TORAH:
Genesis
Exodus
Leviticus
Numbers
Deuteronomy

THE FORMER PROPHETS:
Joshua
Judges
1 and 2 Samuel
1 and 2 Kings

THE LATTER PROPHETS:
The major prophets:
Isaiah
Jeremiah
Ezekiel

The minor prophets—The Twelve (counted as one book):
Hosea
Joel
Amos
Obadiah
Jonah
Micah
Nahum
Habakkuk
Zephaniah
Haggai
Zechariah
Malachi

THE WRITINGS:
Psalms
Proverbs
Job
Song of Solomon
Ruth
Lamentations
Ecclesiastes
Esther
Daniel
Ezra-Nehemiah
1 and 2 Chronicles

The Jewish Old Testament numbers 24 books, not the 39 of Christian Bibles, because of the books that are combined or numbered together. The order is also different.

The Septuagint
The word 'septuagint' comes from the Greek word for seventy. The Septuagint is a translation of the Hebrew Old Testament into Greek, made between 284 and 247BC, for the benefit of Jews living outside Palestine, whose everyday language was Greek and not Hebrew.

According to one tradition, seventy men were shut up in separate cells and given seventy days in which to translate the Scriptures. At the end of that time it was discovered that they had all produced the same translation, word for word!

That is the legend. What is nearer the truth is that Jews living in Alexandria were responsible for the translation, or rather for a number of versions in Greek, and that these evolved over several generations. Each book would be written on a roll and the rolls were stored in different boxes, often with other books to do with the same period or subject.

The Apocrypha

The word 'apocrypha' means hidden things, and it refers to the books that at one time were considered for inclusion in the Old Testament canon. Although none of them was accepted in Palestine as part of the Hebrew canon of scripture, they were kept alongside the rolls of the Greek Septuagint scriptures.

Early Christians found these books when they took over the Septuagint as their Bible, and they included them. The list of books accepted by Roman Catholic Christians, called Deuterocanonical, differs slightly from the books known in the Protestant churches as the Apocrypha. Other branches of the church consider them valuable to read but do not recognize them as an authoritative source of belief. Many of these books are different in quality from the Bible books.

Wisdom books

The books of the Apocrypha belong to different types of literature, just as the rest of the books of the Old Testament do.

There is Wisdom literature—books of poetry and philosophy—represented by Wisdom of Solomon and Ecclesiasticus. **Wisdom of Solomon** was probably written by an Alexandrian Jew. It has echoes of Greek thought which includes a belief in life after death. It contains these lovely words:

'But the souls of the righteous are in the hand of God, and no torment will ever touch them.
In the eyes of the foolish they seemed to have died, and their departure was thought to be an affliction, and their going from us to be their destruction; but they are at peace.' (3:1–3)

Ecclesiasticus is the Greek name given to the Wisdom of Joshua Ben-Sira. He lived in Jerusalem probably around 180BC. The Greek translation of his work is by his grandson who went to Egypt. Perhaps the most familiar verses in it are those in praise of famous men, beginning:

'Let us now praise famous men, and our fathers in their generations.' (44:1)

There are splendid words, too, in the previous chapter:

'Though we speak much we cannot reach the end, and the sum of our words is: "He is the all".
Where shall we find strength to praise him?
For he is greater than all his works.' (43:27–28)

Apocryphal stories

Some of the books in the Apocrypha are stories, rather in the vein of Esther but often with more supernatural ingredients. In **Tobit**, the liver, heart and gall of a fish are able, under the guidance of a guardian angel, to drive away demons and cure blindness.

Judith tells the story of a young widow who enters the tent of Nebuchadnezzar's general, Holofernes, supposedly to give him military secrets. She manages to cut off his head when he is drunk and so rescues the Jewish people, whose land he was going to attack. Unfortunately the writer constantly refers to Nebuchadnezzar as King of Assyria, not Babylon, which throws doubt on the accuracy of the whole story.

History books

There are history books, such as **1 and 2 Maccabees**. 1 Maccabees recounts the struggle of the Jews against a persecuting Syrian king called Antiochus Epiphanes, the courage of the Maccabee champions, and the rule of the Jewish king, John Hyrcanus. It covers the years 175–134BC and was probably written soon after the death of John Hyrcanus in 103BC.

Other parts of the Apocrypha link up with existing books of the Old Testament. There is a letter said to be from **Jeremiah** to the exiles in Babylon, warning them against idolatry. The **Book of Baruch** is said to be by the prophet's scribe, who is mentioned in the book of Jeremiah.

There are several additional Daniel stories. In **Susannah**, Daniel obtains justice for a virtuous Jewish wife who is falsely accused of adultery. In **Bel and the Dragon**, Daniel uncovers the deception of the worshippers of Bel. They insist that he eats the food set out for him each night. Daniel exposes their trickery and reveals that it is the priests and their families who feast on the offerings. Daniel also kills a great dragon worshipped in Babylon. For doing so he is put in the lions' den. But the prophet Habakkuk feeds him—having been miraculously transported there from Judea. The lions do not kill Daniel and he is rescued next day.

Apocalyptic

There is another kind of literature which occurs in the Apocrypha and also in the Bible itself. It is known as apocalyptic. **2 Esdras**, also known as the **Apocalypse of Ezra**, is an example of this kind of writing.

Hebrew prophets did not see life in terms of a cycle, repeated like the changing of the seasons. Nor did they believe that the world and its inhabitants were at the mercy of blind fate. They believed strongly that God was in control and that history marched forward under his direction. They always looked ahead to the climax of history when God's purposes would be completely fulfilled.

Early prophets, like Amos, looked forward to the coming Day of the Lord. They warned Israel and Judah that it would not be a nice cosy time of vindication and reward for them but a day of justice and righteousness. In view of its coming there was need for national repentance.

Deuterocanonical Books		Books of the Apocrypha
3 Esdras[1]	=	1 Esdras
4 Esdras[1]	=	2 Esdras
Tobias	=	Tobit
Judith	=	Judith
Additions to Esther [2]	=	Additions to Esther
Wisdom of Solomon	=	Wisdom of Solomon
Ecclesiasticus	=	Ecclesiasticus
Baruch	=	(Letter of Jeremiah
		(Baruch
Additions to Daniel [3]	=	(Song of the Three Young Men
		(Susannah
		(Bel and the Dragon
		Prayer of Manasseh
1 Maccabees	=	1 Maccabees
2 Maccabees	=	2 Maccabees

Notes:
1 These books form part of the New Testament canon of scripture in the Vulgate (Latin) Bible
2 These are included as part of the book of Esther
3 These are included as part of the book of Daniel

BETWEEN THE OLD AND NEW TESTAMENTS

But in the two centuries before Christ there emerged a new kind of writing about the end-times which was far more vivid and colourful. It included visions of symbolic monsters and supernatural happenings, disturbances in heaven and earth. The imagery was strange and dramatic. The chief example of this kind of writing in the Old Testament is the later chapters of the book of Daniel. There are snatches of the same kind of writing in Isaiah, Ezekiel and Zechariah.

The word 'apocalypse' comes from the Greek, meaning to uncover or reveal. But apocalyptic writing hides as well as uncovers. It was often used in times of persecution.

The great struggle pictured in the clash between dragons and monsters, angels and the stars in their courses, gave the scene a cosmic dimension. Those suffering persecution for their faith could see their battle against a bigger backcloth. The struggles of God's persecuted people were part of the great universal struggle between God and the forces of evil. But the end was certain. God would be victorious, the forces of good would prevail and his people would be vindicated.

The last glimpse of the Jewish people in the Old Testament comes in the books of Ezra, Nehemiah and Esther—when the Persian Empire ruled their country. For 200 years the Persians maintained their empire and that time seems to have been a fairly tranquil one for the Jewish nation—although we know very little of what was going on, especially in the fourth century.

The book of Esther hints at periods when their enemies made threats against the Jews living in Persia. But for most of the time those who remained in exile probably lived at peace. In Palestine, as we have seen, the small remnant of the nation who returned began to rebuild, and to study the Law again.

Jews and Samaritans

When the returned exiles began the work of rebuilding the Temple they made it only too clear that they did not want help from the people now living in the territory that had once belonged to the northern tribes of Israel. These 'Samaritans' (from Samaria, the capital city of Israel) were despised by pure-blooded Jews. They were a half-caste breed—a mixture of Israelites and the nations sent in by the Assyrians to repopulate the land—who had not even kept the religion pure.

The Samaritans saw things differently. They believed that they were true followers of Moses and the Law, and when their offers of help were rejected they did all they could to hinder the work of rebuilding. Rivalry and tension between these two groups quickly grew. In time the Samaritans built their own temple on Mount Gerizim, which had been a holy mountain since the time of Moses. The

enmity between Jews and Samaritans lasted hundreds of years. By New Testament times, Jews would make a lengthy detour rather than go through Samaritan territory. Feeling was bitter in the extreme.

The rise of Greece

As the Persians and their empire spread westwards, the Greeks fought hard to keep them off their soil. The famous battles of Marathon, Thermopylae and Salamis took place at this period in the fourth century BC.

Then an outstanding figure came upon the scene.

Alexander the Great was only twenty years old when his father, Philip of Macedon, was assassinated, but even at this age he began to win one victory after another. His armies swept as far as present-day Pakistan and the tale is told that Alexander sat down on the banks of the Indus river and wept because there were no more worlds to conquer. He died before he was thirty-three, probably the greatest military

Rulers of Palestine Between the Testaments

GREEK/HELLENISTIC RULE 333–166

333–332	**Alexander the Great** conquers Palestine
300	Egyptian kings—the **Ptolemies**
200	Syrian kings—the **Seleucid** dynasty
175–166	**Antiochus IV Epiphanes**, defiling the temple in 168

JEWISH INDEPENDENCE 166–63

166	Mattathias and his sons, the **Maccabees**, rebel against Antiochus
166–160	**Judas Maccabeus**
165	Rededication of the temple by Judas
160–143	**Jonathan** (Judas' brother)
142–134	**Simon** (Judas' brother)
134–104	**John Hyrcanus**
104–103	**Aristobulus**
103–76	**Alexander Janneus**
76–67	**Alexandra Salome** (his widow)
67–63	**Aristobulus II**

ROMAN RULE 63–4

63	**Pompey** takes Jerusalem: Judah is added to the Roman province of Syria
63–40	**Hyrcanus II**
48	Pompey overthrown by **Julius Caesar**
44	Julius Caesar assassinated
40–37	**Antigonus**—Jewish ruler under Rome
37–4	**Herod the Great**
27	Octavian given title of **Caesar Augustus** and control of the Roman Empire

leader that has ever lived.

Alexander had studied under the famous Greek philosopher Aristotle and his one great desire was to spread Greek culture throughout the world he conquered. When he died there was feuding among his generals. In the east, Seleucus inherited Mesopotamia and Syria. Ptolemy had Egypt. Palestine was once again in the middle of a power struggle, for the two generals were fierce rivals. Both wanted to make their capital cities the most magnificent. Both, too, shared Alexander's vision for the spread of Greek culture.

Hellenism

'Hellas' was the old name for Greece, and Hellenism is the name given to the Greek culture of Alexander's time and later. Hellenization meant the spread of Greek thought and philosophy as well as the use of the Greek language. The kind of Greek used, known as *koine* Greek, was different from that spoken in classical times. It took over from Aramaic as the language of international affairs. Greek architecture and buildings flourished and soon there were Greek-type gymnasia, theatres and stadia everywhere. Well-to-do men and women wore Greek-style clothes.

Alexandria, the city in Egypt named after Alexander the Great, was a superb example of Hellenism. It had a museum and a huge and justly famous library. Research was encouraged. Both Euclid the mathematician and the physicist Archimedes lived and studied there. A great many Jews lived in Alexandria and it was probably under the Ptolemies that the Jewish Scriptures were translated into Greek (see *The Old Testament Books*: the Septuagint). Greek thinking influenced some Jewish writing, for example the apocryphal book, the **Wisdom of Solomon**.

Antiochus Epiphanes: oppression

Palestine came under the rule of the Ptolemies during the third century BC, shortly after Alexander's empire was divided. These rulers were easy-going and did not try to force their views on the Jewish people. Many of the Jews were attracted by Hellenism, even so. But there was also a revival of religious and national feeling, mainly among those who lived outside the towns. This group of zealous people was known as **Hasidim**, which means loyal or pious ones. They were devoted to the Torah and against Hellenization.

While the atmosphere was tolerant this group of loyal Jews remained in the background. But things were not to remain undisturbed for much longer. In 223BC Antiochus III came to the throne of the Seleucid (Syrian) Empire. He fought and won a victory against Ptolemy V, gaining the right to rule Palestine. His successor is usually called Antiochus Epiphanes. Epiphanes means 'shown forth' or 'manifested' and Antiochus believed that he was Zeus, the chief Greek god himself, made manifest. He was not the first ruler to consider himself divine but he was one of the most ruthless. He carried out a campaign of Hellenization with obsessive zeal.

According to Antiochus, worship of Zeus was the test of a citizen's loyalty. This also included utter obedience to himself—the king who represented the god. He began to tamper with the affairs of the Jewish people. He wanted more money, so he increased taxes and actually auctioned off the sacrosanct office of High Priest to the highest bidder. Not surprisingly there was some underhand dealing in the arrangement. In the end, two rivals jostled for this prime post.

As a result of the rivalry Antiochus came in person with his army to reinstate his favourite candidate. He plundered the Temple and declared the Jewish faith illegal. He imposed the death penalty on any mother who had her son circumcised—the sign of the covenant faith—and on anyone who possessed a copy of the Torah or who kept the Sabbath.

In 168BC he marched his troops into Jerusalem and put an altar to Zeus over the altar of burnt offering in the Temple court. As if this was not blasphemous enough in Jewish eyes, he then sacrificed pigs on it. To the Jew the pig is an unclean animal and an abomination. Jewish people were then ordered to eat pork and to offer sacrifices to Zeus. Antiochus' troops policed the country to see that his edicts were carried out.

The suffering that followed was very great. Some were not strong enough to resist and obeyed the cruel king's orders. Others resisted and died for their faith—or went into hiding.

Jewish resistance: the Maccabees

Before long an act was committed which fanned the spark of resistance into a flame. A village priest named Mattathias was ordered to make a sacrifice to Zeus and steadfastly refused. He killed the Syrian officer who had given the order and a fellow Jew who had tamely obeyed. Then he and his five sons fled to the hills and went into hiding. A loyal band of Jews joined them, united in the battle cry: 'Let everybody who is zealous for the Law and stands by the covenant come out after me!'

These were no trained soldiers but a band of determined guerillas. Before Mattathias died in 166BC he handed over leadership to his eldest son, Judas. He was nicknamed Maccabeus, which probably means the Hammer, in recognition of the heavy blows he struck against the enemy. In spite of the enormous odds against them, Judas and his followers actually won a victory against Antiochus and demanded a peace treaty.

In 165BC Judas rebuilt the Temple altar, rededicated it and restored worship there. That event is still celebrated by Jewish people every December, at the Festival of Hanukkah or Lights.

When Judas was killed, the war of resistance was carried on in turn by his two brothers, Jonathan and Simon. They were helped by the fact that Syrian attention was focused more and more on Rome. Antiochus fought against the Romans in 190BC, and lost the battle.

The rise of Rome

In the early centuries of its history Rome had only local importance. But by 338BC the Romans controlled about half the western part of the Italian peninsula and went on to rule the whole area. After defeating Carthage in the second century BC Rome's power expanded rapidly in all directions.

In 63BC the Roman general Pompey took over the eastern Mediterranean lands, including Palestine. The Mediterranean Sea was now ringed by Roman provinces and areas of Roman control.

Jewish independence

In Palestine the Maccabees, or Hasmoneans, had won a century of independence for the Jewish nation (from 166 to 63BC). They ruled more or less free from foreign interference. They took the title and office of High Priest as well as ruler. Some took the title of king too.

Sadly, the early ideals were lost and a less lofty style of leadership followed. The Jewish ruler Alexander Janneus was not above using mercenaries and many Jews supported Syria rather than him. He was succeeded by his widow, Alexandra and when she died her two sons fought for the throne.

Then trouble came from nearby Idumea and Nabatea. To resolve their quarrels Alexandra's sons called for the help of the Roman general, Pompey, who was in Syria at the time. When he arrived in Jerusalem he took the city for Rome, and ended Jewish freedom once and for all.

Roman rule

Pompey put the whole region under the supervision of Rome's representative in Syria. He reduced the Hasmonean kingdom to the region of Judea, Idumea, Perea and Galilee and made Hyrcanus II High Priest and ethnarch—ruler of the people—instead of his brother. The Samaritans were allowed to keep a small area which included their temple on Mount Gerizim.

But Rome now had troubles of its own. In 48BC Pompey was defeated by Julius Caesar, who was himself assassinated in 44BC. After many crises, Octavian, with the title of Augustus Caesar, became the first Emperor of Rome in 27BC.

During these changes in power those who had been appointed by Rome to rule the provinces had to be careful to keep in with the right people. Hyrcanus and his adviser, Antipater of Idumea, hastily transferred their loyalty from Pompey to Julius Caesar and so survived. Antipater was then murdered and his two sons, Phasael and Herod, who had helped him rule, took over. But there was intrigue and infighting, so Herod appealed to Rome for help. In 47 he was made governor and in 40BC he was declared king of Judea by Rome. It took him three years to establish his rule with Rome's help but he then reigned, under Rome's overall control, until his death in 4BC.

The Herods

Herod the Great was an Idumean (Idumea was the name used by Greeks and

The most famous of the palace-fortresses built by King Herod is Masada, close to the Dead Sea. Here the Jewish resistance made its last stand against the Romans in AD73. Their mass suicide made the Roman victory an empty one.

99

Romans for the land of Edom). Edomites and Israelites had long been enemies. After the fall of Jerusalem in 586BC the Idumeans gradually pressed north. But the Hasmoneans (or Maccabean kings) conquered Idumea and forced the people to adopt the Jewish faith.

Herod, as an Idumean, was not popular with most Jews. But at least he made and kept peace: the only ruler to succeed in doing so. He was also a magnificent builder. His projects ranged from strong fortress palaces to a beautiful winter palace near Jericho. Josephus the historian tells us:

'He built a fortress in the hills facing Arabia and called it Herodium after himself and seven miles from Jerusalem he gave the same name to an artificial hill . . . He encircled the top with round towers, filling the enclosed space with a palace so magnificent that in addition to the splendid appearance of the interior of the apartment the outer walls, copings and roofs had wealth lavished on them without stint. At very heavy cost he brought in an unlimited supply of water from a distance.'

Herod's greatest undertaking was the rebuilding of the Temple with enormous splendour and magnificence.

Herod was an insanely jealous man. He murdered his loved wife, Mariamne, as well as her mother, and also ordered

the assassination of three of his sons whose rivalry he feared. The story of the slaughter of the children in Bethlehem, told in Matthew's Gospel (chapter 11), is certainly in keeping with his cruel nature.

The Herod family is notorious for its marriage tangles. For example, Herod Antipas took his brother Philip's wife, Herodias and married her himself. As well as being his sister-in-law, Herodias was the daughter of Herod's half-brother and therefore also his niece.

When Herod the Great died in 4BC Rome allowed his kingdom to be divided among his three remaining sons.

Judea, which included the capital city of Jerusalem, went to Archelaus. He was not allowed the title of king but was called ethnarch. Ten years later, in AD6, Rome removed him from office and put in his place a Roman procurator ruling under the Roman governor of Syria. The best-known procurator of the period, through the New Testament accounts, is Pontius Pilate, who governed Judea from AD26–36. (From this time, trouble constantly flared up in the region. It led at last to a general revolt which was ruthlessly punished by the destruction of Jerusalem in AD70.)

The northern part of Palestine was allotted to Antipas, who was given the title of tetrarch of **Galilee and Perea**.

(Tetrarch originally meant ruler of a fourth part but could be used of any subordinate ruler.) Antipas was like his father. He enjoyed luxury and also had his own building projects—among them Sepphoris near Nazareth and the town of Tiberias on the shore of Lake Galilee. He is mentioned in the New Testament as the one who imprisoned and beheaded John the Baptist and before whom Jesus stood trial (see chapter 9).

The third ruler was Philip, who was given land in the north-east. He was a good ruler and remained tetrarch of **Iturea and Trachonitis** until AD34.

THE GREEKS

The golden age of Greece began about 500BC. The city of Athens provided a model for democracy. But the real era of Greek power and influence began when Philip of Macedon welded together the previously warring states of Greece in 338BC. His son Alexander defeated the Persians in 334 and led his victorious armies through Syria and Egypt (founding Alexandria) and east through Persia to the river Indus. All this by the age of 32, when he died and his empire was divided amongst his generals — with Ptolemy taking Egypt, and Seleucus ruling Palestine and the east from Syria.

Wherever the armies went, they spread Greek ('Hellenistic')

ideas and Greek as language. Towns were built to the Greek pattern, with theatres and gymnasia.

The influence of Greece was lasting. When Rome became the major power (from 146BC) Greek remained the common language. The Romans absorbed Greek ideas, even adopting the Greek gods under new Roman names. The New Testament was written in Greek in the first century AD when Rome ruled supreme. Jewish people — not only in Egypt, where the Hebrew scriptures were translated into Greek, but also in Palestine — felt the impact of Greek ideas and customs on their life and culture. For Paul, choosing strategic centres for spreading

the good news about Jesus Christ, the cities of Greece — Philippi, Thessalonica, Corinth, Athens — were prime targets.

MACEDONIA

The Parthenon, built on the Acropolis at Athens, is one of the world's most famous sites. The scenes which decorate the Parthenon's frieze seem about to spring into life—a tribute to the consummate skill of Greek sculptors.

This Greek merchant ship, sixth century BC, is modelled on a vase painting from Athens.

One permanent legacy of Greek civilization is the Games. This vase-painting shows competitors in the Pentathlon—a long jumper, javelin and discus throwers (520BC).

Black Sea

Caspian Sea

ARMENIA

PHRYGIA

CAPPADOCIA

PARTHIA

MEDIA

PISIDIA

CILICIA ● Antioch

CYPRUS

SYRIA

SELEUCID EMPIRE

Ephesus

DIA

● Damascus

● Seleucia

Babylon ●

● Susa

Alexandria

● Jerusalem

● Persepolis

Memphis

EGYPT

PTOLEMIES' EMPIRE

Red Sea

Persian Gulf

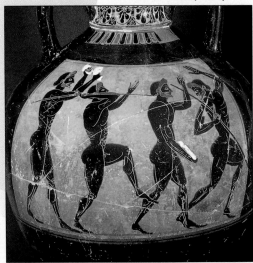

Remains of Greek theatres can be found all over the former Greek Empire. Tiered seating gives everyone a good view, and even a whisper from the stage can be heard at the furthest level. The amphitheatre in Athens continues to be used today.

The head of a woman, from the city of Palmyra, gives a close-up of the kind of headdress, earrings and necklaces a wealthy Greek woman might wear for a special occasion.

The world to which Jesus came was dominated by the Roman Empire. In 27BC Augustus Caesar became its first Emperor. He travelled widely, finding out trouble spots and organizing and settling problems in the Empire.

The backbone of the Empire was its army. Wherever there might be trouble Augustus stationed a legion—or two—of his standing army. There were about ten thousand men in a legion. Each legion was made up of ten cohorts of infantry (480 men to a cohort) as well as cavalry and artillery. The key men were the centurions, non-commissioned officers, each in charge of a band of soldiers originally numbering 100 men. It was the army that kept the peace for which Rome was famous.

The Romans tended, especially at first, to rule indirectly: they appointed or approved rulers popular at local level who would be under Rome and friendly towards them. Herod the Great in Judea was given the support of Rome and in turn recognized Rome's authority. Other areas, known as imperial provinces, were under the direct rule of the emperor, who would appoint a Roman to rule on the spot. He was often given the title of legate or procurator.

Some fortunate cities were made colonies of Rome. These were very special outposts of the Empire, little bits of Rome set down in a far-off place. There were too many Roman citizens to live in Rome itself, so the overflow was settled in colonies. For example, veteran soldiers would be put in a colony with their own bit of land to tend. The local people would also be granted Roman citizenship. Colonies were

fiercely loyal to Rome and helped check discontent or uprisings.

The Romans liked to call the Mediterranean 'our sea' (*mare nostrum*) and ships were used to transport grain and other commodities as well as to control the Empire. Routes for sailing ships had to be planned to make use of winds and currents. In wintertime it was too risky to sail at all. Ships had to be laid up for a few months in safe harbours.

Even more important than sea routes was the wonderful network of Roman roads. They were well-built and well-kept hard roads, marked by milestones. They made travel throughout the Empire easy and safe.

The Romans still encouraged the Greek way of life and although educated people would know Latin, Greek was the common language of the Empire.

Jewish groups

All good Jews were agreed on the authority of the Torah, or Law of Moses, and the importance of the sacrifices at the Temple. But different groups within the nation had different ideas as to how these beliefs should be worked out in daily life.

The Sadducees

The group known as Sadducees (possibly after the priest Zadok) came from upper-class priestly families. They had political standing. They believed in tolerance and compromise with the ruling power.

Their chief loyalty was to the Torah, the first five books of the Old Testament, and it was only that part of Scripture that they revered. They would not even accept the many traditions that by this time had grown up

around the Torah. They rejected any beliefs which they thought were not definitely taught in the Law.

On those grounds they did not believe in resurrection, angels or demons. Nor did they hold with the apocalyptic predictions of the end-times. They laid great emphasis on the sacrifices at the Temple and on the importance of the priests.

The Pharisees

The party of the Pharisees grew out of the Hasidim of an earlier age. They were a much larger group than the Sadducees, and more popular with the ordinary people. There were probably 6,000 of them at the time of Jesus. Some were full-time students of the Jewish Scriptures, though others had ordinary jobs as well. They too were devoted to the Torah, but also to the other books of Scripture which the Sadducees rejected.

As well as the written books of the Law they accepted the oral law which had grown up around it: the 'tradition of the elders'. They tried very hard to live according to all these explanations and rules that accompanied the Law. Pharisees believed in angels and resurrection and the apocalyptic foretellings of a coming kingdom.

The word Pharisee means 'separated one'. The Pharisees wanted above all else to keep God's rules and separate themselves from any 'uncleanness' which might come from breaking the ritual and moral laws. They were against violent opposition to the ruling powers.

The Zealots

The Zealots went along with the beliefs of the Pharisees, but they differed from them in their

attitude to the powers-that-be. They were much more like the Maccabean revolutionaries. They believed that they should have no master but God and planned how best to get rid of Rome by guerilla tactics.

The Essenes and the community at Qumran

About one kilometre from where the first Dead Sea scrolls were found (see feature) are the ruins of a Jewish settlement at Qumran. The men who lived there belonged to the sect of the Essenes, a Jewish group dedicated to keeping the Law. The sect may have begun in Babylon, in reaction to the loose attitudes to religion that had brought about the exile.

It was in about 150BC that a group split off and settled in the desert at Qumran under the leadership of a deposed high priest who was known as the 'Teacher of Righteousness'. They studied the Law diligently as they waited for the coming of the Messiah. They supported themselves with flocks and crops and lived in tents or in the nearby caves, using the formal buildings for religious and social purposes.

Because the Law was so important to them, they made copies of it and of the other holy books, all of which were housed in their library. The remains of the scriptorium can still be seen today.

In AD68 news reached them that the Roman legions had begun their advance. Hastily they wrapped their precious manuscripts in linen, put them in jars and hid the jars in the caves round about. When Qumran was excavated, similar jars to those in the caves were found, and traces of ink in the inkwells matched that used on the manuscripts.

The Essenes were a sect that

resembled the Hasidim. The commune at Qumran seems to have been one of their groups and because of the finds there we know more about them than we do about other Essenes. They looked forward to a day of crisis when God would intervene in history and they alone in Israel would be recognized as God's covenant people. Most Jewish people were expecting a Messiah, though there were different ideas as to the kind of king he would be. The Essenes were expecting three: the prophet that Moses had foretold; a royal Messiah descended from David; and a priest-Messiah, who would be the most important of them all.

The scribes
The scribes, sometimes called lawyers, were first employed in writing down the words of others, as Baruch did for Jeremiah. Then, like Ezra, they became copyists and interpreters of the Law. By New Testament times the scribes were professional interpreters of the Law. They studied civil and religious law and decided how it should be applied. These decisions became the oral law or 'tradition of the elders' mentioned in the Gospels. Every scribe had his own disciples. Scribes were influential people. Many belonged to the Sanhedrin.

The Sanhedrin
The Persians had given the Jews the right to rule their own affairs and the Sanhedrin was the supreme Jewish court, continuing until it was swept away by the Roman authorities in AD70. It was made up of seventy members and the High Priest, who was chairman or president. It had its own police force and could arrest and try people and carry out sentences. It could pass the death sentence, but this had to be endorsed by Rome before the sentence could be carried out.

The synagogue
The Temple in Jerusalem had been the centre of Jewish worship since the time of King Solomon. So what were the people to do when they were taken into exile hundreds of miles away? It is very likely that synagogues began as a solution to this problem, although we have no written evidence for their existence before the third century BC.

The synagogue itself was a plain, straightforward building, not trying in any way to be like the magnificent Temple. The worship practised there did not imitate the Temple worship either. There were no sacrifices, but simply the reading and explanation of the Torah, and prayers. The rolls of the Torah were kept in a special case and taken out to be read every week.

In cities outside Palestine the synagogue became a focal point for Jews to meet and to share life. Courts sat there; school was held there; sometimes a hostel for visitors would be attached.

After the exile, synagogues were set up throughout Palestine as well as being in every city throughout the Empire where there were enough Jews. Sometimes there were a number of synagogues in one city, catering for different groups of Jews. Synagogues varied too in their strictness. Some were readier than others to adopt Hellenism or the local culture.

The synagogue was never seen as a substitute for the Temple. Jewish people would try to go to the Temple for the annual festivals, and animal sacrifices were offered only there.

The Dispersion
As we have seen, many Jews never returned to their own land after the exile. They went on living in different parts of the Persian Empire. Many Jews went to live in Egypt too. In New Testament times there were probably more Jews living in Alexandria than in Jerusalem. Other Jews travelled and settled in many other countries to live and trade there.

These Jews who were dispersed from Palestine were known as the Jews of the Dispersion or the **Diaspora**. Their faith was kept alive by synagogue worship. Their language was Greek, the language of the Empire, and they used the Septuagint or Greek version of the Old Testament. Sometimes they were less strict than Jews in Palestine, absorbing, as they did, some of the local culture.

Produce of Palestine
Olives and olive oil, wines and cereals were all produced in Palestine in the time of the Herods. Most people would eat beans, peas and pulses rather than expensive meat, but fish was part of the diet too. Fish from the coast and from Lake Galilee was salted and exported.

Pottery was manufactured throughout the country, flax was grown and flocks provided wool for cloth. Balsam trees gave a harvest of aromatic gum which was exported. Cheese was made from sheep's and goats' milk.

Tyrian purple, the costly dye used for expensive material, was produced along the coast of Judea. The Dead Sea provided salt and asphalt used in the building of ships. Rice was grown in Judea from the time of the Herods. Dates were exported too, and Judea was known for its fruit drinks!

THE ESSENES
AND THE DEAD SEA SCROLLS

Mohammed the Wolf was a bedouin boy who looked after goats in the valley of the Dead Sea. One day in 1947 he idly threw a stone into the mouth of one of the many caves in the cliffs around and was startled to hear the sound of breaking pottery. He took to his heels and ran off in fright but later returned with a friend to explore further.

Within the cave were a number of clay jars and inside them were lumps of cloth coated with pitch. The linen cloths were wrapped around manuscripts. The boys decided to keep their finds and try to sell them later.

It was several years before the full value and extent of the manuscripts was realized. That first cave was not the only one to hold the written treasure. By the time the caves had been thoroughly searched, copies of all the books of the Old Testament, except Esther, had been found. The Isaiah scroll, dating from about 100BC, was one thousand years older than any previously known manuscript of the Old Testament. Carbon dating has confirmed the estimated age of these rolls. Work still continues on evaluating the manuscripts.

The scrolls were the work of a community of strict Jews, called Essenes (see *World of the New Testament*).

The famous Dead Sea Scrolls, from the Qumran community's library, were placed in storage jars and hidden in these inaccessible caves close to Qumran at the time of the Roman invasion (AD70).

Excavations at Qumran revealed much about the life of the Essene community who settled there in about 150BC. This is the writing-room, where copies of precious manuscripts were made.

Part of the commentary on the book of Habakkuk, one of the manuscripts discovered at Qumran.

THE NEW TESTAMENT

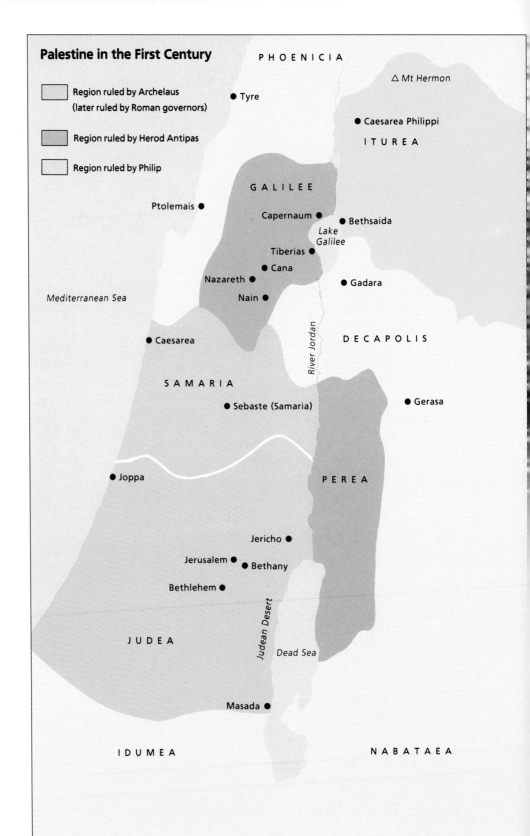

Palestine in the First Century

Region ruled by Archelaus
(later ruled by Roman governors)

Region ruled by Herod Antipas

Region ruled by Philip

PHOENICIA

△ Mt Hermon

● Tyre

● Caesarea Philippi

ITUREA

GALILEE

Ptolemais ●

Capernaum ●   ● Bethsaida

Lake Galilee

Tiberias ●

● Cana

Nazareth ●

Nain ●

● Gadara

Mediterranean Sea

River Jordan

DECAPOLIS

● Caesarea

SAMARIA

● Sebaste (Samaria)

● Gerasa

● Joppa

PEREA

Jericho ●

Jerusalem ● ● Bethany

Bethlehem ●

Judean Desert

JUDEA

Dead Sea

Masada ●

IDUMEA

NABATAEA

GOOD NEWS

The four Gospels: Matthew, Mark, Luke and John

When we read about the life and teaching of Jesus we have not one but four accounts to follow. The story about Jesus — the 'gospel' or 'good news' as the writers describe it — is told in four different books: the gospel according to Matthew, Mark, Luke and John.

It is generally believed that Mark was the first of these Gospels to be written and was a source for Matthew and Luke. So we are using Mark as our chief guide. But because each Gospel writer has his own purpose and readership and the four do not contain exactly the same material, we shall use the other Gospels too.

Why there are four Gospels

Although the Gospels share some material, each one gives us a unique introduction to the person of Jesus. Each was written for a particular readership and brought out some special aspect of Jesus and his work.

MATTHEW

Matthew wrote for Jewish readers. His is a very well-organized piece of writing, with passages about the life of Jesus followed by sections of teaching. It is the most comprehensive of the Gospels, beginning the account before Jesus' birth and ending with Jesus' words to the disciples before returning to God his Father: 'Go and make disciples of all nations baptizing them ... and teaching them to obey everything I have commanded you.' (28:19–20)

Matthew quotes the Old Testament when he recognizes an event as a 'fulfilment' of some passage there — which may or may not have been a prediction. For example, when Gabriel announces the forthcoming birth of Jesus to the virgin Mary, Matthew quotes from the Septuagint (Greek) version of Isaiah 7: 'The virgin will be with child and will give birth to a son, and they will call him "Immanuel" — which means, "God with us".' This link-up would especially interest Jewish readers. Matthew shows how the new revelation of God in Jesus is complete and perfect, compared with the revelation of God in the Old Testament. He is interested too in what is going to happen in the future and records several parables concerned with the last judgment.

Tradition is the only evidence that Matthew, one of the twelve apostles, is the author of this Gospel. The Gospels tell us that Matthew was a tax collector when Jesus called him from his work to follow him. No one knows exactly when the Gospel was written. Perhaps it was late in the first century — around AD84 to 100. Others, however, think it was as early as ten to thirty years after Jesus' death — AD40–60.

MARK

Mark, on the other hand, was written for Gentile, or non-Jewish readers. Papias, writing about AD130, refers to Mark as 'Peter's interpreter' who 'wrote down accurately ... all that he remembered of what Christ had said or done'. This is an exciting suggestion, for it means that Mark had his information straight from the lips of one of Jesus' closest disciples.

Perhaps Peter's Greek was not good enough and Mark translated the apostle's Aramaic into Greek when he wrote the account down. Sometimes Mark leaves a word that Jesus spoke in the Aramaic. In the story of the raising of Jairus' daughter, Mark preserves the actual words of Jesus: '*Talitha koum*', meaning 'Little girl, get up!'

Mark gives us a very human picture of Jesus. He shows him tired out, falling asleep in the boat, or angry when the disciples turned away the children who came to him. Perhaps Mark wanted to correct a heresy

108

which said that Jesus was not truly human. Mark may also have written his Gospel to prepare Christians for the persecution that was soon coming to them. He shows them a suffering Jesus.

In Mark's Gospel Jesus' identity is a mystery: there is no record of his birth. The disciples gradually begin to discover who he is, and halfway through the book Peter declares that he is God's Messiah. Then, for the second half of the Gospel, Jesus tries to prepare them for his brutal death. He is not going to be a military Messiah — but one who will suffer and die and be raised to life for evermore.

John Mark, to give him his full name — again, the person named by tradition as the author — may have put himself into the Gospel story. He describes a young man who was there when Jesus was arrested. He took to his heels, leaving his sole garment behind when the soldiers tried to catch him too. We certainly know that Mark's mother's home was an early headquarters for Jesus' followers. Perhaps the Last Supper was held there (see Acts 12:12).

LUKE

Luke is probably the only non-Jewish writer in the New Testament. His Gospel is part one of a two-volume account of the Christian faith, the book of Acts being part two. Luke, as we discover from Paul, was a doctor, an educated man who wrote very much more polished Greek than Mark. He says in his prologue that he is writing to give the full facts about Jesus to a high-ranking official called Theophilus. Perhaps his Gospel is a defence of the Christian faith to the Roman world.

We learn a lot about Luke from what he includes in his Gospel. He has a special care and concern for the poor and for women (underprivileged too). He emphasizes prayer, especially in the life of Jesus. He also includes three parables about prayer which none of the other writers has. He alone gives us Mary's song of thanksgiving to God when she was pregnant, the stories of the baby Jesus cradled in the manger and of the visit of the shepherds. Perhaps Luke heard them

The Synoptics and Q

Matthew, Mark and Luke are sometimes called the synoptic Gospels. The word synoptic means 'able to be seen together'. It is possible to put the contents of these three Gospels alongside one another and to compare them. Much of the material is shared. Although the accounts vary they are alike enough for readers to conclude that they must come from a common source. Scholars believe that Mark was the first Gospel and that Matthew and Luke used Mark when they were preparing their Gospels. They often soften some of Mark's strong words used to describe Jesus' emotions and improve his rough-and-ready Greek.

Q is the first letter of the German word for source (*Quelle*). It is the name given to the unknown document from which many scholars think Matthew and Luke took their sayings of Jesus which do not appear in Mark's Gospel. Q seems to have been written in Aramaic in about AD50. No copy has ever been found.

from Mary herself. Some put the date of this Gospel at AD57–60 but others place it after AD70.

JOHN

John's Gospel, according to tradition, was written by John the apostle. Instead of mentioning John by name, the Gospel writer refers to 'the disciple whom Jesus loved'. Some scholars think that it was not John himself but a disciple of his, probably called John too, who wrote the Gospel. For a long time John was thought to be the last Gospel written — about AD90–95 — but there are those who now believe it to be much earlier, say 40–65.

John's Gospel is very different from the other three, both in the material included and the way it is treated. Jesus is recognized as Messiah from the beginning. There are no story parables but instead some sayings of Jesus about himself: 'I am the good shepherd', 'I am the bread of life' and others, along with the discussions that followed these claims.

The 'I AM' claims of Jesus in John's Gospel:

- I am the Bread of life (6:35)
- I am the Light of the world (8:12)
- I am the good Shepherd (10:11)
- I am the Door of the sheep (10:7)
- I am the Resurrection and the Life (11:25)
- I am the Way, the Truth and the Life (14:6)
- I am the true Vine (15:1)

Only a limited number of miracles is recorded by John and these are always spoken of as signs. Often they are followed by Jesus' claim to be able to meet the spiritual need of which the physical miracle has been the sign. For example, Jesus fed 5,000 with bread and fish before claiming to be the bread of life — the one who could meet a person's innermost need. He raised Lazarus from death, and claimed to be the resurrection and the life — the one who could give eternal, never-failing life to those who trust him.

Miracles — or signs — of Jesus recorded by John:

- Water turned into wine (2:1–11)
- The official's son at Capernaum healed (4:46–54)
- The sick man healed at the pool of Bethsaida (5:1–9)
- The man born blind given his sight (9)
- Jesus walking on the water (6:19–21)
- 5,000 people fed (6:5–13)
- Lazarus raised from death (11:1–44)
- A miraculous catch of fish (21:1–11)

John is a Gospel marked by contrasts. The most striking is that of darkness and light. Jesus and his truth are the light which darkness can never put out. The wonderful first fourteen verses, known as the Prologue, contain many of the themes that recur throughout the Gospel:

'In the beginning was the Word, and the Word was with God, and the Word was God . . . The Word became flesh and dwelt among us, full of

Jesus described himself as the door or gate for the sheep, keeping them safe in the fold. It was a promise of care and protection for his followers.

On another occasion he used the picture of himself as the vine. His followers are the branches, drawing their life and ability to bear fruit from the main stem.

grace and truth. We have beheld his glory, glory as of the only Son from the Father.' (1:1, 14)

John mentions several different occasions on which Jesus was at Jerusalem. But for him, we would not know of these journeys to the capital. John seems to be writing for Jews and Gentiles. His Prologue speaks of Jesus as the Word who was with God and was God from the beginning, echoing the language of Genesis 1. This idea is one that can be understood in terms of Greek as well as Jewish thinking.

Preparations for Jesus' coming

The Old Testament ended, in the book of Malachi, with the hope of a coming day in which the Lord God would suddenly appear in his temple — a day of judgment:

'Then suddenly the Lord you are seeking will come to his temple . . . But who can endure the day of his coming? . . . See, I will send you the prophet Elijah before that great and dreadful day of the Lord comes.' (Malachi 3:1, 2; 4:5)

Some 400 years passed with no sign of that coming, but when the Gospel records

A coin of Augustus, the Roman emperor ruling at the time of Jesus' birth. It was Augustus who ordered the tax census which took Mary and Joseph to Bethlehem.

begin there is a buzz of excitement. Something is stirring: the promises of God made long ago are about to be fulfilled.

Mark begins his Gospel with the appearance of the striking and charismatic figure of John the Baptist. He was the son of a faithful and god-fearing couple — Zechariah the priest and his wife Elizabeth — who had long been childless.

John the Baptist

Before his birth an angel had declared that John would be the messenger who would prepare the way for the coming Saviour and king. John grew up to become a prophet. He reminded his listeners of the fiery outspoken prophet Elijah, the one Malachi had said would return. Even John's rough homespun clothes were like the prophet's.

Crowds flocked to the Judean desert to hear John preach about the need to repent and turn back to God. He gave the hypocritical religious leaders a lashing with his tongue and he told people of all walks of life how they ought to behave. He described himself simply as a 'voice crying in the wilderness' as he announced the coming of someone greater, who would baptize them with the Holy Spirit instead of the water John used. He attracted a close group of followers who listened intently to what he had to say about the coming deliverer.

Then one day John pointed excitedly at a man who was approaching them.

'Look!' he exclaimed: 'There is the Lamb of God!' His hearers were so intrigued by these

John baptized the repentant crowds who flocked to him. The cleansing waters of the River Jordan symbolized the washing away of past sins and misdeeds, ready for a fresh start.

mysterious words that they followed the man, spending the day with him. In this way they introduced themselves to Jesus.

John called everyone to repentance — not even Herod, the king of Judea, was spared. John had rebuked Herod for marrying his brother's wife, and Herod put John in prison. It was then that Jesus himself began to preach.

'The kingdom of God is near! Turn away from your sins and believe the Good News!' (Mark 1:15)

The beginning of the story

If we want to know the beginning of the story of Jesus we have to turn to Matthew and Luke, who tell us about his birth. Matthew begins even earlier, with a family tree (genealogy) which firmly connects Jesus to Old Testament history. Mary, Jesus' mother, was betrothed to a man called Joseph. But before they were married God sent his messenger-angel, Gabriel, to tell her that she was to have a son:

'He will be great and will be called the Son of the Most High God.' (Luke 1:32)

Mary was mystified. She was still a virgin. But Gabriel told her that this birth would come about through 'the power of the Most High': the Holy Spirit would 'overshadow' her.

Mary hurried south from Nazareth to Jerusalem to take the news to her relative Elizabeth, who was expecting a child — John the Baptist.

An angel reassured an anxious Joseph of the reason for Mary's pregnancy, and he gladly married her.

Baptism

The Jews used water for many religious ceremonies and baptism was one: the outward cleansing indicated an inner 'washing' too. The word means 'to dip'. Gentiles who wanted to take on the Jewish faith were baptized or dipped under water as an initiation rite. John the Baptist used baptism as an outward sign that those who had heard and followed his teaching had truly repented. Jesus, in turn, told his disciples to baptize those who became Christians following their preaching.

Baptism, carried out in various ways, has been a practice in the Christian church at all times.

John the Baptist prepared for his life's work in the Judean desert. Here, too, Jesus faced great testing before his public ministry. Alone in the desert, away from all the distractions and preoccupations of normal life, he was able to focus on the purposes of God.

Jesus' birth

The Roman Emperor Augustus had ordered a census for tax throughout his empire, including Palestine. Joseph and Mary travelled to Bethlehem to register, as this was the city of David, Joseph's ancestor. While they were there, Mary had her baby. The only inn — a rough and ready place — was already full. So Jesus was born in a cave or in the part of a family room where animals were sheltered, with a manger for a crib. There was no palace welcome for God's promised king.

On the night that he was born, shepherds on the terraced hillsides around Bethlehem saw a choir of angels and were given the good news of a Saviour's birth. They hurried to find the baby and to worship him. Later, wise scholars from the East journeyed to find him, bringing rich gifts. So the poor and the rich, the Israelite and the foreigner, welcomed Jesus at his coming into the world.

Jesus as a boy

Only one story about Jesus' boyhood is recorded in the Gospels. Luke tells us that when Jesus was twelve, on the verge of becoming a man by Jewish law, he went to Jerusalem with his parents to celebrate Passover. On the journey home he went missing. Mary and Joseph went back to the city to search for him, and found him in the temple. 'Why were you searching for me?' he asked. 'Didn't you know I had to be in my Father's house?' Already he recognized who his real Father was.

Jesus baptized

According to Luke's Gospel, Jesus was about thirty when he came to his relative, John, in the Judean desert and asked to be baptized. John knew that Jesus was a better man than he was but still had not recognized Jesus as the one whose coming he had been proclaiming.

But God had given John a sign to watch for. The one on whom the Holy Spirit came to rest, like a dove, would be the promised king. John saw this happen when he baptized Jesus. The voice of God was heard too, saying:

'You are my Son, whom I love; with you I am well pleased.' (Mark 1:11)

These words combine two Old Testament verses. One (Psalm 2:7) describes the Messiah as coming from David's line. The other (Isaiah 42:1) shows him as the servant in whom God delights.

The testing of Jesus

With his Father's words at his baptism ringing in his ears, Jesus felt himself impelled by the Holy Spirit to go deep into the Judean desert alone. For forty days he fasted. When he was weak with hunger Satan — the old enemy of mankind who had caused his downfall at the beginning — tempted him. Satan tried to persuade Jesus to substantiate his claim to be the Messiah through wonder-working and spectacular signs.

But Jesus refused to be diverted from the path he knew God wanted him to take. He was to be a Messiah who was humble and obedient to God, meeting the needs of others and not advertising himself. His path would be that of the suffering servant of Isaiah's prophecies, who finally died on behalf of his people, taking their punishment on himself.

After this time of testing, Jesus set out for three years as a travelling teacher.

Peter had his home at Capernaum on the shores of Lake Galilee and Jesus often taught there. The remains of a synagogue from the fourth century AD, with a mix of Roman style and Jewish symbols, still marks the site.

Jesus' disciples

A Jewish rabbi, or teacher, had his own group of disciples or pupils. Jesus chose twelve men to be his close disciples and friends, although many others — women as well as men — also followed him.

These twelve were a mixed bunch. Some were fishermen: Peter and his brother Andrew, and their friends, the brothers James and John. Jesus called them when they were by their boats, saying, 'Follow me.' Levi, also called Matthew, one of the hated taxmen — Jews who collected taxes on behalf of the Romans — was a disciple too. So was Simon, a member of the strong nationalist party who wanted to wrest Israel from Rome's power.

These are the twelve: Simon, renamed Peter; James son of Zebedee and his brother John; Andrew, Philip, Bartholomew, Matthew, Thomas, James son of Alphaeus, Thaddaeus, Simon the Zealot and Judas Iscariot. Jesus called them apostles — those that were to be sent out in his cause.

Working out the order of events

Matthew and Luke tell us about Jesus' birth and all four Gospels recount Jesus' baptism and the beginning of his public life. All of them have a lot to say about the momentous last week of Jesus' life and what followed. But in between those events the timing is vague.

The Gospels are not biographies, dealing with the whole of Jesus' life in detail and in order. Even when we read the same incidents in several Gospels they often happen at different times. Each Gospel writer chose a sequence and pattern that suited his purpose in writing.

So although we can describe the beginning and ending of Jesus' life in time order, we cannot describe the rest of it in this way. We shall look at different aspects of Jesus' public life and then continue the chronological account of his life at the point when the Gospels do so.

One day in the life of Jesus

Mark tells us of a very busy Sabbath day early on in Jesus' public life. He was in Capernaum, a fishing village beside Lake Galilee where

Peter lived and which Jesus made his headquarters. Jesus went, as usual, to the synagogue, where he preached with such authority that the congregation was amazed. But his sermon was rudely interrupted when a demon-possessed man came into the building, shouting and raving. With equal authority Jesus commanded the evil spirit to be quiet and to come out of the man — and it obeyed him.

Jesus went home to Peter's house with Peter, Andrew, James and John. Peter's mother-in-law was lying ill with a high fever, so they told Jesus and he went to her. He held her hand and helped her up. She was completely cured, and began to look after them all.

That evening, after the Sabbath had ended, people from all around brought their sick friends and relatives to Jesus and he healed them all.

Very early next morning, before it was light, Jesus went out and found a quiet place where he could pray. But his disciples soon found him. They tried to persuade him to stay longer because everyone wanted him. But Jesus knew that there were many others who needed to hear the good news that God's promises were to be fulfilled at last; God's kingdom was at hand — spelling freedom and release. So he moved on and travelled throughout Galilee, preaching and healing.

Jesus the teacher

Jesus often taught in brief, pithy sayings that are more like poetry than prose and he often used picture language. In this way what he said could easily be remembered and thought over afterwards. His teaching was usually surprising, turning accepted ideas on their heads.

Matthew and Luke provide us with two parallel blocks of teaching (Matthew 5; Luke 6). They are sometimes called the 'Beatitudes', which means 'Blessed' (because each statement begins with 'Blessed') or 'truly happy':

Blessed are the poor in spirit,
for theirs is the kingdom of heaven.
Blessed are those who mourn,
for they will be comforted.

Blessed are the meek,
for they will inherit the earth.
Blessed are those who hunger and thirst for
righteousness,
for they will be filled.
Blessed are the merciful,
for they will be shown mercy.
Blessed are the pure in heart,
for they will see God.
Blessed are the peacemakers,
for they will be called sons of God.
Blessed are those who are persecuted because of
righteousness,
for theirs is the kingdom of heaven.'
(Matthew 5:3–10)

Most people think happiness is to be found in health, wealth, popularity and self-fulfilment. But Jesus said that true happiness

is reserved for the humble, the merciful, those who know they have no goodness of their own and who are truly sorry for the wrong things they have done and said. He also rated highly the happiness of those who would be persecuted for being his followers.

Jesus taught about prayer, almsgiving and fasting, which were the three chief religious exercises of good Jews. They were meant to be private encounters with God, not public ways of showing off a person's piety, as they had often become. (See Matthew 6.)

Teaching in the open air, Jesus turned familiar sights into vivid object lessons. In springtime the hillsides of Galilee are ablaze with flowers. 'Look what God provides,' Jesus said. 'Not even King Solomon had clothes as beautiful as these. So don't worry! God cares much more for you. He will give you all you need.'

For most of his life Jesus lived and worked in the area around Lake Galilee. He travelled from place to place, teaching and healing. The photograph above is typical of the Galilee countryside.

A possible order of events from the four Gospels ▷

It is not easy to see how the accounts given in the four Gospels fit together chronologically. The beginning and the last week of Jesus' life are clear but what comes between is less easy to place in date order. It is especially difficult to relate John's account, with its very different scheme, to the other three. The order below is based on the three-year ministry suggested by the fact that John records three occasions when Jesus was in Jerusalem for Passover (an annual event).

John's Gospel, particularly, focuses on Jesus' periodic visits to Jerusalem, the nation's capital city and religious centre. In Jesus' day, Herod's Temple—built on the area *now occupied by the Dome of the Rock mosque (gleaming in the sun in the photograph below, taken from nearby Mt Scopus)—drew every eye.*

Events	Matthew	Mark	Luke	John
Announcement of the birth of John the Baptist			1:5–23	
Announcement of the birth of Jesus	1:18–24		1:26–38	
Jesus' mother, Mary, visits Elizabeth			1:39–56	
Birth of John the Baptist			1:57–79	
Birth of Jesus	1:25		2:1–39	
Visit of the Wise Men	2:1–12			
Flight into Egypt and return to Nazareth	2:13–23			
Jesus' boyhood visit to the Temple			2:41–50	
John the Baptist's preaching	3:1–12	1:1–8	3:1–18	1:19-28

Year 1

Events	Matthew	Mark	Luke	John
Jesus' baptism	3:13–17	1:9–11	3:21–22	1:29–34
The temptation of Jesus	4:1–11	1:12–13	4:1–13	
The first Passover				2:13–25
Meeting with Nicodemus			3:1–21	
Meeting with Samaritan woman				4:1–42
John the Baptist imprisoned	14:3–5	6:17–20	3:19–20	
Jesus rejected in Nazareth			4:16–30	
Call of the disciples Andrew, Simon, James and John	4:18–22	1:16–20	5:1–11	
Call of Matthew (Levi)	9:9–13	2:13–17	5:27–32	

Year 2

Events	Matthew	Mark	Luke	John
The second Passover			5:1–47	
Twelve apostles chosen	10:2–4	3:13–19	6:12–16	
Sermon on the Mount (Plain)	5:1—7:28		6:20–49	
The Twelve sent out	10:1—11:1	6:6–13	9:1–6	
Death of John the Baptist	14:1–12	6:14–29	9:7–9	

Year 3

Events	Matthew	Mark	Luke	John
The third Passover			6:1–71	
Peter acknowledges Jesus as the Christ	16:13–20	8:27–30	9:18–21	
Jesus foretells his death and resurrection	16:21–28	8:31—9:1	9:22–27	
The Transfiguration	17:1–13	9:2–13	9:28–36	
The seventy disciples sent			10:1–20	
Jesus at Jerusalem at the Festival of Tabernacles				7:5–52
Jesus with Martha and Mary			10:38–42	
Jesus in Jerusalem at the Festival of Dedication				10:22—38
Last visit to Jerusalem	20:20–28	10:32–34		
In Jericho			19:1–10	
Bartimaeus	20:29–34	10:46–52		

The last week

Events	Matthew	Mark	Luke	John
Triumphal entry into Jerusalem (Palm Sunday)	21:1–11	11:1–11	19:28–44	12:12–16
Judas' betrayal and rulers' plots	26:1–5, 14–16	14:1–2, 10–11	20:19, 22:1–6	11:45–57
Passover/Last Supper	26:17–29	14:12–25	22:7–20	13:1–30
Gethsemane	26:36–46	14:32–42	22:39–46	
Jesus arrested	26:47–56	14:43–52	22:47-53	18:2–12
Jesus' trial by Annas and the Sanhedrin	26:57–27:1	14:53–15:1	22:54–71	18:13–24
Peter's denial of Jesus	26:69–75	14:66–72	22:54–62	18:15, 25–27
Jesus before Pilate	27:2–30	15:1–19	23:1–25	18:28–19:15
Jesus crucified and buried	27:31–66	15:20–47	23:26–56	19:16–42
Resurrection and resurrection appearances (a 40-day period)	28:1–15	16:1–8, 9–14	24:1–49	20:1–21:23
The Ascension		16:19–20	24:50–53	

In answer to their questions about how to pray, Jesus gave his disciples a 'model' prayer, to use just as it was or as a basis for their own prayers.

'Our Father in heaven,
hallowed be your name,
your kingdom come,
your will be done
    on earth as it is in heaven.
Give us today our daily bread.
Forgive us our debts,
    as we also have forgiven our debtors.
And lead us not into temptation,
    but deliver us from the evil one.'
        (Matthew 6:9–13)

Jesus' prayer begins with a reminder that God is a loving Father, but one who is in heaven — that is, far greater and more wonderful than human beings can imagine. His people owe him honour and reverence. Prayer should be concerned first with God's glory and the establishing of his rule in the hearts of men and women. It is right, too, to pray for everyday material needs. Prayer must also include asking God's forgiveness and recognizing the need to respond by forgiving others. Finally there is a prayer for God's help against the temptation to stray from his ways.

Jesus' teaching set people free from narrow legalism. He emphasized not the keeping of strict ceremonial rules but the need to show mercy and love towards others in order to be like the Father in heaven.

Teaching by parable

Much of Jesus' teaching was given in the form of stories, known as parables. They all have two levels of meaning. Some parables can be taken as allegories. An allegory is a story where every person and incident stands for something else, with deeper significance. Jesus interpreted the parable of the sower in this way. But most parables do not carry this detailed meaning. They highlight one main truth dramatically and vividly. It helps in understanding a parable to look at the setting in which Jesus told it.

Mark gives the impression that Jesus spoke in parables in order to keep the truth from his hearers. Jesus says:

'The secret of the kingdom of God has been given to you. But to those on the outside everything is said in parables so that
    "they may be ever seeing but never perceiving,
    and ever hearing but never understanding;
otherwise they might turn and be forgiven!"'
(Mark 4:11–12)

But Matthew words the passage differently: here the result of the parable, not its purpose, is that hearers do not understand. It is a figure of Jewish speech to express a consequence as if it were deliberate intent.

Parables keep the kernel of truth in a nutshell that must first be cracked. They were not for idle listeners but for those intent on discovering Jesus' meaning. Once grasped, they lit up the subject and made understanding deeper and more profound.

The kingdom of God

Jesus preached that the kingdom of God had come, and told parables about it. Someone has said that when we understand what Jesus meant by the kingdom of God (or the kingdom of Heaven as Matthew puts it) we have the key to the Gospels and the whole of the New Testament.

The Greek word for kingdom means 'rule' or 'reign' and the kingdom of God is 'God acting in his kingly power, exercising his sovereignty'.

Jewish people believed that God was supreme over the whole world. Many psalms express this thought. But only God's people, the Jews, who obeyed God's law, recognized this kingly rule. They also believed that one day God would break into history and display his kingly power to all the world, overthrowing evil and showing mercy to his people. That was the day to which the Old Testament prophets had looked forward.

As soon as Jesus began to preach he announced that God's kingdom had arrived. With his coming, God himself had at last broken into history. But for the time being only those who accepted Jesus and his teaching would become his subjects. There

	Matthew	Mark	Luke
Lamp under a bushel	5:14–15	4:21–22	8:16, 11:33
Houses on rock and sand	7:24–27		6:47–49
New cloth on an old garment	9:16	2:21	5:36
New wine in old wineskins	9:17	2:22	5:37–38
Sower and soils	13:3–8	4:3–8	8:5–8
Mustard seed	13:31–32	4:30–32	13:18–19
Tares	13:24–30		
Leaven (yeast)	13:33		13:20–21
Hidden treasure	13:44		
Priceless pearl	13:45–46		
Drag-net	13:47–48		
Lost sheep	18:12–13		15:4–6
Two debtors (Unforgiving servant)	18:23–34		
Workers in the vineyard	20:1–16		
Two sons	21:28–31		
Wicked tenants	21:33–41	12:1–9	20:9–16
Invitation to the wedding; man without a wedding garment	22:2–14		
Fig-tree as herald of summer	24:32–33	13:28–29	21:29–30
Ten 'bridesmaids'	25:1–13		
Talents (Matthew) Pounds (Luke)	25:14–30		19:12–27
Sheep and goats	25:31–46		
Seedtime to harvest		4:26–29	
Creditor and debtors			7:41–43
Good Samaritan			10:30–37
Friend in need			11:5–8
Rich fool			12:16–21
Alert servants			12:35–40
Faithful steward			12:42–48
Fig-tree without figs			13:6–9
Places of honour at the wedding-feast			14:7–14
Great banquet and the reluctant guests			14:16–24
Counting the cost			14:28–33
Lost coin			15:8–10
Prodigal son			15:11–32
Dishonest steward			16:1–8
Rich man and Lazarus			16:19–31
Master and servant			17:7–10
Persistent widow and unrighteous judge			18:2–5
Pharisee and tax collector			18:10–14

was still a further day to be awaited. Jesus would conquer sin and death by his own death and resurrection. Then, at a future time, he would return and usher in the universal rule of the kingdom in all its power.

Stories about God's kingdom

'The kingdom of God is like . . .' That is the way Jesus often began his teaching. Then, to describe the kingdom, he would tell a parable.

One day he told the crowds that followed him a story about a man who went out to sow corn. As he broadcast the seed, some fell on the hard path, some fell on rocky ground, some among the thorn hedges and some on good soil. The seed on the hard path was soon swooped on by birds. The seed on rocky ground sprouted quickly but had no deep roots so it shrivelled in the hot sun. The seed in the hedges was quickly choked by the thorns. Only the seed sown on good ground was successful. And that brought a bumper harvest.

Later Jesus explained the meaning behind this story to his puzzled disciples. The seed, he said, is the word of God. The seed on the path stands for those who hear God's word but the message is quickly taken away by the enemy — the Devil. The seed on rocky ground represents those who hear and receive the word but do not take it deep into their lives. The seed among thorns stands for the word that is is choked by worries and riches. The seed on good soil represents listeners who hear, accept and obey God's word, persisting until there are results.

Jesus told many other stories to illustrate the kingdom. He described a woman putting leaven (yeast) into her dough — that shows how the kingdom grows quietly but rapidly.

The story of the little mustard seed that grew into a huge shrub shows how the kingdom will grow and spread from small beginnings.

One of the best-loved stories Jesus told is about the way God loves and welcomes everyone who turns to him. There was a man who had two sons. The younger asked for his share of his father's fortune and set off to spend it and enjoy himself. The older son stayed at home farming for his father. The young son used up his money and fell on hard times. He was reduced to feeding pigs. At last he came to his senses and decided to return home and ask for his father's forgiveness. But when he was still a long way off his father saw him, came running towards him and welcomed him home.

The older son was not well pleased. He refused to join the celebration party that was

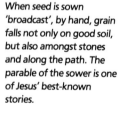

When seed is sown 'broadcast', by hand, grain falls not only on good soil, but also amongst stones and along the path. The parable of the sower is one of Jesus' best-known stories.

in full swing. His father came out to plead with him and to assure him of his love:

'"We had to celebrate and be glad, because this brother of yours was dead and is alive again; he was lost and is found."' (Luke 15:32)

Jesus told this story to law-keeping religious leaders who, like the older brother, were angry and contemptuous that Jesus taught and received the outcasts and sinners who came to him.

In another well-known story Jesus told of a man who was attacked by thieves on the desolate rocky road from Jerusalem to Jericho. They left him half dead. Two religious men went down the road — and passed him by. But a Samaritan, one of the people most hated by Jews, took pity on the victim, bathed his wounds, put him on his donkey, took him to an inn and paid the innkeeper to care for him. In Matthew's Gospel Jesus summarizes God's law as loving God wholeheartedly and loving our 'neighbour' as ourself.

He told this story in answer to the question, 'Who is my neighbour?'

Jesus the healer

Great crowds followed Jesus. They loved to hear his teaching, but even more to see the marvellous deeds that he performed.

One day a local person of importance, president of the synagogue, broke through the crowd to implore Jesus' help for his dying daughter. Jesus set out with him, hampered by the milling crowd.

Somewhere, somehow, a woman pushed her way through and silently touched Jesus' cloak. She had faith that if only she could touch him her haemorrhage, which had lasted twelve years, would stop. Sure enough, she was immediately healed. She turned to steal quietly away, but Jesus stopped, and asked who had touched him. The disciples thought the question was ridiculous, when the crowds pressed so tightly, but Jesus knew that power had left him. The woman came shyly forward and admitted what she had done. She told him her whole story. Jesus wanted to come face to face with her: a personal encounter was part of the whole healing process.

While all this was happening, messengers

Jesus' story of the 'good Samaritan'—explaining God's command to 'love our neighbour'—had a real-life setting. The road from Jerusalem to Jericho passes through bandit country. The isolated inn provided travellers with a safe place to stop.

arrived to tell Jairus, the synagogue leader, that his daughter had died. Jesus told him: 'Don't be afraid, only believe,' and they continued on their way to Jairus' home. There Jesus turned out the professional mourners and went into the child's room, taking with him only her parents and Peter, James and John. He went to the bed and called to the dead child, *'Talitha koum'* — 'Little girl, get up.' She got up at once and began walking around. Jesus told her parents to give her something to eat but not to spread the story far and wide.

The feeding of the 5,000

All four Gospel writers tell us of the day when Jesus preached to enthralled crowds for many hours. Rather than let them go hungry to their homes, he told his puzzled disciples to give them something to eat. All that could be found were five small barley loaves and two fish, provided by a boy. But when Jesus took this gift and gave thanks there was ample food for the whole crowd, which numbered more than 5,000 men, beside women and children.

John tells us in his Gospel how Jesus used this miracle as a sign to point to himself. He said: 'I am the Bread of life.' Just as bread can sustain the body, so Jesus claimed to be able to nourish and give life to the whole person.

THE MIRACLES OF JESUS

	Matthew	Mark	Luke	John
Healing of physical and mental disorders				
Leper	8:2–3	1:40–42	5:12–13	
Centurion's servant	8:5–13		7:1–10	
Peter's mother-in-law	8:14–15	1:30–31	4:38–39	
Two Gadarenes	8:28–34	5:1–15	8:27–35	
Paralyzed man	9:2–7	2:3–12	5:18–25	
Woman with a haemorrhage	9:20–22	5:25–29	8:43–48	
Two blind men	9:27–31			
Man dumb and possessed	9:32–33			
Man with a withered hand	12:10–13	3:1–5	6:6–10	
Man dumb, blind and possessed	12:22			
Canaanite woman's daughter	15:21–28	7:24–30		
Boy with epilepsy	17:14–18	9:17–29	9:38–43	
Bartimaeus and another blind man	20:29–34	10:46–52	18:35–43	
Deaf and dumb man		7:31–37		
Man possessed, synagogue		1:23–26	4:33–35	
Blind man at Bethsaida		8:22–26		
Woman bent double			13:11–13	
Man with dropsy			14:1–4	
Ten lepers			17:11–19	
Malchus' ear			22:50–51	
Official's son at Capernaum				4:46–54
Sick man, pool of Bethesda				5:1–9
Man born blind				9
Command over the forces of nature				
Calming of the storm	8:23–27	4:37–41	8:22–25	
Walking on the water	14:25	6:48–51		6:19–21
5,000 people fed	14:15–21	6:35–44	9:12–17	6:5–13
4,000 people fed	15:32–38	8:1–9		
Coin in the fish's mouth	17:24–27			
Fig-tree withered	21:18–22	11:12–14, 20–26		
Catch of fish			5:1–11	
Water turned into wine				2:1–11
Another catch of fish			21:1–11	
Bringing the dead back to life				
Jairus' daughter	9:18–19, 23–25	5:22–24, 38–42	8:41–42, 49–56	
Widow's son at Nain			7:11–15	
Lazarus				11:1–44

Jesus' miracles

Jesus' miracles are called 'mighty works' in the first three Gospels and 'signs' in John's Gospel. They are not later additions, added to make the story of Jesus seem more wonderful. They are an early and necessary part of the Gospel story. For the mighty works are intended to demonstrate that God really has intervened in history in the person of Jesus. They are the sign that the new age has begun. Someone has remarked that you can no more remove the miracles from the Gospels than you could remove the watermark from a sheet of paper. Jesus said, 'If I drive out demons by the finger of God, then the kingdom of God has come to you.' Jesus' miracles are presented as proof that the kingdom has arrived.

C.S. Lewis suggested that Jesus' miracles were often a speeded-up version of something that happens regularly, which we take for granted. For example, the multiplying of food at the feeding of the five thousand, or the turning of water into wine which Jesus did at a wedding feast, happens every year in nature at a slower pace. But we do not call that miracle.

Whether or not people think the miracles are plausible depends in the end on what they believe about Jesus. If he is God — the one who made the world — come in the flesh, miracle is not only possible but even to be expected.

Jesus' identity

Jesus did not tell his disciples that he was the Messiah, the one chosen by God and the king whose kingdom had arrived. He left them to discover the fact for themselves.

Once, when they were crossing the lake, a storm blew up. There was real danger that their fishing-boat would sink. The frightened disciples appealed to Jesus for help and with a word he quietened the wind and waves. They whispered together about who such a person could be. They had seen Jesus control sickness and demon possession. But now he was controlling the elements. They were beginning to believe that he was more than just an ordinary man.

One day, when they were on their own,

In many parts of the world bread is a staple food. Jesus knew the importance of feeding hungry people. He provided bread for a crowd of 5,000. He also described himself as the 'bread of life'—for there is more to life than satisfying physical hunger.

Jesus asked the disciples point blank who they thought he was. Peter answered for them all with calm conviction: 'You are the Christ.' 'Christ' is the Greek word for Messiah. Jesus told Peter that God himself had revealed that truth to them.

From that moment of recognition Jesus began the next stage of what he had to teach the disciples. He told them that he must suffer and die at the hands of the religious leaders but that he would rise again after three days. Peter spoke up again, telling Jesus he must not say such things. But Jesus knew that his chosen path must lead to death. From time to time he explained to his disciples about his coming suffering and death. But they did not want to hear such things and did not take it in.

The Transfiguration

One evening Jesus took his close disciples — Peter, James and John — up a high mountain to pray. The Gospels record that while they were there, away from the crowds, Jesus was

It may have been on the slopes of Mt Hermon, in the far north of Palestine, that the disciples saw Jesus in his glory at the 'transfiguration'.

changed. His whole body, and his clothes too, shone with an unearthly splendour. While they watched, two others appeared whom they knew to be Moses, the great Law-giver, and Elijah, the mighty prophet. Luke tells us that the conversation centred on Jesus' coming death.

Peter, hardly knowing what he was saying, suggested that it would be good to make three tents — one each for Jesus and his special visitors. But the bright cloud of God's presence covered them and God spoke from the cloud:

'This is my Son, whom I love. Listen to him.'
(Mark 9:7)

The terrified disciples fell flat on the ground. But Jesus touched them on the shoulder: 'Get up' he said, 'Don't be afraid.'

When they looked around there was no one to be seen but Jesus.

Jesus told them to tell no one about this special experience until after he had risen from the dead.

Growing opposition

Jesus spent three wonderful years healing and teaching. He helped the crowds but he also dealt with people one-to-one. A blind man would come begging for his sight, or a group of people would bring a sick friend to Jesus to be healed. He not only met the physical and mental needs but also the spiritual needs of the men and women he encountered. He forgave their sins and started them on a completely new kind of life.

Surely such a person would be loved and accepted by everyone! But from the outset the writers tell us that Jesus made enemies. His very presence divided people into two camps. They had to choose whether to believe him and take their stand with him or to be against him. There was no middle course. His teaching made enemies too. It was so different from that of the other religious leaders.

He did not quote traditional interpretations of Scripture but spoke on his own authority. This displeased most of the Jewish leaders. After all, in their eyes he was a nobody and an upstart, challenging their carefully formulated body of laws. But Jesus did not soft-pedal his approach to them. He publicly warned the people against the hypocrisy and hard-hearted legalism of their teachers.

Several incidents brought the jealousy and hatred of the religious leaders to the point where they were ready to arrange his death.

The raising of Lazarus

Jesus had three good friends who lived in the village of Bethany, near to Jerusalem. They were two sisters and a brother — Martha, Mary and Lazarus. One day the sisters sent an urgent message to Jesus telling him that Lazarus was ill. Jesus did not rush to his bedside but let two days pass before he and his disciples set out for Bethany.

When they arrived Lazarus had been four days in the grave. Martha and Mary could not understand Jesus' delay, because they were sure that he could have healed their brother had he come earlier. But Jesus had a greater miracle to perform. He spoke words of assurance to Martha:

'I am the resurrection and the life. He who believes in me will live, even though he dies; and whoever lives and believes in me will never die.'
(John 11:25, 26)

Jesus was talking about something even more real and lasting than a return from physical death. He was making it plain that as well as raising the dead he could give life that lasted beyond the grave.

At Lazarus' tomb Jesus called with authority, 'Lazarus, come out!' and the dead man appeared, his life restored.

The Jewish authorities were very concerned because this much-publicized miracle made Jesus even more popular and well-known. They plotted to kill him.

Jesus the Messiah

The Hebrew word *Messiah* means anointed one. 'Christ' comes from *Christos*, the Greek form of the word. In Old Testament times people were anointed when they were appointed by God for a special task, such as the role of prophet, priest or king. It was usually a prophet who poured oil on the person's head to mark them out as chosen by God.

The king in particular came to be known as 'God's anointed', and in time the title was used for the ideal king whom God would one day send. There were very different ideas about what kind of king he would be. Some imagined a warrior and national hero, like Judas Maccabaeus. Others expected a second and greater King David, or looked for a supernatural Saviour who would carry out God's rule as head of his people.

Jesus did not call himself Messiah. He knew that the popular idea of the Messiah clashed with what he had come to do. But he accepted Peter's declaration.

Son of God
Although Israel was known as God's son in the Old Testament (see, for example, Exodus 4:22), this title is linked with the idea of Messiahship. It occurs in Old Testament verses relating to kings of Israel but was also recognized by Jewish teachers as foretelling the Messiah. In Psalm 2, for example, God says of the coming Messiah: 'You are my Son.' Jesus recognized himself as God's son in a unique way. The emphasis was on his obedience to his Father's will and plan for him.

Son of Man
This title is the one most used by Jesus about himself. Perhaps that is because it was not linked with ideas of political or military might. Often in the Old Testament the phrase 'son of man' is just another way of saying a human being. However, Daniel 7 depicts a scene where one 'like a son of man' comes with clouds and is presented to God, who is in awesome splendour. God invests him with never-ending power and authority. Jesus quoted this passage as referring to himself at his trial before the Sanhedrin. By claiming this title Jesus emphasized his genuine humanity yet asserted his place of power and honour, coming from God.

The Servant
The servant who suffers for his people was described by Isaiah in four poems. They were not at that time linked with the Messiah but Jesus took the role upon himself. He said:

'The Son of Man did not come to be served. He came to serve and to give his life to redeem many people.' (Mark 10:45)

In Isaiah 53, the last of the Servant songs describes the death of the servant on behalf of his people. His mission would extend to the nations (Isaiah 42, 49).

Palm Sunday

When Jesus was ready to go into Jerusalem he rode in on a donkey amid the delighted cheers of the pilgrims who had begun to gather in the city for Passover. The crowds waved palm branches and strewed their coats on the path.

Jesus was immensely popular and the crowd hailed him in the words of a Messianic psalm:

'Hosanna!
Blessed is he who comes in the name of the Lord!
Blessed is the King of Israel!'

Later on the disciples understood the significance of Jesus' action. The prophet Zechariah, foretelling the coming of the king, said he would ride peaceably — on a donkey, not a war-horse. The crowds seemed to be welcoming their king and the Jewish leaders were furious.

When Jesus arrived in the city he went into the temple. He was angry to see how the traders had turned the court for Gentiles into a bazaar. There was bargaining and cheating as birds and animals were sold for sacrifice and money was changed for the special temple coinage. Jesus drove out the animals and overturned the tables of the money-changers. This act may have been a prophetic sign, by which Jesus signalled the end of the old order and the coming of the new Messianic Age.

'Is it not written,

"My house will be called
a house of prayer for all nations"?

But you have made it "a den of robbers".'
(Mark 11:17)

The temple, with its provision for Gentiles, had been intended by God to be an instrument of their mission to the rest of the world. Instead Jesus saw that it was a centre for Jewish exclusivism and national fanaticism.

The wicked tenants

Jesus told a parable which aroused the hostility of the rulers. He described how a vineyard was let out to tenants who were to pay rent to the owner. But when the servants came to collect the rent the tenants attacked them and even killed some. Finally the owner decided to send his own son, thinking they would respect him. But instead they put him to death.

The rulers who were listening understood only too well what Jesus meant by his story. A vineyard was a common picture for Israel. They were the tenants, the owner was God and his servants were God's prophets. The son was no other than Jesus himself. But instead of taking warning from the story, they only hastened their plans to arrest and kill Jesus.

Judas the betrayer

The religious leaders were plotting Jesus' death but it was one of his own close followers who betrayed Jesus to them. Perhaps Judas Iscariot was a nationalist, disillusioned by the fact that Jesus showed no signs of setting up a kingdom in Jerusalem and wielding power in which his followers could share. He was certainly keen to get money. He decided to turn Jesus over to his enemies and did so for thirty pieces of silver. He promised to tell them when and where Jesus could be found and arrested quietly, away from the crowds.

The Passover and the Last Supper

Passover time had come and Jesus told two of his disciples to get ready the meal that they would share in an upstairs room in Jerusalem. There was no slave to wash their feet, so Jesus took the towel and the basin of water and washed the disciples' feet himself. It was a lesson for them in humility and unselfishness.

During the meal, knowing he was soon to die, Jesus took some bread and passed it to the disciples to eat, saying:

'This is my body.'

Then he handed them a cup of wine, saying,

'This is my blood which seals God's covenant, my blood poured out for many for the forgiveness of sins.' (Matthew 26:26–28)

He told them to do these things in memory of him.

A close-up of the temple, from a scale model of Jerusalem in AD66, at the Holyland Hotel, Jerusalem.

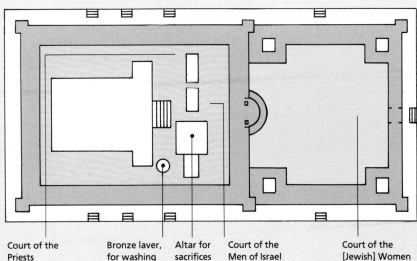

Court of the Priests

Bronze laver, for washing

Altar for sacrifices

Court of the Men of Israel

Court of the [Jewish] Women

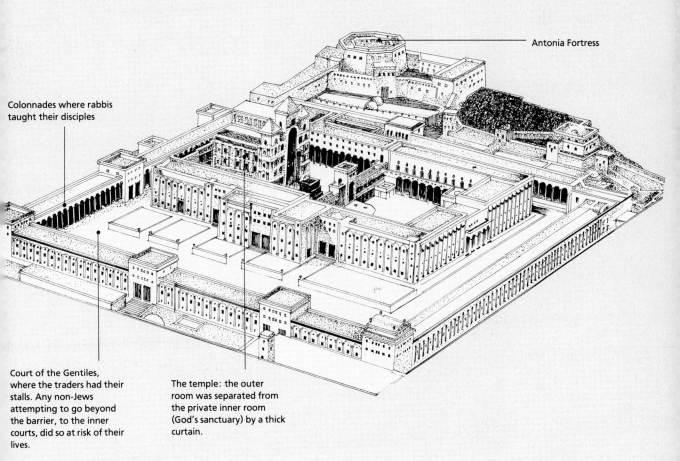

Antonia Fortress

Colonnades where rabbis taught their disciples

Court of the Gentiles, where the traders had their stalls. Any non-Jews attempting to go beyond the barrier, to the inner courts, did so at risk of their lives.

The temple: the outer room was separated from the private inner room (God's sanctuary) by a thick curtain.

Gethsemane

After supper, Jesus and the disciples went to an olive grove called Gethsemane, where they could be quiet and private. Here Jesus prayed in great agony. He foresaw and dreaded the death that lay ahead:

'Father, if you are willing, take this cup from me; yet not my will, but yours be done.'

The arrest

Judas knew where Jesus was going and after supper he had slipped away to tell the priests where they could find him. Scarcely had Jesus finished praying when the light of torches pierced the darkness of the trees. A band of soldiers came and took Jesus prisoner.

Jesus' trial

Jesus was led away captive to the High Priest's house — and the disciples all took to their heels and ran away. In spite of Jesus' repeated warnings that he would be arrested and put to death they had not taken it in.

Peter and John later followed and watched Jesus from the courtyard as he was being interrogated. Here Peter was three times asked if he was one of Jesus' followers, but in panic he denied that he even knew him. Jesus had warned him earlier that this would happen, but Peter could not believe it. Now he wept bitterly.

All night Jesus was cross-questioned. The accounts say that none of the bogus witnesses could agree on their evidence. At length Jesus was asked on oath whether he was the Messiah and he replied that he was and that, in the words of Daniel 7, they would see him seated at the right hand of the Almighty and coming with the clouds of heaven.

This was pronounced to be blasphemy and Jesus was condemned to die. Meanwhile he was handed over to be ill-treated by the soldiers.

Next morning the Roman governor, Pilate, was approached to ratify the death sentence, which the Jews could not carry out without his authorization. He did his best to release Jesus but he was terrified of demonstrations at Passover, when Jerusalem was crowded and feelings ran high. In the end he gave in to the Jewish leaders' wishes and ordered Jesus' crucifixion.

Why Jesus died

It might seem as if Jesus died as a result of the evil plots of jealous men. But in the Bible Jesus' death is viewed as part of God's deliberate purpose. Jesus' own decision to die was the Son's consent to his Father's plan.

The Gospels record that Jesus foresaw his death from the outset of his ministry. As soon as Peter declared his belief in Jesus as Messiah he began to teach the disciples that he must suffer and die. He spoke of his death as a 'ransom for many'. At that time a ransom was paid in order to free a slave, and Jesus understood his death as the means of setting people free and bringing them back to God.

Many other statements that he made about his forthcoming death echo the words of Isaiah 53, where the servant, who is innocent, dies to bring his people relief and pardon for their sins.

In John's Gospel, John the Baptist referred to Jesus, at the outset of his ministry, as 'the Lamb of God who bears away the sin of the

The gnarled trunks of the ancient olive-trees in the Garden of Gethsemane express the anguish of Jesus' 'dark night of the soul' before his crucifixion.

Crucifixion

The Romans did not invent crucifixion but refined it to the cruellest form of execution. In Palestine it was reserved for runaway slaves or the worst kind of criminals against the state.

Before being crucified the prisoner was flogged with a metal-tipped whip which caused horrific injury and loss of blood. He was then expected to carry the cross-beam through the streets to the place of execution. The upright post was already in place.

The prisoner's arms were stretched out and nailed to the cross-beam before it was attached to the upright—to which the victim's feet were nailed. An inscription was put up with the prisoner's name and crime written on it.

Death was extremely slow and excruciating, sometimes taking several days, and was finally caused by asphyxiation.

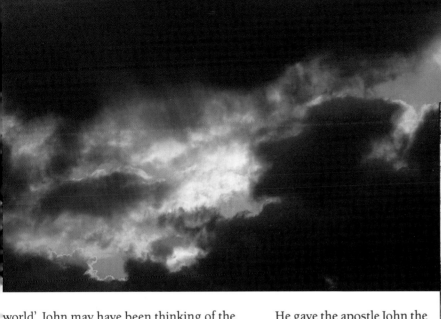

Matthew, Mark and Luke all note that from noon until three, as Jesus hung on the cross, the sun disappeared. The portent of darkness marks a turning-point in human history.

Jesus was buried in a rock-cut tomb, with a stone to seal the entrance. But the good news declared by the Gospel writers is that neither death nor the tomb could hold him. The picture is of Herod's Tomb in Jerusalem.

world'. John may have been thinking of the Passover lamb, which had to be sacrificed on that first occasion long ago in Egypt to save the people of Israel from death. It also brings to mind the lamb sacrificed as a sin-offering. In that ceremony the guilt of the offerer was transferred to the innocent animal which was slaughtered on the offerer's behalf.

Jesus' death is explained in the Bible as a death on behalf of others, a death to free men and women from sin and the spiritual death which is the inevitable consequence of wrongdoing. Jesus saw his death as essential to his Messiahship, not an unfortunate accident or simply the end result of hatred and opposition.

Jesus' death and burial

Jesus was crucified with a criminal on either side of him. At first both cursed him, but one put faith in him even while he was dying. Some of Jesus' enemies came to taunt him, but a small group of faithful disciples, mostly women (his mother among them), stayed close to the cross.

In spite of extreme pain and difficulty in breathing, Jesus spoke several times from the cross. He prayed for his executioners:

'Forgive them, Father! They don't know what they are doing.' (Luke 23:34)

He gave the apostle John the care of his mother, Mary.

The Gospel writers tell us that there was darkness for three hours while Jesus endured the agony of the cross. Jesus used the words of a psalm to express his own sense of dereliction:

'My God, my God, why have you forsaken me?' (Matthew 27:46)

Just before he died he shouted triumphantly: 'It is finished!' He knew that he had perfectly completed the work that his Father had given him to do. Then he prayed the evening prayer of all Jewish children:

'Father! In your hands I place my spirit!' (Luke 23:46)

We read that at the time of Jesus' death the curtain that completely screened the most holy part of the temple was ripped from top to bottom. The Gospel writers understood by this that Jesus, by his death, had opened the way into God's presence.

Two leading Jewish men, who had not agreed to Jesus' death, took care of his burial. One, called Joseph, buried him in the rock tomb prepared for his own use. The women who had witnessed his death watched where Jesus' body was put.

The Gospel writers affirm that Jesus came from God and, forty days after his death and resurrection, returned to God. He was 'taken up to heaven', Luke says, and a cloud hid him from the sight of the watching disciples.

The resurrection

The day after Jesus' death was the Sabbath, when all must rest. But very early on the Sunday morning some of the women who had seen where Jesus was buried hurried back to the place in order to embalm his body with spices. To their amazement the huge stone at the cave mouth had been rolled away. An angel told them that Jesus was no longer there. He had risen.

Athough Jesus had repeatedly told his disciples that he would rise on the third day, none of them had taken it in. Not surprisingly they were sceptical when the women told them of their experience.

But when the disciples were together that evening Jesus himself appeared to them. They were terrified at first, thinking they were seeing a ghost. But when Jesus had calmed and reassured them they at last took in the wonderful reality that Jesus was alive. Their joy and excitement knew no bounds.

The forty days of appearances and the ascension

Over a period of about six weeks Jesus appeared from time to time to his disciples and those who believed in him. On one occasion, the apostle Paul tells us, he appeared to over 500 believers at one time.

His body was real — they could touch him and he ate food in front of them — and yet it was different. He could come through locked doors and appear and disappear at will. His earthly body had been transformed.

During this period Jesus taught his disciples many things that they still did not understand. He explained how it had been necessary for him to die before he could rise in triumph. He proved from the Scriptures that it was part of God's plan that the Messiah should suffer and die, then rise again, and at last be vindicated by God.

Then, one day, Jesus parted from his disciples for the last time. He blessed them and was taken from them. Luke describes how a cloud — the sign of God's presence — received him out of their sight. Jesus was returning to his Father's glory. Seeing him go convinced the disciples that his appearances were now at an end. Jesus' earthly ministry was finished. Their own was just beginning.

THE YOUNG CHURCH

The Acts of the Apostles

The author of Acts is Luke, who also wrote one of the four Gospels. He dedicates this book to Theophilus — the same high-ranking official for whom he wrote his Gospel. His first volume described what Jesus had said and done. Now he continues the story of Jesus' work or acts through the eleven remaining apostles (Judas, the traitor, had hanged himself) who were equipped and given power by the Holy Spirit. The book is normally known as Acts.

Luke is meticulous in his research and a skilled storyteller. He was a travelling companion of Paul — perhaps his doctor? He was a firsthand witness of some of the events of the book.

The book may have been written between AD70 and 80 although some suggest an earlier date in the sixties.

The ascension

During the days following Jesus' resurrection he appeared to his disciples from time to time and taught them from the Jewish Scriptures to understand more about the meaning of his death and resurrection. He would be there with them — and just as suddenly he would disappear. But this state of affairs was not to continue.

Luke begins his story six weeks after the resurrection, with what was to be the last of these appearances of Jesus.

When he talked to his disciples in the upper room on the night before his death, Jesus had promised to send them his Holy Spirit — 'another Helper', who would be with them always, in his place. The Holy Spirit, because he too was God but had no bodily form, could be closer to them even than Jesus.

'You will receive power when the Holy Spirit comes on you; and you will be my witnesses in Jerusalem, and in all Judea and Samaria, and to the ends of the earth.' (1:8)

Luke takes these words as his theme for Acts. He tells his story of how the good news about Jesus was spread from Jerusalem through the lands around, and on to the capital of the Roman Empire, mainly through the experiences of two men: Peter, the apostle Jesus chose to lead the Twelve, and a new convert who became the apostle Paul.

The arrival of the Holy Spirit

On the Mount of Olives, before the eyes of the watching disciples, Jesus was 'taken up to heaven', returning to his Father. The disciples went back to Jerusalem to await the Spirit's coming. There they met to pray, joined by the women and Jesus' family.

Before long Jerusalem was packed with visiting pilgrims. They had come for the festival of Pentecost (fifty days after Passover). Suddenly there was a huge stir in the house where the disciples were meeting. The sound of a great gust of wind swept through it and a tongue of fire lighted on the head of every disciple. These were the outward signs that the Holy Spirit had come.

Crowds of pilgrims, hearing strange sounds, came rushing together to the house. When the excited disciples went out and spoke to them about Jesus, the people understood the words they heard, whatever their native language. But some accused the disciples of being drunk, which Peter hotly denied. He stood up in front of them all and preached to them about Jesus.

Many must have witnessed Jesus' crucifixion and it was startling news to be told that he was alive. Peter quoted from the Old Testament to convince them that Jesus' resurrection had been foretold by their own prophets and that his death was not just the result of human wickedness but was part of God's great plan to save mankind. He declared:

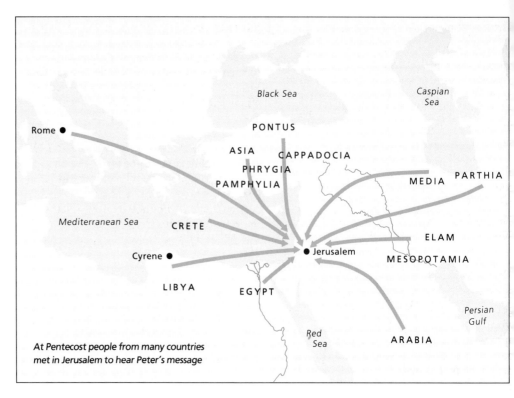

At Pentecost people from many countries met in Jerusalem to hear Peter's message

'God has made this Jesus, whom you crucified, both Lord and Christ.' (2:36)

Many of his listeners were filled with remorse: 'Brothers, what shall we do?' they demanded of the apostles. Peter was ready with the answer:

'Repent and be baptized, every one of you, in the name of Jesus Christ for the forgiveness of your sins. And you will receive the gift of the Holy Spirit.' (2:38)

About three thousand were baptized that day. They formed the nucleus of the new church. The church was not a building or an institution but the close-knit company of those who were committed to Jesus.

Persecution begins

The new group of Christians flourished; every day more people joined them. But trouble soon came. The authorities who had brought about Jesus' crucifixion were not prepared to hear it proclaimed that he was alive and still at work through his followers. The Sadducees in particular were angry, because they did not believe in life after death.

When Peter and John healed a lame beggar in Jesus' name, and boldly announced that it was through the power of Jesus that they had performed this act, the religious leaders could bear it no more. They arrested them but could not decide how to punish them, because the man who had been healed was living proof of the miracle. So they let them go, warning them to stop preaching about Jesus.

But the disciples refused to be silenced. Gone were the frightened, unnerved followers of Jesus who had run away when he was arrested and left him in the lurch. The resurrection of Jesus and the strengthening power of the Holy Spirit had transformed them. They were full of eagerness and courage. But they were soon in trouble again. The leaders were even prepared to put them to death, but the counsel of Gamaliel, a wise and good rabbi, prevailed:

'Leave them alone. Nothing will come of their efforts if they are imposters. But if not, we may find ourselves fighting against God himself.' (5:38, 39)

The apostles were not downcast. They rejoiced 'because they had been counted worthy of suffering disgrace for the Name'.

The Christian church

Meanwhile the new Christians gave themselves wholeheartedly to meeting together, learning what the apostles had to teach them, and praying. Their shared meals no doubt included the act of Communion that Jesus had taught them to keep at the last supper.

These first Christians voluntarily shared all their possessions and had everything in common. When anyone was in need, the others would sell their goods or land to provide for them. It was a caring, loving community — a major factor in its growth.

Ananias and Sapphira

But it seems this ideal way of life was too good to last. Two disciples, a husband and wife, sold their land to give the money to the apostles for the common good. But they held back part of the proceeds, pretending they had given it all. They wanted to look after their own interests, yet to be thought more generous and wholehearted than they were. Peter told the man, Ananias, that he had lied not just to the other Christians but to the Holy Spirit. Ananias fell dead at Peter's feet. Some hours later his wife Sapphira arrived, not knowing what had happened to her husband. In answer to Peter's question she repeated the lie, and she too died.

There have been many attempts to soften the seeming harshness of this judgment. But Ananias and Sapphira were guilty of a very serious breach of the love and integrity of the ideal community. Sharing and mutual trust could never be the same again.

Stephen

As the church grew, so did the administration. The apostles therefore asked the church to choose seven good men who would take care of such matters, in particular the distribution of funds to poor widows.

Stephen, one of the men chosen, was also an outstanding preacher and one who performed miracles. He was farsighted and recognized that the days of keeping the law and worshipping at the temple were over. Jesus had brought salvation and a far-reaching new morality which did not depend on these rituals.

The authorities recognized this challenge to their worship and way of life, and arrested him. He was brought before the Sanhedrin, where his well-reasoned defence only made them more angry. They took him out and stoned him.

'Look, I see heaven open and the Son of Man standing at the right hand of God.' Stephen cried out. Then he entreated, 'Lord Jesus, receive my spirit,' and like his Master added, 'Lord! Do not hold this sin against them.' When he had said this, Luke writes, 'He fell asleep.'

Samaria

So far, the followers of Jesus had remained in Jerusalem, except for those converted at Pentecost, who had returned to their homes taking the good news with them. After Stephen's murder, persecution forced most

---

The Message of the Apostles

Throughout Acts Luke gives brief summaries of several sermons preached by the apostles. One scholar, C.H. Dodd, put together the main themes of these sermons. He called this body of material the *kerygma*, which means the herald's message. These early preachers were called heralds because they proclaimed God's message for all to hear. This was what they preached:

- The age of the Messiah, foretold by the prophets, had arrived with the coming of Jesus and his kingdom.

- Jesus had spent his life doing good. He had demonstrated his power. He had died not only through the plots of his enemies, but as part of God's salvation plan. Jesus had been raised to life and was now exalted by God to a place of authority and power. He would come again as judge of all.

- The Holy Spirit had now come and would be given to all who repented and put their trust in Jesus.

- All who repented would receive forgiveness of sins. They would be baptized as an outward sign of belief.

Before he left his disciples Jesus instructed them to spread his message, from Jerusalem through Judea and Samaria (the country pictured here) to the ends of the earth. The story begins in Acts.

Christians to leave the city and only the apostles stayed behind. Wherever Christians went they talked about Jesus. One of them, called Philip, took the bold step of preaching in a city of Samaria.

For hundreds of years there had been hatred between Jews and Samaritans. But Jesus had preached in Samaria and he had told his followers to preach there too. There was widespread joy in the city as they heard that the Messiah they were expecting had come, and saw the amazing miracles Philip performed.

News of the mission spread to Jerusalem and the apostles sent Peter and John to see what was happening. They prayed that these new believers would receive the Holy Spirit, certain that this mission was part of the programme Jesus had given them for the spread of the gospel beyond Jerusalem and the immediate territory of Judea — and their prayers were answered.

The Ethiopian official

After preaching to huge crowds in Samaria, Philip was told by God to go to the help of one person who was travelling the desert road to Egypt. He was a high-ranking Ethiopian official. As Philip came near to his chariot he discovered that he was reading from an Old Testament scroll.

'Do you understand what you are reading?' Philip asked him.

'How can I unless someone explains it to me?' he replied.

Philip gladly climbed up beside him and preached the good news about Jesus, starting at the very verse the official was reading. It came from Isaiah's account of the suffering servant who died for his people's sins. The Ethiopian was converted and baptized, and went joyfully on his way back to Africa, taking the good news with him.

Saul's conversion

One of the chief enemies of the new Christian faith was a brilliant young scholar called Saul. He was a man of action too. He had watched while Stephen was murdered and had voted for his death. Saul's determination to suppress this new sect grew even stronger. He organized house-to-house searches and arrests and when some of the Christians escaped he obtained an extradition order so that he could bring them from Damascus to Jerusalem for trial.

He set out for Damascus. But in the burning heat of noon, as they travelled the hot road, a blinding light suddenly flashed before Saul. He fell to the ground and heard a voice say:

'Saul, Saul, why do you persecute me?'
'Who are you, Lord?'
'I am Jesus, whom you are persecuting.' (9:4, 5)

Saul knew now that Jesus was real and alive and that in persecuting his servants he had been persecuting Jesus himself. In that moment Saul's anger and enmity vanished. He submitted with all his being to his new Master, humbly asking, 'What shall I do, Lord?'

His sight had gone, and he was led into the city where for three days he was blind and ate no food. But God called Ananias, a Christian living in Damascus, to go to Saul. At first he was fearful, having heard of all the harm this enemy of the Christians had done, but he obeyed instructions and found Saul. He spoke to him:

'Brother Saul, the Lord — Jesus, who appeared to you on the road as you were coming here —

has sent me so that you may see again and be filled with the Holy Spirit.' *(9:17)*

He laid his hands on Saul and Saul's sight returned. He received the Holy Spirit and was baptized.

At once Saul began his new task of preaching about Jesus, arguing powerfully in the synagogues that Jesus was the Messiah. Outraged, some of his fellow-Jews tried to kill him. At last he had to be let down over the city wall in a basket in order to escape.

Jews and Gentiles

So far, the gospel had been preached to Jews, to Samaritans, and to those who had adopted the Jewish faith. Many non-Jews admired the high standards of the Jewish religion and worshipped Israel's God. They were known as God-fearers. Others went further: they received the covenant sign of circumcision and promised obedience to the whole Jewish Law.

It is hard to imagine just how big the gulf was between Jews and Gentiles at that time. Good Jews had as little contact as possible with Gentiles. They certainly would not eat with them or set foot in their houses. Any utensil used by a Gentile had to be specially purified or destroyed. Gentiles were 'unclean', Jews believed, and outside God's covenant which he had made with Israel alone.

It did not occur to the first Christians, who were all Jews, that Gentiles could possibly have a share in God's plan of salvation. The barriers seemed too great. Soon they must learn to break down these prejudices.

Cornelius

Cornelius was a Roman centurion, stationed at the military headquarters of Caesarea. He was a good man and a God-fearer. One day he was amazed by a vision of an angel, who told him that God had accepted his prayers and pious deeds and that he was to send for a man called Peter who was staying in Joppa.

While messengers were on their way there, Peter had a vision too. He had gone onto the flat roof of the house to pray, while he waited for the meal to be cooked. Perhaps he looked out to sea and saw the white sails of a ship — or perhaps it was the awning above him — because he had a vision of an enormous sheet being let down from heaven. It was full of every kind of animal that Jews had been taught not to eat. A voice commanded:

'Get up, Peter. Kill and eat.'

Peter protested,

'Surely not, Lord, I have never eaten anything impure or unclean.'

But the answer came,

'Do not call anything impure that God has made clean.' *(10:14, 15)*

In the sea-port of Joppa, Peter had a dream with far-reaching consequences. God's message through Jesus was not for the Jews only but for everyone.

The vision was repeated three times. Then Peter heard a loud knocking at the door. Messengers from Cornelius were waiting to speak to him. When Peter heard what they had to say he began to put two and two together. God had been telling him through the vision that he must not call unclean those people God had accepted.

He began by inviting the Gentile soldiers into the house. Next day he set off with them.

When he arrived, he told Cornelius and the invited crowd the good news about Jesus. They eagerly drank in what he had to say, and to Peter's amazement the Holy Spirit came to them. They began to speak in tongues — unknown ecstatic languages — and to praise

Antioch in Syria was the first great centre of Christianity after Jerusalem. Here the followers of Jesus were first called Christians—and it was the church at Antioch that commissioned Paul and Barnabas for their missionary journey. Antioch (Antakya) today is a large and important city, as it was in New Testament times.

The ancient city was founded in 300BC by a general of Alexander the Great. It became part of the Roman Empire and capital of the imperial province of Syria. According to the historian Josephus, Antioch was the third city of the Empire, after Rome and Alexandria. It was famous for its boulevard and colonnade with trees and fountains, and known as 'Antioch the Beautiful' because of its fine buildings. It was also called 'Queen of the East' because its population included people from Persia, India and even China. It had a Roman population too and a large Jewish colony.

God. When Peter saw that God had accepted these Gentiles he was sure that he should baptize them. So Gentile believers became part of the Christian church.

When Peter returned to Jerusalem he was criticized at first for going into a Gentile home. But when the church heard Peter's story they accepted the fact that God was offering salvation to Gentiles too.

This is a crucial event in Acts and in the history of the church. There are echoes of it all through the New Testament (for example, Ephesians 2 and 3). It launched the mission to Gentiles.

Antioch

Some of the Christians who had been scattered after the killing of Stephen found their way to Antioch. There they told the good news about Jesus to Jews and possibly to Gentiles too. It is difficult to know from the text just who these converts were, but they were certainly Greek-speaking, and perhaps God-fearers, like Cornelius. They were from varied cultural backgrounds and proved that the gospel could meet the needs of those from very different cultures.

A large number of converts began to meet together in Antioch and Barnabas, a Christian Jew from Cyprus, was sent from Jerusalem to oversee affairs. He was satisfied

that God was at work but recognized that this young church needed to be taught the new faith more thoroughly. So he fetched Saul — or Paul as he became known in the Gentile world.

For a year they taught the church, which became a great centre, counterpart to the original church in Jerusalem. But from the beginning Antioch had a more open attitude and found the integration of Jewish and Gentile believers easier to accept.

Paul's first missionary expedition

When the church in Antioch was praying and fasting together, the Holy Spirit said:

'Set apart for me Barnabas and Saul for the work to which I have called them.' (13:2)

The church responded by fasting, praying, laying their hands on these two as a sign of commissioning, then sending them to spread the gospel further afield.

They took with them John Mark, a young nephew of Barnabas, and set sail from Seleucia, the port of Antioch, which was fifteen miles inland up the River Orontes.

First they visited Cyprus, Barnabas' home where the proconsul — in spite of opposition from his sorcerer — was attracted to their message.

They left Paphos in Cyprus and crossed

the Mediterranean to Perga in the province of Pamphylia. They did not linger in this low-lying coastal plain — perhaps, as some suggest, because Paul caught malaria and the area was too unhealthy for them to remain. Whatever the reason, they pressed on to the healthier northern highlands. But the route from Perga to Antioch in Pisidia, which was their next stop, was mountainous and bandit-ridden.

John Mark had already left them at Perga and gone home to Jerusalem. No one knows why, but Paul felt keenly that Mark had let them down.

In Pisidian Antioch, Paul preached first in the synagogue. This became his usual habit. He believed that Jews had first right to hear the gospel. He could also appeal to them from their Hebrew Scriptures (the Old Testament).

When the Jews in Antioch rejected him he turned to the Gentiles. Many were converted and a new little church was formed. Paul's aim was always to establish and nurture new churches or groups of Christians.

Some of the Jews were jealous of his success and stirred up opposition. The same thing happened at Iconium, nearly a hundred miles south-east, and the next place on their route. Threats were made to stone them and they fled to Lystra, then Derbe.

When Paul preached at Lystra he caught sight of a man who had been lame from birth. Paul realized that he had faith in what was being said. He called out: 'Stand up straight on your feet!' and the man was healed.

Paul and Barnabas were quite unprepared for what followed. Hasty preparations were made to offer sacrifice to them because the local people decided that they must be gods visiting the earth. The two men tore their clothes in horror and cried out, 'Men, why are you doing this? We too are only men, human like you.'

But they used this opportunity to explain that they were bringers of good news about the true God who provided the crops and who made heaven and earth. Paul suited his message to his hearers' background and understanding. This explanation was very different from the Scripture-based sermons that he preached in the synagogues.

Antagonistic Jews from Antioch and Iconium had followed the two and they set the crowds against them. Paul was stoned and left for dead but amazingly he recovered. He and Barnabas bravely retraced their route, encouraging all the converts they had made on their way out and choosing leaders to oversee the new churches.

On their way back they stopped in Perga to preach, then sailed back to Syrian Antioch to report to the church there.

The Council of Jerusalem

The church at Jerusalem was very different in outlook from that in Antioch. At Jerusalem a large number of priests had become Christians, whereas Antioch was composed of Greek-speaking Jews and Gentiles. These Hellenist Jews, as they were called, tended to be much less narrow and legalistic than the Jews who lived in Judea and Jerusalem. Many of the stricter Jews still believed that although Gentiles could be converted it was necessary for them to become Jews too. After all, they argued, God made his covenant with Jews, so any who wanted to be in relationship with him must receive the covenant sign of circumcision and become part of the Jewish nation.

Some of these Judaistic Christians came to Antioch and spread their teaching there. Paul and Barnabas argued fiercely with them. Paul believed fervently that salvation was through faith in Christ alone, and in no way depended

Cyprus was the first stop for Paul and Barnabas on their missionary journey. It was Barnabas' home. From the harbour at Paphos (pictured here), they set sail for the south coast of present-day Turkey.

THE ROMANS

The Romans are perhaps best-remembered today (at least in western Europe) for their roads. Roman roads were built to last. But the long, straight highways were not in the first instance for trade: they were for conquest and control. These were the solders' roads in war — and, in the peace that followed, they made for an ease of travel unknown before.

Following the Greeks with their culture, ideas and language came the practical Romans with their roads and aqueducts, plumbing and heating, baths and spectator sports. From 146BC when Carthage was destroyed, the Romans extended their rule all around the Mediterranean Sea.

Palestine, in New Testament times, was under Roman occupation. Roman army officers and officials move in and out of the Gospels, Acts and Letters. Paul was a Roman citizen, although he was a Jew by birth. He draws imagery from Roman charioteers and the Games. Jesus lived his life in the confines of Palestine, where Jewish Zealot guerrillas harrassed the Roman troops. Paul travelled the Empire — to Rome itself, where a Christian church was already established.

Many gladly turned from the old gods to the new gospel of Jesus. But later in the first century, as the cult of emperor worship grew stronger, Christians paid dearly for their faith. They were made a public spectacle in the arena, fighting wild animals and turned into human torches by the Emperor

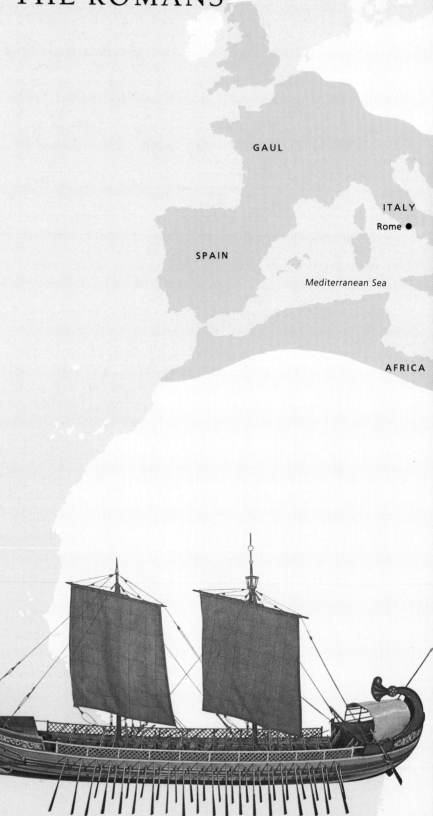

GAUL

ITALY
Rome ●

SPAIN

Mediterranean Sea

AFRICA

The swift and manoeuvrable warship was a significant factor in Roman conquest and control.

Beautiful examples of Roman glass have been found in many places.

Dawn illuminates the ancient city centre of Rome. At this hour no traffic hurtles past as yet on the modern road.

CEDONIA
● Philippi
Thessalonica
● ASIA   CAPPADOCIA
CHAIA
Corinth ● Ephesus   CILICIA
● Athens   PISIDIA GALATIA ● Syrian Antioch
REECE   Tarsus   SYRIA
CRETE   CYPRUS   ● Palmyra
Damascus ●
Caesarea ● ● Jerusalem
PALESTINE
EGYPT

☐ The Roman Empire (at its greatest extent, around AD 100)

Stone-carvings depict scenes from daily commerce: a money-changer and his servant (above); farmers paying for the lease of land (left).

on any outward rituals. He spoke out strongly to correct those who believed that salvation was gained by good deeds as well as faith.

It was decided that Paul and Barnabas should go to Jerusalem and see the apostles there. So a council was held at which James, the brother of Jesus, took the chair. After a long discussion Peter spoke of his experience with Cornelius. Not even Jews could bear the burden of keeping the Law, he argued. Why expect Gentiles to do so?

'We believe it is through the grace of our Lord Jesus that we are saved, just as they are.' (15:11)

James quoted from the Old Testament to support his argument and concluded:

'It is my judgment, therefore, that we should not make it difficult for the Gentiles who are turning to God.' (15:19)

Finally it was agreed that Gentile Christians should not be required to follow Jewish practices, but they were asked to keep certain rules, mainly to do with Jewish food laws. In this way Jewish Christians, still sensitive to their upbringing, would have no qualms in sitting down to share meals with Gentile fellow-Christians.

Paul's second journey

Paul and Barnabas planned to set out on a second missionary expedition and Barnabas was all for giving his nephew, John Mark, another chance and taking him with them. Paul would not hear of it and the two disagreed so strongly that in the end they split up.

Barnabas sailed for Cyprus again with John Mark, and Paul set off with Silas, like himself a Roman citizen. At Lystra Paul and Silas chose Timothy to join the team. First he was to be circumcised. It seems surprising that Paul agreed that Timothy should be circumcised in view of his strong arguments against the rite for Gentile Christians. But Timothy was Jewish through his mother, though his father was Greek. Perhaps Paul felt that Jews would take notice of Timothy's preaching only if, as a Jew, he had submitted to the covenant rite.

On this journey the team was somehow prevented from preaching in Asia, so they pressed on to Troas, the Aegean port near the site of the ancient city of Troy. Here Paul had a vision in which a Macedonian man begged 'Come over to Macedonia and help us.' So a momentous decision was made. For the first time Christian missionaries set foot on the continent of Europe.

At Philippi

There was no synagogue in Philippi, either because there were too few Jewish men or because they were too poor to afford one. But Paul and his team found a place by the river where prayers were held and they went there to preach on the Sabbath. Lydia, a wealthy businesswoman, was converted and at once invited the missionaries to stay in her home.

The next convert Luke tells us about was a poor, demon-possessed slave who brought profit to her masters by fortune-telling. Whenever she saw Paul and his party she shouted at the top of her voice, 'These men are servants of the Most High God who are telling you the way to be saved.' Eventually Paul told the evil spirit in Jesus' name to come out of her. But, dismayed at their loss of income, her employers dragged Paul and Silas before the magistrates and had them thrown into prison. Both were flogged, in spite of being Roman citizens, and left in the innermost cell. But instead of cursing or bemoaning their fate, Paul and Silas sang praises and prayed to God.

At midnight a strong earthquake shook the whole prison, loosening the chains and

Philosophies of the Day

By Paul's day belief in the old Greek gods was failing and various philosophies had sprung up. But even these had lost their original freshness and did not fill the spiritual emptiness.

The **Stoic** philosophy was founded by Zeno of Cyprus who settled in Athens in about 300 BC. He taught in a *stoa* or porch, so his followers were dubbed Stoics, meaning 'porch people'. Zeno emphasized the importance of reason. The good life was life lived in harmony with nature, which was also founded on reason. The aim was to be self-sufficient and to endure pain without fear. It was more important to be virtuous than to enjoy pleasure.

The **Epicurean** philosophy was founded by Epicurus at about the same time. Pleasure was the chief aim, but pleasure found in friendship, in good morals or things of the mind. Not surprisingly, some followers interpreted pleasure in a different way and gave all their attention to enjoying the pleasures of the flesh.

John Stott succinctly sums up the differences between the two philosophies: 'It was characteristic of Epicureans to emphasize chance, escape and the enjoyment of pleasure and of the Stoics to emphasize fatalism, submission and the endurance of pain.'

Luke passes over 100 miles of journeying in one sentence as the missionaries travel along the great Roman east-west highway, the Egnatian Way. They preached in Thessalonica — still a great city today — but they met strong opposition from angry Jews, who followed them to Berea. Finally Paul had to leave quickly for Athens, where he waited alone for the rest of the party.

At Athens

In Athens, at the intellectual centre of the world, Paul argued with the Stoic and

stocks by which the prisoners were fastened to the wall. The jailer was terrifed. If the prisoners escaped, his life would be forfeit. He was about to kill himself when Paul shouted out that no one was missing. The jailer called for lights and came rushing in, crying out to Paul:

'What must I do to be saved?'

Paul answered:

'Believe in the Lord Jesus Christ and you will be saved — you and your household.' (16:30, 31)

The jailer and all his family believed and were baptized, but not before he had washed the wounded backs of his prisoners.

Next morning the authorities were keen to get rid of Paul and Silas but Paul refused to leave without a proper apology. As Roman citizens they had been wrongfully flogged. Probably it was for the sake of the young church that he made this stand.

It was Paul's strategy to preach the gospel in key places. He often chose cities that stood at crossroads from which travellers would journey throughout the Empire. In this way the gospel would continue to spread through the converts he made.

From Thessalonica in the north, on the great Egnatian Way, he travelled to Athens. He held discussions in the public square and addressed the city council (the Areopagus). This picture is taken from the market-place of ancient Athens, looking towards the Acropolis.

Athens had its golden age in the fifth century BC when the great Greek sculptors, playwrights, philosophers and architects flourished. But even in Paul's day it was regarded as the Roman Empire's intellectual centre. The buildings and monuments were unrivalled. The city was so full of sculptures of the gods that one Roman satirist remarked it was easier to find a god there than a man.

The ancient citadel, the Acropolis, was high enough to be seen for miles around. North-west of the Acropolis was the Areopagus, or Hill of Mars. The court was originally held there, but it had become a council whose members were guardians of the city's morals, religion and education.

The Agora, or market-place, had many porticoes painted by famous artists. Here philosophers argued and discussed.

Epicurean philosophers in the marketplace, where such discussions were the order of the day. At their invitation he spoke about his faith on the Hill of Mars. He quoted from their own poets, preaching in terms that they could follow. But he made little headway when he told them about the resurrection and a coming day of judgment.

At Corinth

Paul moved on from Athens to Corinth, where he earned his keep by tent-making until Silas and Timothy arrived with a gift of money from the churches. He was then able to preach full-time and stayed for eighteen months establishing a church and teaching converts.

Paul's third journey

Luke rapidly sketches the end of the second missionary journey and the beginning of the third, when Paul began by revisiting the churches he had founded during his first journey. Then he went to Ephesus.

At Ephesus

Paul returned to Ephesus, as he had promised when he called there at the end of his second journey. He spent two years there,

Corinth, in the south of Greece, was refounded as a colony by Julius Caesar; in 27BC it became capital of the province and residence of the Roman pro-consul. It was very important commercially, with a harbour that straddled the isthmus and a port on either side: Cenchreae looked towards Asia, and Lechaeum towards Italy.

Attempts to build a canal had failed (though there is one today), but small boats were dragged across a slipway and other cargoes taken overland.

It was a very cosmopolitan place with a reputation for immorality and drunkenness. On a rocky height nearly 600 metres/2,000 feet above sea level stood a temple to Aphrodite, goddess of love. A thousand female slaves served her and roamed the streets at night as prostitutes.

The Isthmian Games were held here and attracted visitors from all over the Greek-speaking world.

Today the great columns of the Temple of Apollo (about 540BC) stand out against the background of the hill-top citadel.

longer than anywhere else. He preached to the Jews first, in the synagogue. When they rejected him he hired a lecture hall as his headquarters. He could only have it when its owner was not using it — at the hottest time of the day — but people flocked to listen to him.

Paul seems to have performed many unusual miraculous cures in this city. Perhaps he felt this was the 'language' the Ephesians best understood.

Ephesus was swarming with tourists, many of whom came to visit the famous temple of Artemis. Local silversmiths had made a good living selling silver souvenirs of the goddess, but Paul's preaching was so successful that trade fell off. One of them, Demetrius, summoned a meeting of other craftsmen to voice their complaints. He stirred up so much feeling that a mob gathered and they all began to chant the slogan 'Great is Artemis of the Ephesians!' over and over again.

The whole city was in an uproar by the time they made their way to the theatre. The Christians held Paul back forcibly when he wanted to go and address the rioters. The event turned into a mass demonstration with half the people not even knowing why they were there. It was a long time before the city clerk could restore order.

The collection for the poor

Paul left Ephesus and spent time with the churches in Macedonia and Achaia. No doubt he was collecting the churches' contribution for the poor Jewish Christians in Jerusalem.

Paul never forgot that the Gentiles owed a great deal to their Jewish fellow-Christians. That was why he had organized this collection. It would also demonstrate — again — the reality of Jew and Gentile being one in Christ. He took this gift with him when he went up to Jerusalem. He also took along with him representatives of the different churches that had contributed, so that they could present the gift in person.

Journey to Jerusalem

Paul could not spare time to call in at Ephesus again on his way to Jerusalem. But he sent a message to the leaders of the church and they met the ship at Miletus. He warned and encouraged them, quoting some words of Jesus himself: 'It is more blessed to

Ephesus was ideally placed as a centre of trade located on the main route from Rome to the East. It was a good centre for the whole Roman province of Asia (western Turkey). It was famous for its shrine to Artemis, which was one of the seven wonders of the world. Artemis was not the virgin huntress of Greek and Roman mythology but the many-breasted Asian mother goddess.

Ephesus was a centre of magic and magical arts, and books on magic were often called 'Ephesian writings'. It had a vast theatre that could seat 20,000 spectators.

The city's spectacular ruins attract many visitors today.

Accused of taking a non-Jew into the temple area, Paul was in danger of his life. A barrier between the Court of the Gentiles and the inner courts carried notices forbidding non-Jews to enter, on pain of death. This one was found intact in Jerusalem in 1871. A fragment of another, its letters showing traces of the original red paint, was found in 1936.

give than to receive.' They knelt down on the beach together and prayed.

'They were all crying as they hugged him and kissed him good-bye,' Luke wrote. 'They were especially sad because he had said that they would never see him again.'

Paul knew that he would probably face trouble in Jerusalem. On his journey a prophet called Agabus warned him not to go to Jerusalem. He bound his own hands and feet with Paul's belt as an acted prophecy of what would happen to Paul. But Paul's mind was made up:

'Why are you weeping and breaking my heart? I am ready not only to be bound but also to die in Jerusalem for the name of the Lord Jesus.' (21:13)

Jerusalem and after

Paul was warmly welcomed in Jerusalem but the Christian leaders warned him that he was suspect in the eyes of many of the Jews who had been converted there. Some of these had been priests and had a strict background. Paul, on the other hand, had the reputation for throwing out Jewish customs. So they recommended that he should disarm their suspicions by paying for four Jewish Christians to complete the vows they had taken.

Paul agreed, but when he was attending to the matter at the temple he was seized by onlookers who mistakenly thought he had taken Gentiles into the temple court reserved for Jews. The penalty for this was death. The ringleaders whipped the crowds into a frenzy of fury against Paul. It was no good for him to protest that he was innocent. At last the Roman commander intervened and rescued Paul. When he discovered that he was a Roman citizen he allowed him to address the crowd.

The next day Paul was brought before the Sanhedrin — the Jewish Council. He knew what he was doing when he told them that he was being charged in connection with the resurrection. That subject was an old battleground betweeen Pharisees and Sadducees, both of whom were present. The Council was soon in an uproar.

Later Paul's nephew discovered that some of the Jews were plotting to murder Paul. He reported the matter to the commander and Paul was sent off by night to the military headquarters at Caesarea, into the custody of Felix the Governor. Paul stated his case before him, but Felix allowed it to lapse for two years, after which Festus took over as Governor. He immediately began to deal with the case. The Jewish accusers wanted Paul brought back to Jerusalem for trial but Festus refused, perhaps suspecting that they might ambush and kill him.

Paul eventually used his privilege as a Roman citizen, appealing to Caesar to have his case heard in Rome. Before he was sent there he had a further chance to speak of his faith before King Agrippa, grandson of Herod the Great, and his sister Bernice, who were visiting Festus.

They agreed that Paul was innocent and that, but for his appeal to Caesar, he could have been set free. But perhaps Paul knew that he would never be safe from Jewish plots while he remained in Palestine. Also his appeal meant that his ambition to reach Rome would be fulfilled at last. He would be a prisoner, but he might find opportunity to witness to his faith in the capital of the Empire.

Journey to Rome

Luke describes with graphic detail the eventful journey to Rome. Against Paul's advice, the captain of the ship decided to sail, risking the lateness of the season. There were

errible storms but Paul encouraged
everyone on board:

*Take heart! Not one of you will lose his life;
only the ship will be lost . . . For I trust in God . . .'
(27:22, 25)*

After a gruelling voyage the boat was
eventually wrecked close to the coast of
Malta. All managed to reach shore on bits of
wreckage or by swimming. They spent the
winter there and Paul healed and preached to
the islanders. Then they continued their
journey to Rome.

It must have cheered Paul greatly when
some Christians from Rome walked thirty to
forty miles from the city to meet him and
accompany him into Rome. There Paul was
kept under house arrest but given
considerable freedom. He called the Jewish
leaders to visit him so that he could tell them
the truth about himself, as well as preaching
to them about Jesus the Messiah. For the rest
of his stay he was able to use his house as a
place where people could gather to hear the
good news.

Luke's account comes to a sudden end.
We leave Paul in Rome in his rented house
under Roman guard. Luke says that he stayed
there for two years. Perhaps his Jewish
accusers did not come in person to take up
their case and it was therefore dismissed. We
know that Paul was freed for at least another
two years to carry on his travels. After that he
was arrested again and finally put to death
for his faith in AD64.

Following a plot against
his life, Paul was kept
prisoner in Caesarea for
two years, until his appeal
to Caesar took him to
Rome. The theatre of the
ancient city has survived to
be restored and used
today.

PAUL'S LIFE AND JOURNEYS

It was Paul's strategy to preach the gospel in key places. He often chose cities that stood at crossroads from which travellers would journey throughout the Empire. In this way the gospel would continue to spread through the converts he had made.

● Rome

ITALY

● Puteoli

● Rhegium

● Syracuse

MALTA

GREECE

Beroea ● Thessalonica ● Philippi

Troa

Mity

Corinth ● ● Athens

CRETE

● Lasea

For many years Paul longed to go to Rome. In the end he went as a prisoner, aboard a Roman grainship.

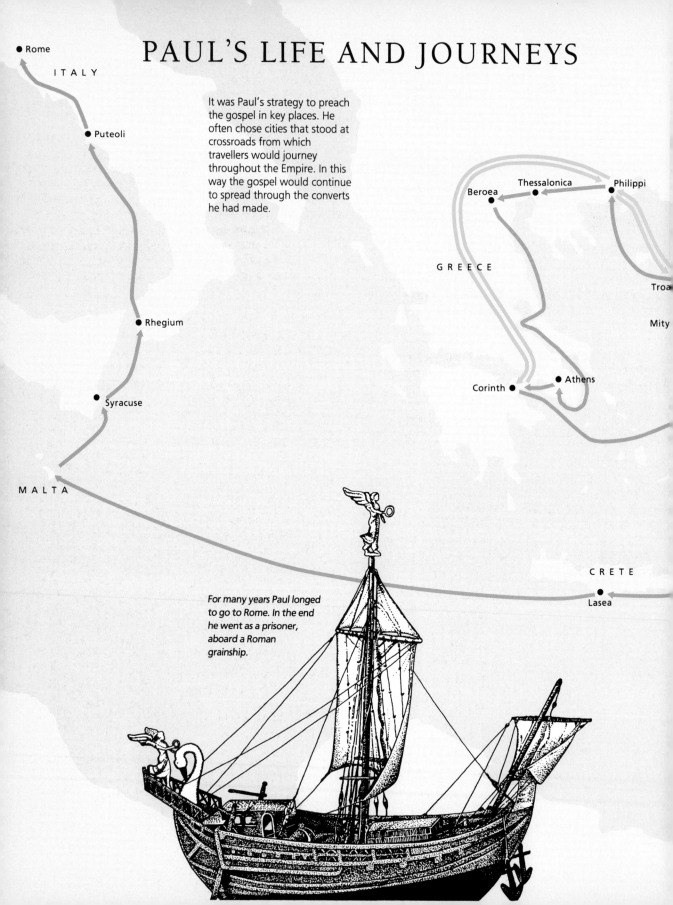

Biography of Paul

Saul was born in Tarsus, capital of the Roman province of Cilicia (now southern Turkey). He had a strict Jewish upbringing but he must have learned much from the Greeks and Romans he mixed with there, and from the culture of the city, which rivalled Athens and Alexandria in learning.

Saul's chosen career was the study of the Law but, like all Jewish students, he also learned a trade. Tarsus was famous for its leather work and Saul became a tent-maker or worker in leather goods.

He went to Jerusalem to study under Gamaliel, a great rabbi whose grandfather, Hillel, had been an outstanding teacher. Saul was a Pharisee, extremely zealous for the Jewish Law. He was also a Roman citizen and is usually known by his non-Jewish name of Paul.

At some time soon after his conversion, according to his own account, he spent a long period in Arabia. Perhaps he needed the quiet and solitude of the desert in order to think through the implications of his new faith.

Paul's contribution to the Christian church was tremendous. He was the chief apostle to the Gentiles, or non-Jews, and travelled many hundreds of miles, always breaking fresh ground in his preaching. He was often imprisoned, beaten and ill-treated for his faith, on top of all the usual hardships of travel in that age.

The letters Paul wrote to young churches provided the theological framework for the new faith.

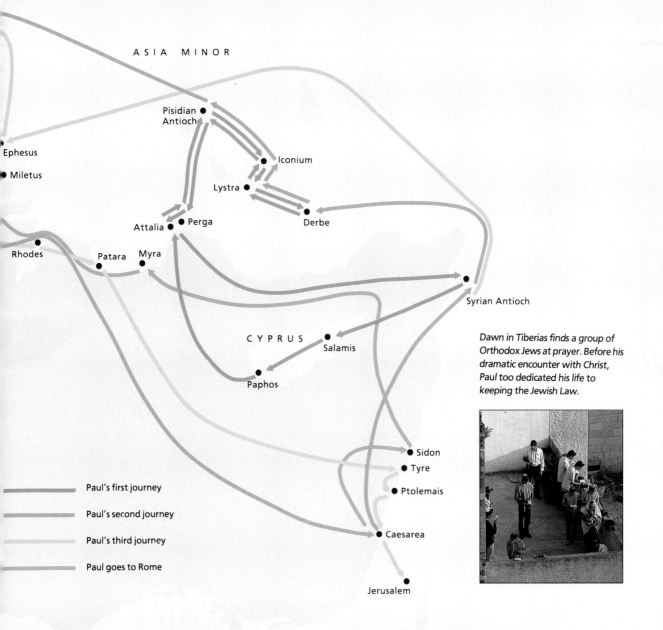

ASIA MINOR

Ephesus
Miletus
Pisidian Antioch
Iconium
Lystra
Attalia • Perga
Derbe
Rhodes
Patara Myra
Syrian Antioch

CYPRUS
Salamis
Paphos

Sidon
Tyre
Ptolemais

Caesarea

Jerusalem

Paul's first journey

Paul's second journey

Paul's third journey

Paul goes to Rome

Dawn in Tiberias finds a group of Orthodox Jews at prayer. Before his dramatic encounter with Christ, Paul too dedicated his life to keeping the Jewish Law.

11
LETTERS FROM PAUL
Romans to Philemon

A letter written in Greek. It begins with the name of the sender, greeting the recipient. It closes with further greetings and farewell.

Wherever Paul went he preached the Gospel, and as a result little groups of new Christians sprang up in many cities throughout the Roman Empire, forming local churches. Paul sometimes chose leaders for them.

Often Paul had to continue on his journey leaving behind a young church with very little experience or information about their new-found faith. Sometimes other teachers would arrive after Paul had left and pass on all kinds of wrong ideas. When it was impossible for Paul to visit in person and put things right, he wrote letters to the churches, setting them straight where they were muddled or confused and answering any questions they were asking.

Paul was very busy and constantly on the move but when he was put in prison because of his preaching there was plenty of time to write. He generally had a helper with him who acted as scribe and wrote at Paul's dictation.

The letters he wrote were greatly treasured by the Christians who received them and were probably passed round to nearby churches too. In time, some of them came to be recognized as inspired writings. They were accepted as God's own word to Christians. These are the thirteen letters that

Letter Writing, Greek Style

Paul's letters follow the standard letter-form of the time. John Drane sets this out as follows:

1. The letter began with the name of the sender, followed by that of the person he was writing to.
2. Next came a greeting, perhaps in a single word. Paul often combined the Hebrew *Shalom* or peace with the Christian greeting of 'Grace'.
3. Then came thanks for the good health of the person addressed. Paul often thanked God that his friends were flourishing in their Christian lives.
4. The main body of the letter came next. Paul usually devoted the first part to teaching and the second to the practical outcome of that teaching in terms of Christian living.
5. Personal news and greetings were given. Paul sent messages to individual men and women in the church.
6. At this point Paul often added a little note in his own handwriting, to prove that he was the writer. The rest would be written by a scribe or secretary.
7. The farewell was usually a single word but Paul often expanded this into a fuller blessing and prayer for his readers.

Suggested Dates and Places of Paul's Letters

Letter	Date	Sent from
GROUP 1		
Galatians	AD48	Syrian Antioch
1 Thessalonians	50	Corinth
2 Thessalonians	50	Corinth
GROUP 2		
1 Corinthians	54	Ephesus
Philippians	54	Ephesus?
2 Corinthians 10–13	55	Ephesus
2 Corinthians 1–9	55–56	Macedonia
Romans	57	Corinth
GROUP 3		
Colossians	60–61?	Rome
Philemon	60–61?	Rome
Ephesians	60–61?	Rome
GROUP 4		
Titus	After 62	Ephesus
1 Timothy	After 62	Macedonia
2 Timothy	64?	Rome

we have in the New Testament.

When we come to read these letters we have to do some detective work. It is like hearing one side of a conversation. Sometimes Paul seems to be answering questions his readers have asked. He also gives his views on situations that are not fully explained. We have to pick up the clues and piece the jigsaw together as well as we can. In spite of these hindrances, what Paul has to say about the Christian gospel and the Christian life is clear and straightforward.

Paul's usual pattern is to begin his letter with theory — teaching about the Christian faith — then to follow it up in the second half of the letter with practical help on how this 'head-knowledge' should work out in everyday Christian living.

In some of his letters — Colossians, Philemon, Ephesians, Philippians — Paul refers to himself as a prisoner. It is usually thought that Paul wrote these letters from Rome where he was imprisoned in AD60–62. But he may have been in prison earlier in Ephesus and the chart assumes that Philippians was written at that time. This chapter follows the chronological order given in the chart (the New Testament order is different).

Galatians

The readers. Galatia probably refers to northern Turkey. In that case Paul was writing to the churches he founded in Pisidian Antioch, Iconium and Derbe on his first missionary journey.

The purpose of the letter. Paul was very worried because visitors had come to the Galatian church saying that he was no true apostle and — worse still — giving a different version of the gospel. He wrote to put matters right.

Here is a letter written at top speed and at white heat. Paul is desperately anxious about the young Christians in Galatia. He is afraid that they have been put right off course by the wrong ideas put into their heads by the visiting preachers. He speaks out plainly:

'You foolish Galatians! Who put a spell on you?' (3:1)

Paul had made the gospel crystal clear to them and he repeats the heart of it here:

'We know that a person is put right with God only through faith in Jesus Christ, never by doing what the Law requires.' (2:16)

These wrong-headed teachers had told the Galatians that in addition to putting their trust in Jesus, they must keep the Law, as the Jewish covenant had required. As a sign that they would keep the Law they must also be circumcised. But no one except Jesus has ever lived their whole life without breaking the Law. Paul repeats that God accepts a person who puts faith — trust — in Jesus. That is all that is needed:

'Those who depend on obeying the Law live under a curse... No one is put right with God by means of the Law... But by becoming a curse for us Christ has redeemed us from the curse that the Law brings.' (3:10–13)

Paul also tells these Gentile Christians that, through faith, they have become as much children of Abraham as the Jews were. In other words, they are now part of God's covenant people (Galatians 3). The constant struggle to keep the Law is not only unnecessary but stifles the freedom that Christians should enjoy:

'Freedom is what we have — Christ has set us free! Stand, then, as free people, and do not allow yourselves to become slaves again.' (5:1)

Christians should lead a new kind of life which will please God — but not by their own efforts. Just as they received new life in Jesus through the Holy Spirit's power, so the Spirit will help them now to produce the qualities of 'love, joy, peace, patience, kindness, goodness, faithfulness, humility, and self-control'.

1 and 2 Thessalonians

The readers. These letters were written to the Christians in Thessalonica, the capital city of the Roman province of Macedonia (northern Greece). Paul preached and founded a church there on his second missionary expedition (see Acts 17).

The purpose of the letter. The Thessalonians

GALATIANS

KEYNOTES OF THE LETTER

Paul's authority as an apostle
1–2

The law convicts; faith saves
3–4

Freedom—and responsibility
5–6

1 THESSALONIANS

KEYNOTES OF THE LETTER

Paul's ministry in Thessalonica—news from Timothy   1–3

Sexual standards, and love   4

Jesus' coming again   4–5

148

A Roman arch straddles an arterial road—the ancient Roman east-west highway known as the Egnatian Way—in Thessaloniki (the Thessalonica of Paul's day).

had become muddled about Jesus' return. Paul wanted to clear up misunderstandings and give more teaching on the subject.

Paul often had to remind young Christians that in spite of the easy attitude to sex all around them, they must live pure lives. Casual sex is not part of God's plan:

'God wants you to be holy and completely free from sexual immorality... God did not call us to live in immorality, but in holiness.' (4:3, 7)

Paul deals with a special worry the Thessalonian Christians had in connection with Jesus' return. They recognized that Jesus would come to take his people to be with him but they were anxious about the fate of Christians who had already died. What would happen to them? Paul reassures them that all Christians will be united with Jesus on that day. In fact, those who have died will take priority:

'Those who have died believing in Christ will rise to life first; then we who are living at that time will be gathered up along with them in the clouds to meet the Lord in the air. And so we will always be with the Lord. So then, encourage one another with these words.' (4:16–18)

The way to be ready for that day is to live in obedience to God's commands, and be thankful.

Some argue that Paul did not write 2 Thessalonians, because what he has to say about Jesus' coming again does not match up with 1 Thessalonians. There he writes as if Jesus might come at any time; here he explains that other events must happen first.

Paul encourages the Thessalonians about the way their faith has grown in spite of the

persecution they have gone through. He tells them that when Jesus comes again they will be vindicated and true justice will be done.

It seems that a bogus letter may have arrived, said to be from Paul but giving wrong information. From this letter the Thessalonians understood that Jesus' return had already taken place. Paul tells them not to be misled. Before Jesus returns there will be a final outburst of evil, led by someone Paul calls the 'Wicked One'.

Some of the Thessalonians had opted out and stopped working for their living. Paul tells them plainly:

'In the name of the Lord Jesus Christ we command these people and warn them to lead orderly lives and work to earn their own living.' (3:12)

Paul signs this letter himself, so that they will know it is genuine.

1 and 2 Corinthians

There are problems in sorting out just how Paul's two letters, as we have them in our New Testament, fit into a pattern. It is a bit like doing a jigsaw puzzle. Here is one possible order of events:

- While he was at Ephesus Paul received disturbing news from Corinth and he wrote a letter, particularly about immorality. He refers to this letter in 1 Corinthians 5:9.

- When members of Chloe's household brought news of divisions at Corinth (see 1 Corinthians 1:11) Paul wrote again. This second letter is our 1 Corinthians, in which he also answers questions which the Corinthians had put to him (see 1 Corinthians 7:1).

- Paul then paid a short and painful visit to Corinth (see 2 Corinthians 2:1; 12:14; 13:1). He followed that with another letter, which may be part of 2 Corinthians —chapters 10–13.

- After that, Paul heard with relief and delight from Titus that the Corinthians had had a change of heart (see 2 Corinthians 7:6–7). That was when he

Jesus' Second Coming

Paul uses the word *parousia* for the coming again of Jesus. The word means 'presence' and was used for a royal visit. The early Christians expected the second coming of Jesus to happen very soon. It would be the climax of the Day of the Lord talked about by the prophets, and begun with Jesus' first coming.

wrote his fourth letter, which is our 2 Corinthians 1–9.

The readers. These letters are written to the Christians at Corinth — an important seaport in the south of Greece — where Paul founded a church on his second missionary expedition (see Acts 18).

The purpose of the letter. Paul had a number of reasons for writing to the Corinthians. There was a good deal that he needed to put right in their church life and in their personal lives too. He also wanted to answer the questions that they had fired at him. Above all, he wanted to restore his own relationship with the Corinthians. Outsiders had visited Corinth and given him a bad name. Paul is anxious to set the record straight.

The church at Corinth was very lively, with plenty of gifts and enthusiasm but plenty of problems too.

Paul has been told that the church has split into cliques — each following one leader or another. He brings home to them the importance of being one and reminds them of the central fact of their faith — Jesus crucified for their sakes! That puts an end to all bickering or pride.

Paul is shocked to hear that a member of the church has actually been committing adultery with his step-mother. He reminds them that all sexual misbehaviour is wrong:

'Don't you know that your body is the temple of the Holy Spirit, who lives in you and who was given to you by God? You do not belong to yourselves but to God; he bought you for a price. So use your bodies for God's glory.' (6:19–20)

Question and answer

Paul answers the questions they have put to him:

'Is celibacy a good thing?' Paul assures them that sexual intercourse is good and right between husband and wife. But he does suggest that those still unmarried would do better to remain single — like him. He reminds them that 'there is not much time left': Jesus' coming is very near and Christians should therefore be as free as possible to serve God, without other distractions.

'Should we eat food that has been sacrificed to idols?' Slaughtered meat was usually offered in a pagan temple before being sold in the marketplace. Did this make it unfit for Christians to eat? Paul says that since the gods represented by the idols don't exist, any such ceremony is meaningless.

But he knows that not everyone is able to take such a robust view, and begs the Corinthians to be sensitive to one another's feelings. If it upsets another Christian's conscience, don't eat meat. The good of others comes before personal preference.

The gift of love

Paul has a good deal to say about some of the showier Christian gifts which so preoccupied the Corinthians. They seem to have been so

Marriage versus celibacy was one of the issues in Paul's first letter to the Corinthian Christians. This Greek vase painting shows a girl being dressed for her wedding.

eager to use their gifts that church meetings ended in uproar. Christian worship should be orderly, Paul tells them. He recommends love as the gift that best shows their Christian faith in action. One of the most famous passages in the Bible is chapter 13 of this letter:

'If I speak in the tongues of men and of angels, but have not love, I am only a resounding gong or a clanging cymbal... Love is patient, love is kind. It does not envy, it does not boast, it is not proud... Love never fails... These three remain: faith, hope and love. But the greatest of these is love.' (13:1, 4, 8, 13)

The resurrection

Lastly Paul deals with resurrection. Some Corinthians had been saying that there was no resurrection for Christians after death. Paul argues forcefully that Jesus rose and therefore those who are united to him will also rise to new life. The resurrection of Jesus is the foundation of all faith:

'If Christ has not been raised, then your faith is a delusion and you are still lost in your sins.' (15:17)

He explains that the earthly body will be changed into a spiritual body and looks forward to the future coming of Jesus when all Christians will be changed 'in a flash, in the twinkling of an eye, at the last trumpet'. Death will be swallowed up in victory.

'Thanks be to to God, who gives us the victory through our Lord Jesus Christ!' (15:57)

Paul writes his second letter to the Corinthians with great feeling. There is a strong sense of the pain and difficulties he has had to endure in his mission as an apostle:

'We are often troubled, but not crushed; sometimes in doubt, but never in despair; there are many enemies, but we are never without a friend; and though badly hurt at times, we are not destroyed.' (4:8–9)

We get a fascinating glimpse into the grim facts of his missionary expeditions:

Paul's Thorn in the Flesh

In 2 Corinthians Paul talks mysteriously about his 'thorn in the flesh'. He is clearly referring to some problem which hit him hard. There are many different views as to what this source of trouble may have been. Some think it was an eye disease or recurrent malaria. Whatever the affliction was, it brought Paul low, and he tells the Corinthians that he prayed three times for God to remove it. But God's answer came:

'My grace is sufficient for you, for my power is made perfect in weakness.' (12:9)

Paul gladly accepted his weakness because it was a means of demonstrating God's power.

'We have been beaten, imprisoned, and mobbed; we have been overworked and gone without sleep or food.' (6:5)

And later:

'Five times I was given the thirty-nine lashes by the Jews; three times I was whipped by the Romans; and once I was stoned. I have been in three shipwrecks, and once I spent twenty-four hours in the water. In my many travels I have been in danger from floods and from robbers, in danger from fellow-Jews and from Gentiles; there have been dangers in the cities, dangers in the wilds, dangers on the high seas and danger from false friends. There has been work and toil; often I have gone without sleep; I have been hungry and thirsty; I have often been without enough food, shelter, or clothing. And not to mention other things, every day I am under the pressure of my concern for all the churches.' (11:24–28)

Paul felt deeply concerned about the churches he had founded. At Corinth, as in other places, false teachers had arrived upsetting Paul's work and casting doubt on his apostleship. However much he disliked doing it, Paul had to stand up for himself and make good his claim to be a true apostle sent to them by God and engaged in a ministry of reconciliation:

'If anyone is in Christ, he is a new creation; the old has gone, the new has come!' (5:17)

'God was reconciling the world to himself in Christ.' (5:19)

The Games

In his letters Paul often uses the national games, introduced by the Greeks, as an example of the Christian life. He compares himself to an athlete, competing in the Christian race, and urges Christians to go into training and strive hard to win.

The best known of the ancient games were the Olympics but games were also held on the Corinthian isthmus—the Isthmian games—and at Delphi and Argos. The competitors had to keep strictly to the rules and to train hard and long for the events. These included running, chariot racing, quoits, boxing, wrestling and hurling the spear. Huge crowds watched and, although the prize was no more than a wreath of pine or laurel or olive, the honour of winning was tremendous.

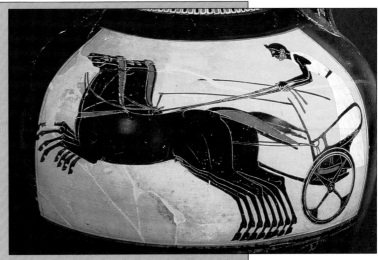

Chariot-racing is pictured on this Greek vase. Paul urges Christians to race for the goal (life in Christ) with the same single-minded concentration.

Paul writes too about the Corinthians' giving. He had begun a special collection of money to help the poor Christians in Jerusalem. He believed that Gentile Christians owed much to their Jewish brothers and sisters and he sees this gift of money as one way of paying the debt. It also proved the genuineness of the Gentiles' obedience to the gospel and demonstrated, in a practical way, the oneness in Christ of Jew and Gentile. Paul spent some time organizing the collection from the different churches. It seems as if the Corinthians had made a good start but their giving had tailed off. Paul writes glowingly about the joy and blessing of giving generously to God. If they need an incentive to give, he reminds them:

'You know the grace of our Lord Jesus Christ; rich as he was, he made himself poor for your sake, in order to make you rich by means of his poverty.' (8:9)

Every other gift fades in comparison and Paul exclaims:

'Let us thank God for his priceless gift!' (9:15)

Philippians

The readers. Paul wrote his letter to the Christians at Philippi, in northern Greece, where he first preached and founded a church on his second missionary journey (see Acts 16).

The purpose of the letter. Paul wanted to thank the Philippians for their gift of money and to beg them to settle differences in the church.

The Christians at Philippi seem to have had a special place in Paul's heart. He writes to them very affectionately. 'I thank my God for you every time I think of you,' he tells them.

He is especially grateful for the way they have helped to support him time and again with their gifts. Now he is writing to thank them for another gift brought to him by Epaphroditus. He was a Philippian Christian who had been a great help to Paul while he was in prison. Epaphroditus had been seriously ill and Paul is now anxious to reassure the Philippians that he is better and to send him back to them — with Paul's letter — safe and sound.

Although Paul is in prison, waiting to know whether he will be sentenced to death or released, he is not taken up with his own affairs. He is more concerned about the Philippians and the need for them to be in harmony. Joy is the keynote of the letter.

He has some wonderful words to say about the example Jesus set, maybe quoting from an early hymn:

'Who, being in very nature God,
  did not consider equality with God
    something to be grasped,
but made himself nothing,
  taking the very nature of a servant,
  being made in human likeness.

And being found in appearance as a man,
  he humbled himself
  and became obedient to death — even death
    on a cross!' (2:6–8)

Paul longs for all the Philippians to be 'one in soul and mind'. In a moving appeal, he begs two women in the church, who have obviously quarrelled, to make it up: 'Euodia and Syntyche, please, I beg you, try to agree as sisters in the Lord.' (4:2)

Paul gives his recipe for a contented and wholesome Christian life:

'Whatever is true, whatever is noble, whatever is right, whatever is pure, whatever is lovely, whatever is admirable — if anything is excellent or praiseworthy — think about such things. Whatever you have learned or received or heard from me, or seen in me — put it into practice. And the God of peace will be with you.' (4:8–9)

ROMANS

KEYNOTES OF THE LETTER

Romans

The readers. Paul wrote to the church at Rome, capital of the Empire, which he had not yet visited. But he knew a number of Christians living there and looked forward to visiting and meeting them all before long.

The purpose of the letter. Paul wrote to prepare the way for the visit he planned to make to them. In the letter he sets out clearly and logically the gospel message he preached. He also gives practical advice about Christian living.

Paul's letter to the Romans has much in common with Galatians, but Galatians was written in the heat of the moment, while Romans was composed at leisure. It is the harvest of Paul's reasoning and thinking about the gospel message he has preached over the years.

A desperate problem — and God's solution

Paul begins with the fact that no one is fit to enter into a relationship with God. He shows how all types of people — pagans, moralists, Jews who had the Law — had failed to meet God's standards:

'There is no difference at all: everyone has sinned and is far away from God's saving presence.' (3:22–23)

But having painted the blackest possible picture, Paul outlines the amazing solution to the problem. Once again, people of every kind have equal opportunity:

'But now God's way of putting people right with himself has been revealed. It has nothing to do with law ... God puts people right through their faith in Jesus Christ. God does this to all who believe in Christ.' (3:21, 22)

Paul insists that there is nothing men and women can do by themselves to get right with God. God has done it all:

'It was while we were still sinners that Christ died for us! By his sacrificial death we are now put right with God ... We were God's enemies, but he made us his friends through the death of his Son.' (5:8–10)

Paul uses the word 'grace' to describe the way God has reached out to men and women. Grace is the gift of God's love, freely given to those who do not deserve it. When anyone responds to God's grace in trust, peace and joy follow:

'Now that we have been put right with God through faith, we have peace with God through our Lord Jesus Christ.' (6:1)

Some had argued from this that it doesn't matter how a Christian behaves, because sin gives God the chance to show more grace. Paul says that nothing could be further from the truth! Once a person has been put right with God the old way of life ends. Paul uses Christian baptism as a picture of life before and after becoming a Christian. Just as Jesus died, so water baptism signifies the death of the Christian's old self. As Jesus rose from death, so the Christian emerges to live a new kind of life, which will be pleasing to God.

The Jewish nation

Chapters 9 to 11 deal with the situation of the Jewish people. These chapters are important because they prove that the God who promises salvation to all in chapters 1–8 is worthy to be trusted because he had kept his promises to Israel. He had not abandoned them — and Christ and his believers were the fulfilment of Old Testament scripture.

Paul reminds his Gentile readers not to be overconfident. It is true that they have become part of God's church — just like a wild olive grafted onto the true stock of the Jewish nation. But although it looks as if God has rejected his own people, the Jews, he still has plans for their salvation. Paul is amazed at God's great mercy to all:

'How great are God's riches! How deep are his wisdom and knowledge! Who can explain his decisions? Who can understand his ways? . . . For all things were created by him, and all things exist through him and for him. To God be the glory for ever! Amen.' (11:33, 36)

Paul uses the rest of the letter to talk about the kind of new life that Christians should lead. At the heart of it is total self-giving to God:

'Because of God's great mercy to us I appeal to you: Offer yourselves as a living sacrifice to God, dedicated to his service and pleasing to him.' (12:1)

The effects of that self-giving will filter through to every area of life. In the church, every Christian is to use their God-given abilities to help others. Paul pictures the church as a body, with everyone representing one part and having a vital role to play if the whole body is to function well.

Christians must be good citizens too. 'Everyone must obey the state authorities' and pay taxes — and respect — to those in control.

In Rome, as in Corinth, there was a clash of cultures in the Christian community. Jewish Christians were not willing to buy meat that had been offered in pagan temples. Gentile Christians did not have the same scruples. In this letter Paul points out how important it is not to sit in judgment on others, just because their conscience reacts differently. Those who think themselves 'strong' and robust should be gentle with those who have scruples, and not cause them any offence. Paul begs them to follow the example of Jesus, who did not please himself. Then there will be unity:

'All of you together may praise with one voice the God and Father of our Lord Jesus Christ.' (15:6)

The last chapter of Romans is taken up with Paul's greetings to all his friends who are living at Rome, the capital of the Empire. 'Greetings to Mary, who has worked so hard for you . . . Greetings to Apelles, whose loyalty to Christ has been proved' — fascinating and tantalising glimpses into the church of Paul's day, notable in the number of women included.

'Let us give glory to God!' Paul concludes. 'He is able to make you stand firm in your faith . . . To the only God, who alone is all-wise, be glory through Jesus Christ for ever! Amen.' (16:25, 27)

The Colosseum at Rome, built in AD70, was the arena where up to 45,000 people could watch the gladiators.

Colossians

The readers. Colossae was a town in the fertile valley of the River Lycus, near Laodicea, in the western part of present-day Turkey. Paul had not visited the church there but it was not far from Ephesus where he had spent three years.

The purpose of the letter. Paul wrote to correct some very strange views about Jesus which the Colossians had picked up. They did not believe that Jesus was unique as the Son of God. He was only one of several manifestations of God. In order to have full salvation it was necessary to worship some of these other powerful beings.

Paul also needed to put them right because they were saying that salvation

The Christians at Colossae who received Paul's letter lived in the beautiful Lycus Valley of present-day Turkey, pictured here.

depended on being circumcised and keeping strict rules.

Jesus — the one who is God's Son — is at the heart of this letter. Paul makes it crystal clear that Jesus is unique. He made the worlds and through his death he brought the whole universe back to God, as well as making men and women God's friends:

'Christ is the visible likeness of the invisible God. He is the first-born Son, superior to all created things... God created the whole universe through him and for him. Christ existed before

Gnosticism

No one knows just when the philosophy of gnosticism began but it was certainly flourishing in the second and third centuries AD. It was a mixture of astrology, reincarnation and Greek science. The name comes from the Greek word *gnosis* or knowledge. Gnosis was not intellectual knowledge but a mystical knowledge or enlightenment which was needed in order to reach the other world in due course.

Gnostics believed in two worlds, the spiritual world, where God existed, and the material world, which was evil. God could have nothing to do with the material world—our world—so human beings must try to escape to the spiritual world. Some were given a spark of divinity to which they must add secret knowledge, so that when they died they would be reunited with God. Without the spark and the enlightenment, they would return in another incarnation.

Gnosticism led to two different ways of life. Some gnostics became very ascetic, turning away from all pleasure. They believed that material things were wrong, so must be avoided. But others decided that, because salvation had nothing to do with behaviour, they could do just as they pleased. Both views cut right across Christian beliefs and behaviour. Asceticism contradicted the Christian acceptance of all good things as coming from God and to be enjoyed. On the other hand, living a life of self-pleasing and indulgence denied the Christian belief that life should be lived to please God and that his moral laws should be obeyed.

The letters to the Corinthians and the Colossians, 1 John and Revelation seem to hint at the fact that Gnostic-type heresies were affecting these churches.

all things, and in union with him all things have their proper place... Through the Son, then, God decided to bring the whole universe back to himself. God made peace through his Son's sacrificial death on the cross and so brought back to himself all things, both on earth and in heaven... By means of the physical death of his Son, God has made you his friends, in order to bring you, holy, pure and faultless, into his presence.' (1:15–22)

Paul warns the Colossians against becoming slaves to rules made up by human beings. The only kind of circumcision

Christians need is what he calls 'the circumcision made by Christ, which consists of being freed from the power of this sinful self'.

They have also been set free by Christ from the crippling 'do's and don'ts' that make life so unbearable. They have been brought to life with Jesus. Now they must take off, like dirty clothes, the old ways of behaving — sexual immorality, lust, greed, lies. Then they can dress themselves in the clean clothes of kindness, humility, gentleness, tolerance and love.

Paul gives guidelines for relationships and sets out the way in which husbands and wives, children and parents, owners and slaves are to behave to each other.

One of the messengers to carry this letter was Onesimus, who had been a runaway slave and whose master, Philemon, was probably a member of the church at Colossae (see below).

Philemon

This letter is written to an individual Christian — a friend of Paul's called Philemon — on a very personal matter. Philemon was a wealthy Christian (the church met in his house, so it must have been spacious) and he owned slaves. One of those slaves, Onesimus, had run away and while he was on the run he had somehow come into contact with Paul, who was in prison because of his preaching. As a result of that meeting Onesimus became a Christian.

Paul knows it is his duty as a citizen and a Christian to send Onesimus back to his master. It was a serious crime to harbour a runaway slave. But Paul does the very best he can for Onesimus and gives him this covering letter to take to his master. In it he tells Philemon that he thinks of Onesimus as his spiritual son — 'who became my son while I was in chains'.

The name Onesimus means 'useful'; Paul comments on how useful Onesimus has been to him in prison and how loth he is to part with him. 'I am sending him back to you now,' he writes, 'and with him goes my heart.'

Paul pleaded with Philemon to welcome Onesimus not as a disgraced slave but as a brother in Christ. Paul promised to pay back any money Onesimus may have stolen.

The New Testament never speaks against slavery — the structure on which contemporary civilization was built. But in this letter we catch a glimpse of the understanding which later led Christian reformers to campaign for the abolition of slavery.

We don't know the end of Onesimus' story. Perhaps Philemon pardoned and freed his slave and sent him back to Paul. As the letter has been kept, a happy outcome seems likely. Ignatius, an early church leader, mentions a man called Onesimus who was leader of the church at Ephesus. Did the runaway slave make good?

Paul ends his letter on a cheerful note. He asks Philemon to prepare a guestroom for him. He has high hopes that he will soon be out of prison and visiting his old friend again.

Ephesians

The readers. This letter may have been intended to circulate around several churches. There are no personal messages in it and not all of the ancient manuscripts mention Ephesus as the place where it was sent.

The purpose of the letter. This is a letter of secrets shared — the great secrets of what God has planned for Jesus, for his people and for the whole universe. God's purposes for his people are so marvellous that they must live lives to suit.

Paul is full of excitement as he shares with the Ephesians some of the secrets of God's plans — hidden down the ages until the coming of Jesus and his church.

At the heart of God's plans is Jesus himself. Everything in the whole universe has its centre in him. When the time is ripe God will 'bring all creation together, everything in heaven and on earth, with Christ as head'.

Paul's readers must have tingled with excitement when they read that they, too, were part of God's cosmic plans:

'Even before the world was made, God had already chosen us to be his through our union with Christ, so that we would be holy and without fault before him.' (1:4)

There were harsh penalties for runaway slaves in the first century. Paul's letter to Philemon is a plea for leniency towards his slave Onesimus. This disc is a Roman slave-badge, inscribed with the words: 'Seize me if I should try to escape and send me back to my master.'

*In his letter to the
Ephesians Paul conjures up
the familiar picture of a
Roman soldier to describe
the 'armour' needed by
Christians—the shield of
faith, the helmet of
salvation, God's word as a
sword for the fight.*

Paul shares another secret. God has chosen Gentiles as well as Jews to be part of his family. Jesus' death on the cross not only reconciles them to God, but has broken down the barrier that existed between Jews and Gentiles, 'in this way making peace'.

Paul overflows with praise and joy as he thinks about God's wonderful grace and love. His praise and thankfulness find an outlet in prayer for the Ephesians — that they may come to know God better and experience his love in all its breadth and depth and height.

Now Paul turns, as he usually does in his letters, from teaching — or Christian theory — to the practice of everyday Christian living. He has described the oneness that was brought about by Jesus' death, now he wants to see unity in action. He wants the church, like a body of many parts, with Jesus as head, to grow together in love. Everyone should use the gift God has given them to help build up the life of the church:

'So when each separate part works as it should, the whole body grows and builds itself up through love. (4:16)

Paul writes about the right way to relate, in the family as well as the church, and gives instructions, as he did in Colossians, for Christian husbands and wives, parents and children, slaves and masters.

'Finally,' he implores them, 'be strong in the Lord and in his mighty power.'

To do so they must be properly armed. Paul uses the pieces of armour that a Roman soldier wore and carried to illustrate the way in which a Christian can defend himself and attack his enemy — not human beings but 'the wicked spiritual forces in the heavenly world'.

Faith is the shield, salvation the helmet, truth the belt and the word of God the sword of every Christian.

'So put on God's armour now! Then when the evil day comes, you will be able to resist the enemy's attacks; and after fighting to the end, you will still hold your ground.' (6:13)

The Pastoral Epistles: 1 and 2 Timothy, Titus

The readers. 1 and 2 Timothy are written to the young man Timothy, once Paul's missionary partner, now leader of the church at Ephesus. Titus is another of Paul's team, now leader of the church in Crete.

Doubt has been thrown on Paul's authorship of these three letters. It is pointed out that they are very different from his earlier ones in style and subject-matter. Others argue that Paul did write them. If so, they are almost certainly his last letters.

The purpose of the letters. 1 and 2 Timothy and Titus are called the 'Pastoral' Epistles because they focus on the needs of the churches as God's 'flock'. Paul wrote to give these two young men guidance in their care (pastoring) of the churches they led.

Paul had a very warm relationship with Timothy — like a father to his son. He showed his confidence in him by giving him responsibility at Ephesus. He encourages him — for Timothy seems to have been shy and under-confident — and tells him not to let anyone look down on him because he is young. He gives him help with the problems at Ephesus.

After Paul has talked about the false teaching that has been going round at Ephesus, he advises Timothy about prayer in the church. Then he gives guidelines for choosing a church leader — and these set a very high standard:

'A church leader must be without fault; he must have only one wife, be sober, self-controlled and orderly; he must welcome strangers in his home; he must be able to teach; he must not be a drunkard or a violent man, but gentle and peaceful; he must not love money; he must be able to manage his own family well and make his children obey him with all respect... He must be mature in the faith... He should be a man who is respected by the people outside the church.' (3:2-7)

Paul describes relationships in the church as family ones:

'Do not rebuke an older man, but appeal to him as if he were your father. Treat the younger men

as your brothers, the older women as mothers, and the younger women as sisters, with all purity.' (5:1–2)

Paul has invested a great deal of affection and trust in Timothy. He ends his letter with the plea: 'Timothy, keep safe what has been entrusted to your care.'

The second letter to Timothy is a very personal one. Paul has a good deal to say about Timothy as well as about his own situation.

In prison, expecting the death sentence soon, Paul thinks about Timothy with deep emotion and longs to see him again. He wants to give him strength and encouragement while he still can. He draws three pictures of the Christian life: as soldier, athlete and farmer.

'Take your part in suffering, as a loyal soldier of Christ Jesus.' (2:3)

Like a good soldier, Timothy must aim to please his commanding officer and not get involved with other matters. Like a good athlete, Timothy must keep to the rules of the race. Like a farmer, Timothy can expect to enjoy a harvest from all the hard work he has put in.

Paul speaks movingly about the end of his life, which is near:

'I have fought the good fight, I have finished the race, I have kept the faith. Now there is in store for me the crown of righteousness, which the Lord, the righteous Judge, will award to me on that day — and not only to me, but also to all who have longed for his appearing.' (4:7-8)

The farmer ploughs and sows in expectation of the harvest. So Paul encourages Timothy to look for the harvest which will result from all his work in Christ's service.

He looks forward to a visit. Timothy is to bring Paul's cloak when he comes, as well as his parchments and books. Something warm to wear and something good to read were needed in prison!

Titus seems to have had a hard job leading the church in Crete. Paul quotes a Cretan poet who describes his countrymen as 'liars, evil brutes, lazy gluttons'.

Paul repeats the instructions he had given to Timothy for the appointing of church leaders and tells Titus to keep a sharp eye open for false teaching and silly talk. He suggests how old and young, men and women, ought to behave in the church and in the community. Paul stresses the importance of living good lives:

'For the grace of God that brings salvation has appeared to all ... It teaches us to say "No" to ungodliness and worldly passions, and to live self-controlled, upright and godly lives in this present age while we wait for the blessed hope — the glorious appearing of our great God and Saviour, Jesus Christ.' (2:11–13)

TITUS

KEYNOTES OF THE LETTER

Appointing church leaders 1

Wrong and right behaviour 1

Christian living 3

WRITING MATERIALS

In ancient times, even before the time of Abraham, writing was impressed on soft **clay tablets**, afterwards baked hard. Broken fragments of pottery (shards) might also be used. The Egyptians were the first to use the pith of **papyrus** reeds from the River Nile as writing material. The pith was pressed out into long strips, then another layer was laid widthways across the top. The two layers were soaked with glue and water, then beaten into one sheet. Finally the surface was smoothed with pumice.

The word **Bible** comes from the town of Byblos, on the Mediterranean coast, which traded in papyrus. The name of the city came to stand for a roll made from papyrus, hence for a book.

But papyrus was difficult to produce, not easy to write on and not very durable, so animal skins which were stronger were also used. The skins of calves, antelope, sheep and goats were scraped and stretched to make **parchment** or vellum. Sheets of writing material—papyrus or parchment—would be joined to make a roll. A typical roll would be 6 metres / 20 feet long and 25 centimetres / 10 inches wide. It was rolled up from each end and gradually unrolled when it was used. We call these rolls **scrolls**.

Because parchment was expensive, the same roll would sometimes be used twice. The scribe would scrape off the first layer of writing before making a second. Manuscripts with two such sets of writing are called **palimpsests**. Using ultra-violet photography it is possible to expose the first layer of writing, which is often of greater interest.

In the first century AD a new way was found to bind sheets together in pages to form a book. Then what is known as a **codex** could be made, with writing on both sides.

Ink was used from early times, made from soot and gum, dried into a cake. It could be moistened with water for use. Egyptians used a rush cut on the slant and frayed into a brush as a **pen**. Early Hebrews used the same type of pen, but later scribes used a reed with its point split to make a nib.

Assyrian and Babylonian scribes used a wedge-shaped stylus on wet clay tablets. This is a Babylonian contract for a sale of land, written in cuneiform.

The paper on which the New Testament documents would have been written was made from papyrus—a reed which still grows in Israel's Hula Valley.

The ancient Egyptians used picture symbols known as hieroglyphs, painted on walls (as here) or on sheets of papyrus.

Paul and his secretaries may have used a pen-case like this Roman one, with spare pens and black ink in the inkwell.

GENERAL LETTERS

Hebrews to Jude

Paul was not the only first-century Christian leader to write letters to Christians. There are eight other letters in the New Testament, some written by Jesus' apostles.

Hebrews

The writer. No one knows who wrote the letter — which is in excellent, polished Greek. There have been plenty of guesses, which include Priscilla or Aquila (tentmakers and friends of Paul), Barnabas (Paul's original companion on his missionary expedition) and Luke — author of one Gospel and Acts. In the King James' Version of the Bible Paul's name appears as author but that is very unlikely.

The readers. The letter seems to be aimed at a group of Jewish — or Hebrew — Christians who were tempted to go back to their Jewish faith.

The purpose of the letter. The letter aims to show that Jesus and all that he has done is way beyond what went before. The Old Testament faith had a great deal of outward ceremony and appeal, but Jesus' way to God is far better. Jesus is a greater prophet than any who came before. He offers a better covenant — or agreement — with God than Moses made. Jesus is a better High Priest than Aaron or his followers and he offered a far better sacrifice — that of his own life — than the Old Testament animal sacrifices.

To return to the old covenant is to grasp at insubstantial shadows instead of holding on to the firm reality of Jesus and the good things he has brought. To try to maintain the Old Testament practices as equally valid alongside the Christian faith is to deny all that Jesus has done.

The greatness of Christ

'In the past God spoke to our ancestors many times and in many ways through the prophets, but in these last days he has spoken to us through his Son.' (1:1–2)

That opening sentence of the letter sums up the whole. Jesus — greater and better than any other, human or heavenly — has come, and nothing will ever be the same again. He has made God known and opened up a free, new way to God. The writer hammers home again and again that Jesus takes first place. Not only is he great in himself, but he has brought a salvation which is greater than anything ever known before. Christians have everything to be glad about and to hold onto in their new relationship with God, forged by Jesus in his death for them.

Jesus is better than any angelic being — he is not one of God's servants, as the angels are:

'He is the one through whom God created the universe, the one whom God has chosen to possess all things at the end. He reflects the brightness of God's glory and is the exact likeness of God's own being, sustaining the universe with his powerful word.' (1:2–3)

The writer slips in a little warning at this early stage. It is a serious matter if his readers think they can play fast and loose with the salvation Jesus offers. He reminds them that there was serious punishment for those who rejected God's message in Old Testament times, so:

'How, then, shall we escape if we pay no attention to such a great salvation?' (2:3)

Moses, the great lawgiver and leader of the people of Israel, pales into insignificance beside Jesus. The writer compares Moses, as a servant in God's house, to Jesus, the Son whose house it is.

The scene switches from Moses, the

lawgiver and leader, to Aaron and those who came after him as High Priest. Human high priests had two disadvantages — their own failings and weakness and the fact that they died and their work ended.

'Jesus lives on for ever... so he is able, now and always, to save those who come to God through him, because he lives for ever to plead with God for them.' (7:24, 25)

'Jesus, then, is the High Priest that meets our needs. He is holy; he has no fault or sin in him... he does not need to offer sacrifices every day for his own sins first and then for the sins of the people. He offered one sacrifice, once and for all, when he offered himself.' (7:26–27)

Although the High Priest went once a year into the inner sanctum of the temple — the Most Holy Place — beyond the thick curtain, he could never make the way into God's presence open to all. But:

'Christ did not go into a man-made Holy Place... he went into heaven itself, where he now appears on our behalf.' (9:24)

So the writer can confidently say:

'We have then... complete freedom to go into the Most Holy Place [which is God's presence] by means of the death of Jesus. He opened for us a new way, a living way, through the curtain — that is through his own body.' (10:19, 20)

Jesus is not only a better High Priest, he also offered a better sacrifice. He is himself

both Priest and sacrifice. The writer emphasizes that 'the blood of bulls and goats can never take away sin'. But Jesus could offer himself as the perfect sacrifice, because he was without sin.

The writer next compares the old covenant — which God made with Israel through Moses at Sinai — with the new covenant that Jesus brings. He quotes the words of Jeremiah, who looked ahead to the day when God would make a new and better agreement. God says:

'I will put my laws in their minds
and write them on their hearts...
I will forgive their sins
and will no longer remember their wrongs.'
(8:10, 12)

The new covenant offers forgiveness of sin

The writer of the letter to the Hebrews encouraged his readers to see themselves as runners in a race. In the watching crowd are men and women of faith from earlier times. In front, as their goal, is Jesus himself, who knows what it is to endure. The runners in this Greek vase painting are competing in a gruelling long-distance race.

Melchizedek

Melchizedek is a little-known Old Testament character who is mentioned in this letter. When the writer wants to compare Jesus to a priest in the Old Testament he chooses Melchizedek as the prototype. Melchizedek appears briefly in Genesis as King of Salem (Jerusalem) and a priest of God. He brought bread and wine to Abraham after he had fought successfully to free Lot from neighbouring kings who had captured him. Melchizedek gave Abraham a blessing and Abraham gave him a tenth part of his possessions. Melchizedek is also mentioned in one of the psalms (Psalm 110) where God says to his anointed: 'You are a priest for ever, in the order of Melchizedek.'

Jewish readers would have found difficulty in thinking of Jesus as a priest, because he was not born into the priestly family of Aaron, of the tribe of Levi. But the writer to the Hebrews sees the priesthood of Melchizedek as having more in common with Jesus than that of Aaron. He finds meaning in both Old Testament references.

Melchizedek's parentage, birth and death are not mentioned so, the writer concludes, he was 'without beginning or end of days'. That makes him like Jesus, who has neither beginning nor end. Melchizedek was, like Jesus, a king as well as a priest. Some people were looking for a Messiah who was both king and priest and Jesus is both the King and the great and never-ending High Priest.

on the grounds of Jesus' sacrifice of himself; the ability to keep God's laws through the help of the Holy Spirit.

The writer reasons that to go back to the old rituals and the old covenant now is to despise Jesus and his sacrifice — a most serious sin.

'By faith . . .'

Like the apostles and other New Testament preachers, the writer has emphasized throughout the letter that the response he wants from his readers is faith in God and his promises. All that men and women are required to do for their salvation is to accept in trust God's provision in Jesus. Now he shows how faith has always been the response God looks for. He sets out a wonderful picture-gallery of Bible portraits — men and women whose faith in God has shone through their daily lives.

He begins with Adam's son, Abel, whose faith made his sacrifice acceptable. He lingers over Abraham — the great father of his nation — who, with his wife Sarah, trusted God so completely that, when God called him, 'he left his own country without knowing where he was going'.

Moses has good coverage:

'It was faith that made Moses, when he had grown up, refuse to be called the son of the king's daughter. He preferred to suffer with God's people rather than to enjoy sin for a little while.' (11:24–25)

When he runs out of time to deal with everyone in detail, the writer outlines the adventures of a whole galaxy of men and women who

'did what was right and received what God had promised. They shut the mouths of lions, put out fierce fires, escaped being killed by the sword. They were weak, but became strong . . . The world was not good enough for them! . . . What a record all of these have won by their faith!' (11:33, 34, 38, 39)

These men and women are a 'cloud of witnesses' to spur on his readers to similar faith. He urges them not to fall by the way or to slacken their efforts in the Christian life.

Like runners in a race, they must get rid of every hindrance and run with determination. Jesus — the centre of his thinking and writing — is the one on whom they must fix their eyes. Jesus went right on to death on the cross. Think of him, the writer says, and don't give up either!

James

The writer. The author may have been James, the brother of Jesus, who was leader of the church at Jerusalem. It was probably written within ten or twenty years of Jesus' death, as James was martyred in AD60.

The readers. Greetings are given 'to all God's people scattered over the whole world'.

The purpose of the letter. Rather like the Wisdom literature of the Old Testament, this letter gives advice on how to live wisely and well. It also encourages Christians facing trials, and those being exploited and badly treated.

This letter is a bit like Proverbs in the Old Testament: it deals with a whole range of topics — often returning to something already mentioned. It is hard to trace a continuous thread through it. It also echoes some of the teaching of Jesus in the Sermon on the Mount. James has the prophet's strong sense of social justice and makes scathing comments about the rich who grind down the poor. He promises the poor and downtrodden that the coming day of the Lord will put right these injustices.

James likes to paint word pictures. There is a thumbnail sketch of a rich man going into the synagogue and being warmly welcomed and conducted to the best seat. But when a poor man slips in he is curtly ordered by the usher to sit at his feet. James disapproves strongly of such snobbishness.

He compares those who bless God and curse other people to a fountain that gushes out both sweet and bitter water. It should be impossible! The tongue is like a ship's rudder or a horse's bridle — very small but very powerful! In another picture he likens the tongue to a forest fire — a tiny spark can cause an enormous amount of damage.

James stresses the importance of genuine

James takes the pictures of a horse, guided by a bit, and a great ship steered by a small rudder, to illustrate what he says about the control of the tongue: if we can control what we say, we are in the control of the whole person.

faith — a faith that works. He has no time for mere head-knowledge about God:

'Faith by itself, if it is not accompanied by action, is dead.' (2:17)

Abraham is a good example: he put his faith in God into action, when he trusted God enough to offer Isaac, his son, as a sacrifice.

James knows that many of his readers are going through tough times and he encourages them:

'My brothers, remember the prophets who spoke in the name of the Lord. Take them as examples of patient endurance under suffering. We call them happy because they endured. You have heard of Job's patience, and you know how the Lord provided for him in the end. For the Lord is full of mercy and compassion.' (5:10–11)

Patience must be linked with prayer. Pray whatever is happening!

'Is anyone among you in trouble? He should pray. Is anyone happy? He should sing praises. Is there anyone who is ill? He should send for the church elders, who will pray for him.' (5:13–14)

Whatever the situation or need, James has some encouragement or warning for the readers of his letter.

1 Peter

The writer. Peter, the apostle and close disciple of Jesus, may well have written this letter. Some think the Greek is too good to have been written by a Galilean fisherman but the polished style may be the work of Silvanus — or Silas — who was Peter's scribe. There is evidence that the letter is an early one and if Peter is the author it was written before 64–68, the likely time of Peter's death as a martyr.

The readers. Peter writes to God's chosen people scattered throughout the provinces of the Roman Empire in Asia Minor (Turkey). Jews who lived outside Palestine were known as the Dispersion or Diaspora. Peter thinks of these scattered Christians as the new Dispersion.

The purpose of the letter. These Christians will soon be facing persecution and Peter writes to give them strength and courage.

'Let us give thanks to the God and Father of our Lord Jesus Christ!' Peter exclaims. He is writing to Christians facing persecution, but he is full of joy and excitement as he thinks about the wonderful salvation Jesus has brought.

Peter encourages them by showing that the trials they are going through have a purpose. Just as gold is purified by fire:

Faith and 'Works' in the Letters of Paul and James

Some people think that there is a clash of views between Paul and James. Paul teaches, especially in Galatians and Romans, that people are saved by faith alone and not by what they do. James seems to be saying that good deeds are necessary. He writes, 'You see then that it is by his actions that a person is put right with God and not by his faith alone.'

Both quote the example of Abraham to prove their point. Paul argues that Abraham was put right with God because he believed God's promise. It was through faith that he was 'accepted as righteous by God' (Romans 4:22). James, on the other hand, says that Abraham was put right with God 'through his actions, when he offered his son Isaac on the altar' (James 2:21).

Paul and James are not really contradicting each other. They are using the words 'faith' and 'works' in different ways. By faith Paul means the total commitment of a person to God. Abraham was saved by his total trust and commitment to God and his promise. James takes faith to mean accepting a fact as true. No one is saved just by believing in the existence of God.

'Works', or deeds, for Paul means the impossible attempt to keep the Law. That is doomed to failure and could never make a person right with God. But James uses 'works' to mean faith in action. Abraham showed that his faith was genuine by acting upon it and offering up Isaac.

Paul and James agree that the kind of faith that God looks for is a trust shown in total self-giving and demonstrated in active obedience.

'So your faith, which is much more precious than gold, must also be tested, so that it may endure. Then you will receive praise and glory and honour on the Day when Jesus Christ is revealed.' (1:7)

Later in the letter he tells them that they are following in the footsteps of Jesus when they put up with undeserved suffering.

'Christ himself suffered for you and left you an example, so that you would follow in his steps. He committed no sin, and no one ever heard a lie come from his lips. When he was insulted he did not answer back with an insult; when he suffered, he did not threaten, but placed his hopes in God, the righteous Judge.' (2:21–23)

Peter gives practical advice, too, on family and church affairs. He advises Christian wives with pagan husbands that if they behave in the right way: 'It will not be necessary for you to say a word, because they will see how pure and reverent your conduct is.' (3:1–2)

Speaking as a church leader himself, Peter begs leaders to be gentle, humble servants of the Chief Shepherd, Jesus. Everyone in the church is to look after others' needs.

He assures them, as he draws to an end, that:

'After you have suffered for a little while, the God of all grace, who calls you to share his eternal glory in union with Christ, will himself perfect you, and give you firmness, strength, and a sure foundation. To him be the power for ever! Amen.' (5:10–11)

2 Peter

The writer. Many think that the writer was a follower of Peter, writing as he would have written, rather than Peter himself. If Peter was the author, it was written before the mid-sixties of the first century, when he met his death. Some of those who do not think Peter wrote it give a date as late as AD120–175.

The readers. The only clue to this is in 3:1 where Peter says that it is the second letter he has written to them. If 1 Peter was the first, this letter was meant for the same readers.

The purpose of the letter. The purpose is to warn against false and immoral teachers.

This letter was not immediately accepted by the church as having the full authority of Scripture, but was later included as part of the inspired writings.

Peter speaks out very strongly against the false teachers who are spreading their beliefs among Christians. It is not only their beliefs that are wrong — their behaviour is too. They are in the business of religion for what they can get out of it. Peter gives strong warnings against them but is sure that:

'The Lord knows how to rescue godly people from their trials and how to keep the wicked under punishment for the Day of Judgement.' (2:9)

Peter draws his readers' attention to people who say that Jesus is not coming again. They laugh at the idea. 'He promised to come, didn't he?' they ask, 'Where is he? . . . Everything is still the same as it was since the creation of the world!'

Just as the flood interrupted ordinary living in Noah's day, so Jesus' return will break into history, Peter assures them. He has two explanations for the delay. In the first place, God does not experience time as we do.

'There is no difference in the Lord's sight between one day and a thousand years; to him the two are the same.' (3:8)

Secondly, God's delays out of love and mercy. He does not want anyone 'to be destroyed but wants all to turn away from their sins'.

Peter picks up on a picture Jesus himself used about his return. The Day of the Lord will come like a thief — at a moment when no one is expecting it. He gives a vivid description of the end of the world:

'The heavens will disappear with a shrill noise, the heavenly bodies will burn up and be destroyed, and the earth with everything in it will vanish.' (3:10)

But Peter confidently looks forward to 'what God has promised: new heavens and a new earth, where righteousness will be at home'. All the more reason for Christians to live good lives, at peace with God and 'to continue to grow in the grace and knowledge of our Lord and Saviour Jesus Christ. To him be the glory, now and for ever! Amen.'

The letters of John

The writer. The same person is thought to have written all three letters and he may also have written John's Gospel. Some think that it was John the apostle and close friend of Jesus. Others believe that there were two leaders in the church called John. These letters might be from John the apostle's follower, a man known as John the Elder (an elder was a church leader). He must have been well known to his readers, for in his third letter he just introduces himself as 'the Elder'.

1 John

The readers. 'I am writing this to you so that you may know that you have eternal life — you that believe in the Son of God.' The letter was to Christians — those who had put trust in Jesus Christ as God's Son.

The purpose of the letter. John wanted to reassure Christians whose faith has been disturbed by false teachers — possibly with Gnostic ideas (see notes on *Gnosticism*). These teachers believed they were on a high spiritual plane, free from sin, and thought they could act as they pleased. Because they considered this world wholly evil they did not believe that God could have entered it in Jesus. He was not really Son of God or Messiah, they said, and only seemed to be truly human.

This letter is more like a piece of music than a reasoned discourse. The three themes of truth, light and love keep chiming in like repeated tunes. God is truth, God is light and God is love. The Christian who wants to follow God must 'walk' in truth, light and love.

John does not believe, as the false teachers did, that anyone can be free from sin in this life:

'If we say that we have no sin, we deceive ourselves, and there is no truth in us.' (1:8)

But full confession results in forgiveness and cleansing through the blood (the death) of Jesus:

'If we confess our sins to God, he will keep his promise and do what is right: he will forgive us our sins and purify us from all our wrongdoing.' (1:9)

John is full of the wonder of God's love:

'See how much the Father has loved us! His love is so great that we are called God's children — and so, in fact, we are.' (3:1)

But it follows that 'if this is how God loved us, then we should love one another'. And love must be practical:

'My children, our love should not be just words and talk; it must be true love, which shows itself in action.' (3:18)

Finally he reassures his readers about eternal life:

'We live in union with the true God — in union with his Son Jesus Christ. This is the true God, and this is eternal life.' (5:20)

2 John

2 and 3 John are the shortest documents in the New Testament; each fitted onto a single sheet of papyrus.

2 John is a brief letter addressed to 'the chosen lady and her children' but most people think the 'lady' was a local church. Perhaps this was a code name, used for safety reasons.

John stresses truth and love once again. He is delighted to hear that these Christians are not caught up with false beliefs. He longs for them to show love to one another. His argument is a circular one, beginning and ending with love:

'This love I speak of means that we must live in obedience to God's commands. The command, as you have all heard from the beginning, is that you must all live in love.' (6)

Another topic dealt with in the second and third letters of John is that of travelling missionaries. There was widespread peace throughout the Empire, because of Roman rule, and there were good roads, too, so people were often on the move. But inns were wretched places. Most were flea-ridden and filthy and some had a bad moral reputation as well. So John encourages his readers to show hospitality to Christians on their travels, especially when they are working to spread the gospel. But they must not welcome or encourage false teachers. If they do, they are siding with them.

John cuts his letter short:

'I have so much to tell you, but I would rather not do it with paper and ink; instead I hope to visit you and talk with you personally, so that we shall be completely happy.' (12)

3 John

This letter is to one person — Gaius, who is a church leader.

This is a very personal letter. John speaks warmly to Gaius:

'My dear friend, you are so faithful in the work you do for your fellow-Christians, even when they are strangers.' (5)

John encourages Gaius to go on helping the travellers who set out to preach the gospel, trusting God to meet their needs.

John warns Gaius against a self-important leader called Diotrophes. But he has high praise for Demetrius, another Christian in the church.

Once more he writes briefly because:

'I hope to see you soon, and we will talk face to face.' (14)

Jude

Jude, the author of this book, calls himself the servant of Jesus Christ and brother of James — who must have been someone well-known. Everyone at that time knew James, leader of the church in Jerusalem, and both James and Jude were brothers of Jesus.

This letter is addressed: 'To those who have been called by God, who live in the love of God the Father and the protection of Jesus Christ'. We do not know where these Christians lived.

Jude and 2 Peter have a substantial amount of material in common. Most people think that Jude's letter came first and the author of 2 Peter borrowed from it.

Both writers are shocked at the way 'godless people have slipped in unnoticed among us, persons who distort the message about the grace of our God in order to excuse their immoral ways, and who reject Jesus Christ, our only Master and Lord'.

It is not surprising that Jude — and Peter — speak very strongly against those who completely contradicted the gospel and the Christian life in this way.

Jude quotes the example of people in Old Testament days who lived bad and immoral lives and points out what happened to them in the end. One example is the cities of Sodom and Gomorrah, where God's judgment fell because of the inhabitants' wickedness.

In spite of such a strong and outspoken message Jude gently encourages his readers:

'But you, my friends, keep on building yourselves up on your most sacred faith. Pray in the power of the Holy Spirit, and keep yourselves in the love of God, as you wait for our Lord Jesus Christ in his mercy to give you eternal life.' (20)

He ends his letter with one of the loveliest prayers of praise to God:

'To him who is able to keep you from falling, and to bring you faultless and joyful before his glorious presence — to the only God our Saviour, through Jesus Christ our Lord, be glory, majesty, might and authority, from all ages past, and now, and for ever and ever! Amen.' (24–25)

13

JESUS REIGNS
Revelation

A coin with the head of the Emperor Domitian, whose demand for universal worship led to persecution for Christians towards the end of the first century.

John, the author of Revelation, was serving sentence on the island of Patmos (pictured here) when he received the visions recorded in the book. However dark things may look, God remains in control of human destiny.

The author of Revelation, according to tradition, is John the Apostle — also thought to have written the Gospel called by his name, and three letters. John is quoted as author of Revelation as early as AD135. Some scholars point out the big differences in style between John's Gospel and Revelation, but there are likenesses in language too. Both refer to the *Logos* or Word, to the Lamb of God and to the water of life.

Irenaeus (who lived about 130–202) said that John wrote his revelation 'not long ago but almost in our own generation, towards the end of Domitian's reign'. This dating fits in with the circumstances of the book. The Roman Emperor Domitian (AD81–96) demanded that all citizens should offer worship to him and this led to the persecution of Christians who refused to do so.

Some scholars disagree with this date and suggest a date in Nero's reign (some time between AD60 and 70).

The readers. The first readers were members of churches in the Roman province of Asia — present-day Turkey. Jesus gives John letters to seven of them, in the cities of Ephesus, Smyrna, Pergamum, Thyatira, Sardis, Philadelphia and Laodicea.

The purpose. Members of the churches in Asia were a tiny minority of the population. What could they hope to achieve against the mighty power of Rome? They accepted that Jesus had died and risen again and that one day he would return to establish his kingdom, making the kingdoms of the world his own. In that day the powers of evil would be destroyed and justice and peace established.

Meantime, Rome continued its oppressive rule and idolatry flourished. Christians who would not acknowledge the Emperor as Lord suffered imprisonment and sometimes death. Was God at work? Or was Rome the only power that really counted?

Revelation was written in that setting, to meet the needs of the perplexed and suffering Christians. It was certainly not intended as an intellectual puzzle for the church to sit back and unravel, as some would see it. The book was meant to bring faith, hope and certainty to a small and needy church, and to encourage their trust in the living Lord of history.

W. C. van Unnik wrote in his book *The New Testament*: 'This is not a book written to titillate or to gratify the curiosity of men anxious to tear aside the veil from the future. It is no book of riddles, although often in the past it has been treated as one. It does indeed draw veils aside and open up a vista of God's actions and his ways; for it proclaims the kingdom of God, which is here and now and yet is still to come in its fulness, bringing with it the overthrow of all that is against him.'

What kind of writing is Revelation?

It is easy to see some similarities between Revelation and apocalyptic writing. There are strange beasts and coded numbers,

angelic messengers and much about the heavenly world. But Revelation is also very different. The writer uses his own name, not that of a figure from the past, and he boldly names his readers. He does not share the gloom of the apocalyptists, nor does he put his hope only in the other world. He believes that God has been at work in Christ bringing salvation in this world.

He writes of the Messiah and his kingdom but, unlike the apocalyptists, he does not see this only in terms of the future. The kingdom of God came with Jesus and his death and resurrection brought salvation. His coming again will bring in the kingdom in all its fulness. So John is firmly rooted in the present as well as the future, in this world as well as the heavenly one. The present suffering of God's people is not without meaning or purpose.

The apocalyptists found no place for ethical teaching, but — especially in the letters to the churches in chapters 2 and 3 — John emphasizes the importance of doing what is right as well as believing the truth.

Revelation may be written in the style of apocalyptic but its message goes far beyond that kind of writing.

John was in Patmos (a small, crescent-shaped island off the coast of present-day Turkey) where he had been deported because of his Christian preaching. He was probably ordered to join one of the gangs set to work in the quarries. Blisters, aching bones and exhaustion were enough to fill the mind and banish thoughts of beauty, peace and joy. Yet against a backcloth of hardship and pain, above the clank of chains and shovels and picks, John was overwhelmed with the dazzling colours, sights and sounds of the world beyond his own.

At the start of his vision in Revelation, John heard a voice, so commanding that it was like the sound of a trumpet or a roaring waterfall. He turned to see a majestic being, clearly human, yet overpoweringly great and awesome. In reassuring and familiar tones, the mighty one told John not to be afraid:

'I am the first and the last, I am the living one! I was dead but now I am alive for ever.' (1:17–18)

John realized that this was Jesus, now glorified and majestic. He describes the one he saw. His hair was white as wool, his eyes blazed like fire and his feet shone like brass. Out of his mouth came a two-edged sword.

This description is important not because it literally describes Jesus, but because of what the images convey. Some of them are taken from the Old Testament which gives

Apocalyptic Writing

As we have already seen (under *Apocrypha*), apocalyptic was a special kind of writing full of strange imagery and coded messages. Many such writings were produced between 100BC and AD100 within the Jewish tradition, at a time when God's people were suffering for their faith and asking the question, Why?

Why did they suffer? Why were they not rewarded for their faithfulness as some of the teaching of the Old Testament led them to expect? Why did God allow the evil powers to prosper?

Apocalyptic writing followed certain accepted patterns. It usually claimed to be a revelation made through an angel or heavenly being to some great person of the past, such as Enoch, Abraham, Moses or Ezra—either to lend the message authority, or to keep the author anonymous for his own safety. Apocalyptists did not follow the Old Testament tradition and see God at work in this world. They believed that God had made two different worlds—this world and a heavenly one. It was the heavenly world that the writer revealed through his angelic interpreters. Apocalyptists were pessimistic about this world, which they believed was heading for ruin. Ethical teaching was beside the point: their purpose was to show how God would eventually bring about his people's deliverance. Sometimes this was linked with God's Messiah who would bring in God's kingdom.

Visions and dreams and revelations were all concerned with the heavenly world. They were full of strange beasts and symbolic numbers. Some of these were a kind of code to protect writer and reader in dangerous times. Some apocalypses consist of history retold in the form of prophecies coming from the lips of the historical 'author'. These prophecies tended to be wonderfully precise and accurate when they dealt with the past but curiously vague in dealing with the future!

the clue to their meaning. When Jesus' hair is described as white as wool or snow, readers familiar with the book of Daniel would remember the same description of God himself. John is saying that Jesus, seen as a man, is also God.

John listened intently as Jesus dictated to him seven letters to be sent to seven of the churches in the Roman province of Asia — to Ephesus, Smyrna, Pergamum, Thyatira, Sardis, Philadelphia and Laodicea. Jesus, the Lord of the churches, speaks with encouragement and warning about their lives and behaviour of these Christians.

The letters follow a pattern. Each begins by introducing Jesus in a way in which the vision has described him. For example, 'These are the words of him who has the sharp, double-edged sword.' Each letter gives Jesus' comment on the spiritual state of that church. There are two that deserve no blame, two that deserve no praise and three that are part good and part bad. Each church is commended for what is good and told to repent of what is bad. Then a thrilling

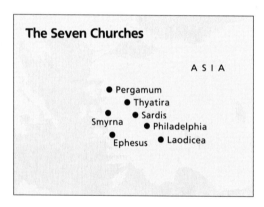

The Seven Churches

A S I A

● Pergamum
● Thyatira
● Sardis
Smyrna
● Philadelphia
Ephesus ● Laodicea

promise of reward is given to those who 'overcome'. Each letter ends with the words that Jesus spoke when he was teaching on earth: 'If you have ears, then listen!'

These letters contain intimate knowledge of the readers and their local situations. Wrong beliefs, leading to wrong practice, needed to be put right in many cases. Total and loving commitment to Jesus was vital if the churches were to survive the persecution that threatened or had already come.

False teachers are called by various names — Nicolaitans, followers of Jezebel, and followers of Balaam. Their wrong behaviour involved sacrifice to idols and sexual immorality. We cannot be sure who they were, but scholars think that all these groups were connected. They may represent an early form of Gnostic teaching (see notes on *Gnosticism*).

The main message of Revelation

Once these early chapters are past, Revelation seems to take off from the world of everyday reality. But we are not plunged into a nonsense or fairy-tale world. J. B. Phillips, who translated the New Testament into modern English, wrote that it was a thrilling experience dealing with Revelation, because the translator is carried 'not into some never-never land of fancy, but into the Ever-ever land of God's eternal values and judgments'.

Revelation is difficult to understand in detail but in its broad sweep the writer is declaring with all the imagery and language at his disposal the facts about God and this world of which he was certain and positive. All the visions that follow confirm these truths:

● God is in charge. Jesus has conquered death, and his rule, already begun, will one day be universal.

● The evil that is so pressing and real in the world around will not have the last say. God is all-powerful and will bring everything under his control.

● Everything that happens is part of God's plan and will lead to ultimate good.

● Christians can look forward to a new earth and heaven where only goodness will live and pain and sadness will be no more.

● God's plan is the salvation of the world — transformed into the kingdom of Christ. Only those who deliberately choose to do so will remain outside the blessings God has in store.

A glimpse into heaven

'After this I looked, and there before me was a door standing open in heaven. And the voice I

had first heard speaking to me like a trumpet said, "Come up here..."' (4:1)

With these words John's readers are taken with him into heaven itself.

The brilliance of jewels and the glory of the rainbow convey the wonder of the throne of God and of God himself. Surrounding the throne are twenty-four elders, perhaps representing the church. Flashes of lightning and rolls of thunder proceed from the throne and the Spirit's light illuminates it. Other created beings surround it, constantly chanting their hymn of 'Holy, holy, holy'. The twenty-four elders sing:

'You are worthy, our Lord and God,
to receive glory and honour and power,
for you created all things.' (4:11)

A written scroll is seen in the hand of God, sealed with seven seals. A search is made for one fit to break the seals and open it. John weeps when he realizes there is no one. Then an angel points him to the Lion of the tribe of Judah. But when John looks towards the centre of the throne he sees not a Lion but a Lamb, one that appeared to have been killed but is now alive. The strong and kingly Lion is also the suffering Lamb. John recognizes that Jesus, the slain Lamb, is the only one worthy to be in control of the future, to open the seals. The death and resurrection of Jesus are the key to all that happens in the world: the central event of history. This great act of salvation has broken the power of evil and death and made it possible for God's good purposes to be unfolded.

The song of praise for creation changes to a song of worship to the one who died:

'Worthy is the Lamb, who was slain,
to receive power and wealth and wisdom and
strength
and honour and glory and praise!' (5:12)

Visions of doom and glory

The central part of Revelation is full of strange visions. At first these picture the doom and punishment coming on wicked leaders and on Babylon — John's code-word for Rome. Seals are broken, trumpets sound, stars fall from the sky, plagues ravage the earth and the four horsemen of the apocalypse ride out.

These visions in Revelation have been compared to a kaleidoscope. In a series of changing and colourful patterns they show how God will finally overcome the powers of evil. God's judgments are like the Old Testament plagues which Moses brought

---

Ways of Interpreting Revelation

Modern readers find Revelation a hard book to read, full of strange visions, and even stranger interpretations. But Revelation has a message for a world where it is easy for the individual to feel helpless against huge organizations and great powers. Revelation reminds readers that God is in control, and the future is in his keeping.

There have been many different ways of interpreting Revelation. These are some of them:

● The book and its events have significance only for those who lived at the time it was written. This view—called the **preterist**—is held by most scholars. It does not give the book much value for later readers.

● Some see Revelation as an inspired forecast of the whole of human history, setting out—in symbolism—the whole history of Western Europe up to the second coming of Christ.
    The disadvantage of this view—the **historicist**—is that the book would not have helped its first readers, nor does it include people outside Western Europe. Also, those who hold this view offer so many different interpretations that none rings really true.

● Another interpretation views the whole book—apart from the first few chapters—as referring to the end of the age. All the visions have to do with the events immediately preceding the second coming. This view—the **futurist**—makes the book valuable only to those who live in the period spoken of.

● Some believe that the book does not refer to actual events, either at the time of writing or in the future. It is not concerned with the early church or with the end of the age. Instead, it sets out the principles on which God works all through history, in poetic terms. This is the **idealist** view.

What matters is to recognize both the meaning of Revelation for its first readers and its abiding value in demonstrating God's control and sovereignty over history.

John in his vision sees God enthroned, in control of the world no matter how dark things may seem— and round the throne he sees a rainbow like an emerald.

The book of Revelation ends with a vision of heaven and earth made new. John sees the new Jerusalem lit not by sun or moon but by the glory of God's presence.

against Egypt. There, as in Revelation, these judgments were not a pointless outpouring of God's anger, but a necessary means to God's salvation of his people — and through them the salvation of all the world.

Satan is finally put down. After his self-glory in heaven, 'the great dragon was hurled down — that ancient serpent called the devil, or Satan, who leads the whole earth astray'. From there he has harried men and women and in particular God's people, but his ultimate ruin is sealed. The effect of his conquest of the first man and woman in the Garden of Eden has been wiped out by the victory of the Lamb's death and resurrection. Soon his power will be broken for ever and he will be cast into the lake of fire, reserved for the Devil and his angels.

New heaven and a new earth

The last part of the book begins with God's promise:

'Now I make all things new!' (21:5)

A description of the new creation, pictured as a city called New Jerusalem, where God is the light and life, fills the last pages. All is perfect where God lives in close intimacy with his people:

'God himself . . . will wipe away all tears from their eyes. There will be no more death, no more grief or crying or pain. The old things have disappeared.' (21:4)

'The city has no need of the sun or the moon to shine on it, because the glory of God shines on it, and the Lamb is its lamp. The peoples of the world will walk by its light, and the kings of the earth will bring their wealth into it. The gates of the city will stand open all day; they will never be closed, because there will be no night there . . . But nothing that is impure will enter the city, nor anyone who does shameful things or tells lies. Only those whose names are written in the Lamb's book of the living will enter the city.' (21:23–27)

Justice is done and all wrongs are righted. Those who wilfully serve evil and ignore God are shut out of the place where God and his Christ are king. But the desire of God's Spirit and of God's people — pictured as the bride of Christ — is that others will come to share the perfect joy and bliss of God's kingdom. The invitation goes out:

'The Spirit and the bride say, "Come!"

Everyone who hears this must also say, "Come!"

Come, whoever is thirsty; accept the water of life as a gift, whoever wants it.' (22:17)

At its close, the book confirms the promise of Jesus to return to earth and to bring in his universal kingdom. Jesus says: 'I am coming soon.' And the writer replies with a heartfelt, 'Amen. Come, Lord Jesus!'

THE NEW TESTAMENT BOOKS

The twenty-seven books that make up the New Testament had nearly all been written by AD100. But how did they come to be recognized as a unified collection, and one that carried the stamp of divine authority? Christians accepted the Old Testament because Jesus himself had used and quoted these books. But who would give authority to their own 'scriptures' or holy writings?

The first documents of the New Testament to be written were the letters from apostles. Professor F. F. Bruce writes: 'Long before the apostolic letters were recognized as elements in a canonical collection they were recognized as divinely authoritative by those for whom they were written . . . authority is the necessary precedent of canonicity.'

In other words, it is true of the New Testament as it was of the Old Testament writings that ordinary people as well as religious leaders recognized the authority of certain writings. It was for that reason that they were included in the canon of scripture.

Until around AD60

eyewitnesses of Jesus' doings and sayings were alive to talk about them. But by then that generation was beginning to die, so Mark, in Rome, wrote down Peter's gospel as he had preached it. Soon after that Matthew's Gospel was produced in the East, based on sayings of Jesus that Matthew himself had probably collected. Then Luke, the companion of Paul, wrote two books, covering the events from the birth of John the Baptist to the time Paul spent in Rome—AD61–62. The first of these is his Gospel and the second the Acts of the Apostles. Finally, towards the end of the first century, John, Jesus' friend and disciple, wrote down his memories of Jesus and his meditations on them.

It was towards the end of the century, too, that the first move began to put together a recognized list. The four Gospels of Matthew, Mark, Luke and John were brought together not long after John had written his Gospel. Before they were collected, the church in Rome had Mark, the churches in the East had Matthew, Greek Christians

had Luke and the church at Ephesus had John. Now all the churches had the four Gospels, known as **The Gospel**.

At the same time, or a bit earlier, Paul's letters to various churches were collected together, known as **The Apostle**. Acts was included too because it was so obviously part of Luke's writing. Also it gave prominence to Paul, writer of the letters. Letters from other apostles and men closely associated with them, as well as Revelation, were also recognized as having divine authority.

In AD140 a man called Marcion began to spread his teaching and to set up his own list of scripture to suit his non-orthodox views. He even edited some of the books he included, to bring them into line. He had a large following. Because of his false teaching the church leaders were even more concerned to draw up an official list of books. These were books that could be used to teach right doctrine and to correct heresy.

The early church was doubtful for some time about

a few books which are now in the New Testament. In the early fourth century Eusebius drew up three lists: one of books recognized as part of the canon, one of those definitely not recognized, and a third list of those that he says were still disputed by some. This list of doubtful books included James, Jude, 2 Peter, 2 and 3 John. The first known list that contains the twenty-seven New Testament books as we have them dates from AD367. In 397 the Synod of Carthage declared this same list as Scripture but they had already been acknowledged by the church as the canon for a long time.

INDEX

Books of the Bible

Biblical References

(Quotations of more than one verse only)

KEY TO BIBLE VERSIONS:

GNB = Good News Bible
NIV = New International Version
REB = Revised English Bible
RSV = Revised Standard Version
KJV = King James (Authorized) Version